UR EXCAVATIONS TEXTS

VI

LITERARY AND RELIGIOUS TEXTS

THIRD PART

UR EXCAVATIONS TEXTS

PUBLICATIONS OF THE JOINT EXPEDITION OF THE
BRITISH MUSEUM AND OF THE UNIVERSITY MUSEUM,
UNIVERSITY OF PENNSYLVANIA, PHILADELPHIA,
TO MESOPOTAMIA

UR EXCAVATIONS TEXTS

VI

LITERARY AND RELIGIOUS TEXTS
THIRD PART

by

AARON SHAFFER

with a contribution by

MARIE-CHRISTINE LUDWIG

THE BRITISH MUSEUM PRESS

© 2006 The Trustees of the British Museum

First published in 2006 by The British Museum Press

A division of The British Museum Company Ltd

38 Russell Square, London WC1B 3QQ

British Library Cataloguing in Publication Data

A catalogue record for this book is available from the British Library

ISBN-13:   978-0-7141-1161-2

ISBN-10:   0-7141-1161-9

Printed in Great Britain

CONTENTS

PREFACE

This volume is the third and last part of the publication of the literary, religious and scholastic texts deriving from the excavations conducted by Sir Leonard Woolley at Ur in the years 1922-1934 under the auspices of the British Museum and the University of Pennsylvania Museum, Philadelphia. It completes the work begun some fifty years ago by our distinguished predecessors Cyril Gadd and Samuel Noah Kramer.

The volume is largely the work of the late Professor Aaron Shaffer of the Hebrew University of Jerusalem, who sadly died after a long illness on 5th April 2004. It is a matter for regret to his many friends that he did not live to see his life's work published.

All the tablets published here and in the first two parts of volume VI were originally sent to the British Museum so that they could be studied preparatory to a final publication. Now that this has been achieved, they will be returned in due course to the Iraq Museum, Baghdad. We are most grateful to the Iraqi State Board of Antiquities and Heritage for facilitating the full publication of the Ur excavations in this way.

Professor Shaffer was originally invited to undertake this project by Dr R. D. Barnett in the 1960s, and the work continued with the active encouragement of my predecessors Dr E. Sollberger and Mr T. C. Mitchell. In recent years my colleague Christopher Walker has been in charge of the project, and it is entirely due to his energy and selfless dedication that this volume will now see the light of day. In this difficult task, Mr Walker has been ably assisted by Dr Marie-Christine Ludwig who has made an invaluable contribution by recopying some tablets and correcting the copies of others.

Dr John Curtis
Keeper

Department of the Ancient Near East
British Museum
November 2005

ABBREVIATIONS

AOAT   *Alter Orient und Altes Testament*

ETCSL   *Electronic Text Corpus of Sumerian Literature* (Oxford)

ISET 1   M. Çığ and H. Kızılyay, *Istanbul Arkeoloji Müzelerinde Bulunan Sumer Edebî Tablet ve Parçaları - I*

JAOS   *Journal of the American Oriental Society*

JCS   *Journal of Cuneiform Studies*

MSL   *Materialien zum sumerischen Lexicon*

NABU   *Nouvelles Assyriologiques Brèves et Utilitaires* (Paris)

OBO   *Orbis Biblicus et Orientalis*

OECT   *Oxford Editions of Cuneiform Texts*

            I, S. Langdon, *The H. Weld-Blundell Collection in the Ashmolean Museum*

            V, O. R. Gurney and S. N. Kramer, *Sumerian Literary Texts in the Ashmolean Museum*

            XIV, Eleanor Robson, *Mesopotamian Mathematics, 2100-1600 BC*

PAPS   *Proceedings of the American Philosophical Society*

RA   *Revue d'assyriologie et d'archéologie orientale*

RIME   *Royal Inscriptions of Mesopotamia, Early Periods* (Toronto)

RlA   *Reallexicon der Assyriologie*

TCL   *Textes cunéiformes du Louvre*

TCS   *Texts from Cuneiform Sources*

UE   *Ur Excavations*

UET   *Ur Excavations, Texts*

ZA   *Zeitschrift für Assyriologie*

INTRODUCTION

The present volume has been in progress for the best part of 40 years, and represents the life work of the late Professor Aaron Shaffer of the Hebrew University of Jerusalem. He was invited to undertake it by Dr Richard Barnett, then Keeper of Western Asiatic Antiquities at the British Museum, while UET VI/2 was still awaiting publication, and the first quotations from the present volume, using Shaffer's provisional numbers, appear already in 1969 (Sjöberg, TCS 3). It was originally intended that following the model of UET VI/1 and UET VI/2 Shaffer would prepare the copies and Samuel Noah Kramer would write the Catalogue, but all the drafts for the Catalogue available to us come from Shaffer alone.

Shaffer's practice for many years was to come to London and spend a month or two in the Students Room of the then Department of Western Asiatic Antiquities searching through the trays of unpublished tablet fragments still remaining from the Ur excavations. The fragments had all already been baked by Cyril Bateman, the Department's Conservator, and Shaffer was given free access to the collection. He would copy anything he found interesting, mark the tablets with his own running numbers for future reference, and return to Jerusalem to search through his files and library for duplicates ofs what he had copied. It is a testament to his knowledge of Sumerian literature that he was able to identify so many small and unpromising looking fragments long before today's electronic databases became available.

Gadd's copies in UET VI/1 and UET VI/2 followed the old British Museum style of copying in a large script with very limited attention to details of palaeography; in fact his copies are virtually useless for palaeographical studies. Shaffer, by contrast, from the beginning of his work attempted to copy his fragments at the same size as the originals and to follow exactly the forms of the signs found on the tablets. The result is that many of his copies can be hard to read, but the interpretation of the text is left to the reader, not dictated by the copyist. In later years, however, Shaffer switched to tracing from enlarged photographs of his fragments; this applies to the fragments numbered by him from 402 onwards and to a few earlier numbers which he recopied. Our impression is that these later copies are somwhat less satisfactory palaeographically, but still superior to Gadd's.

Photocopies of Shaffer's earlier group of copies were for many years available for consultation in the University Museum, Philadelphia, and were used by several other scholars in the preparation of text editions of major Sumerian literary works, mostly with proper acknowledgement of Shaffer's work, but occasionally only referring anonymously to UET VI/3. We have included reference to these editions at the appropriate points in the Catalogue which follows.

Shaffer himself made many visits to Philadelphia, where he would have been able to consult both Kramer and Ake Sjöberg. His copies were also made available to Miguel Civil at the University of Chicago, and are taken into account in Civil's Catalogue of Sumerian Literature (and by extension in Oxford University's recent Electronic Text Corpus of Sumerian Literature). No doubt all of these, and probably other scholars, were able to assist Shaffer in the process of identification of his fragments, but we are no longer able to document this in detail.

A few of the copies had deteriorated over the years to the point that they were no longer fit to reproduce, and these have been replaced by new copies made by M.-C. Ludwig. The same applies to a few of the later tracings which appear to have been made in a hurry. The tablets recopied by M.-C. Ludwig are nos. 434-436, 439-449, 452-453, 475-476, 522, 561, 741, 893 and 913. She has also checked all of the other copies in detail against the original fragments and made changes where necessary.

For the large text of Inana's Descent (no. 433) there was available to us only a poor photocopy of a tracing by Shaffer, so for this tablet, which is too fragile to be handled for recopying, we include here recent photographs of the tablet (Plates A-D).

Some of the fragments which Shaffer copied he recognised as not being literary or scholastic and eliminated them from this publication. We have eliminated a few more which seemed to us to be fragments of economic texts. There are also gaps in the sequence of numbers which Shaffer allocated to his fragments, so no useful purpose is served by a complete index of his numbering system. We have included his numbers in the Catalogue for the sake of cross-reference to preceding publications and to the existing collection of photographs.

The copies which Shaffer made at the same scale as the originals are mostly reproduced here at approximately the same scale; but his tracings were made on a considerably larger scale and these have simply been reduced here to a size convenient for reading and to fit the page without precise reference back to the size of the original fragments. We include a table of dimensions of the fragments.

Many of the copies of smaller fragments are presented at odd angles. This reflects partly Shaffer's preference for copying lines rectilinearly and partly his perception of the irregular shapes of the original tablets. As is inevitable with tablets copied by trainee scribes many tablets have erasures. Often these are marked on the copies by dotted ovals, but in any case innumerable signs were rewritten over erasures.

We also include a list of all those fragments published in the three parts of UET VI which have excavation (U.) numbers together with their provenances, if known. Regrettably, all too many fragments have no U. number. Some brief mention of the provenances of published literary texts was made in UE VII, pp. 108-113, 136-137, and 214 ff., but for a more detailed analysis we refer the reader to P. Brusasco, 'Family Archives and the Social Use of Space in Old Babylonian Houses at Ur', in *Mesopotamia* XXXIV-XXXV (Firenze, 1999-2000), pp. 1-173, and in particular to his analysis of the findspots of tablets from nos. 5 and 7 Quiet Street (pp. 152-154) and from no. 1 Broad Street (pp. 159-161). See also D. Charpin, *Le Clergé d'Ur au siècle d'Hammurabi* (Paris, 1986), pp. 419-486.

In our own work preparing the copies for publication and redrafting Shaffer's Catalogue we have profited from the advice of Bendt Alster, Jerry Cooper, Gertrud Farber, Jo Ferrara, Irving Finkel, Mark Geller, Jacob Klein, Piotr Michalowski, Eleanor Robson, Jon Taylor, Steve Tinney, Konrad Volk and Nathan Wasserman. We were also assisted by Ann Searight in scanning the copies and with other professional advice.

We wish to record our thanks to Aaron Shaffer's family and to his student Nathan Wasserman for their help and encouragement in bringing this volume to publication.

Marie-Christine Ludwig and Christopher Walker

CATALOGUE

Unless otherwise stated all texts are unilingual Sumerian and datable to the Old Babylonian period. The numbering of the copies continues the sequence of UET VI parts 1 and 2 (here cited as UET 6/...). For convenience of cross-reference to earlier publications and privately circulating copies of these texts Shaffer's provisional numbering is added in brackets. For example no. 583 has already been cited as UET 6/3 no. 250. The British Museum's archive of pre-publication photographs is also based on these provisional numbers.

The numbers given after the titles of compositions refer to Miguel Civil's Catalogue of Sumerian Literature, now followed in Oxford University's Electronic Text Corpus of Sumerian Literature.

Nos. 415-503. Epic and Mythological texts.

Nos. 415-416. Enki's Journey to Nippur (1.1.4); see A. H. al-Fouadi, *Enki's Journey to Nippur* (University Microfilms, Ann Arbor, 1969).
No. 415 (66). Fragment of obverse only; lines 6-18.
No. 416 (156). Fragment of a one-column tablet; obv., lines 31-40, rev. blank; same tablet as UET 6/185.

Nos. 417-419. Inana and Šukaletuda (1.3.3); see K. Volk, *Inanna and Šukaletuda* (SANTAG 3, 1995).
No. 417 (15+116+171+179+296) Joined fragments of a three-column tablet; obv. ii = lines 65-81, obv. iii = lines 119-135, rev. iv = lines 226-230, rev. v = lines 280-283. Cited and copied as text Fu in K. Volk, op. cit.
No. 418 (129a). Fragment, one side only; lines 93-103; probably part of the same tablet as no. 419. Cited and copied as text Gu1 in K. Volk, op. cit.
No. 419 (79). Fragment of a one-column tablet; obv. and rev., lines 111-113 and 114-118; probably part of the same tablet as no. 418. Cited and copied as text Gu2 in K. Volk, op. cit.

Nos. 420-436. Inana's Descent to the Netherworld (1.4.1), Ur recension. A. J. Ferrara is now undertaking a new edition of Inana's Descent, based where possible on the material from Ur. Apart from nos. 424 and 428 below all the pieces of Inana's Descent published here appear to have been written by the same scribe in the same small archaizing script.
No. 420 (495). Fragment, one side only; lines 60-66.
No. 421 (559). Fragment, one side only; lines 124-125?/126?-129.

No. 422 (502). Fragment, one side and left edge; lines 128, 129, 129a, 129b; two unplaced lines on the left edge; ruling along the left edge.
No. 423 (414). Fragment, one side only; lines 129a, 129b, 130-137.
No. 424 (580). Fragment of a one-column tablet; obv., lines 129-133; rev., lines 158, 161-164?. This fragment and no. 428 are written in distinctively larger scripts than the other fragments, but do not belong to the same tablet.
No. 425 (320). Fragment, one side only; lines 150-154, 160-162; ruling along the left edge.
No. 426 (269) Fragment, one side and lower edge; lines 164-168, 170, 172, 173, 175; ruling along the left edge.
No. 427 (483). Fragment, one side only; lines 177-180, 182, 184-188, partially in the 'double line' recension.
No. 428 (416). Flake; large script; lines 182, 185-189.
No. 429 (267). Fragment, one side only; lines 187-191.
No. 430 (291). Fragment, one side only; lines 209-212; ruling along the left edge.
No. 431 (306). Fragment, one side and upper or lower edge; lines 246-250.
No. 432 (488). Fragment, upper or lower edge and two sides; lines 339-343 and three unplaceable lines.
No. 433 (1+328). Joins UET 6/10; joined fragments of a large one-column tablet, an imgida according to the colophon:

   1. šu-nigin₂ 2,54(=174)
   2. im-gid₂-da-3-kam zag-til-la
   3. an-gal-ta ki-gal-še₃

'Total, 174 lines. Third imgida, complete, "From the great heavens to the great place"'.
This tablet is thus the third and last imgida of three which contained the complete text of Inana's Descent. See the discussion of UET 6/10 (cited as source S) in W. R. Sladek, *Inanna's Descent to the Netherworld* (University Microfilms, Ann Arbor, 1974), pp. 15f. A transliteration, translation and photographs of UET 6/10 with some newly joined fragments are given by S. N. Kramer, PAPS 124 (1980), pp. 295-312. See also the comments by B. Alster in Acta Sumerologica 18 (1996), 1-18. New photographs are given here on plates A-D and a copy of the lower edge on plate 3. As can be seen from the photographs, the tablet is split and badly distorted, so that the various fragments could not be rejoined in such a way that the different parts of a line are always directly aligned.

Comparing the present state of the tablet with the photograph published by Kramer in PAPS 124, three small fragments, Kramer's Cb, E, and N, have been added by Shaffer at the top left corner of the Reverse. Of the other small fragments copied by Kramer Ba+Bb+Bc+D have been joined together to form a complete upper or lower edge, but this edge appears to be too narrow to be the missing lower edge of UET 6/10+433, so it is presented here separately as no. 436. The main tablet, UET 6/10+433, has Kramer's lines 1-63 and traces of 64 on the obverse, and Kramer's lines 70-end on the reverse. This corresponds to lines 236/237-415 in Ferrara's forthcoming edition

No. 434. Kramer's Fragment A: Kramer's lines 57-61.

No. 435. Kramer's Fragment Ca: Kramer's lines 67-72; ruling along the left edge.

No. 436. Kramer's Ba+Bb+Bc+D: Kramer's lines 62-66 on obverse and 67-70 on reverse; ruling along the left edge. The dotted line to the left of the copy indicates the expected width of the fragment if it were to match the upper edge of UET 6/10+433. The apparent three vertical rulings on the left edge of Ba do not appear to be replicated on UET 6/10+433, which has a single vertical ruling. If UET 6/10+433 and no. 436 belong to two different exemplars, then no. 434 may belong with no. 436 and no. 435 with UET 6/10+433.

Note that the other small fragments copied by Kramer in PAPS 124, p. 302, are recopied below as nos. 439-446. BM 69737 copied by Kramer has been recopied and republished as CT 58, 59. See also nos. 447-463 below.

No. 437 (29+73+89). Extract tablet: joined fragments of a one-column tablet, obverse and reverse. The first extract is from Inana's Descent to the Netherworld (1.4.1); lines 1´-13´ list the temples, lines 7f. of the composition in the 'long version' (cf. W. R. Sladek, *Inanna's Descent to the Netherworld* (University Microfilms, Ann Arbor, 1974) pp. 183f.), with the inclusion here of Larsa (line 5´). The continuation is a variant of the 'double-line' recension with lines 14, 16, 17, 18, 23, and perhaps 22 of the composition; the reverse gives lines 24, 20, 27?, 29, 31, and a variant line; cf. W. R. Sladek, op. cit., pp. 71f., for the order of the paraphernalia. Compare also no. 438 below. The second extract, rev. lines 7f., is an Inana self-praise text, 'a-a-mu an ma-an-ze$_2$-em$_3$', 'My father An has given me', similar to W. H. Ph. Römer, Orientalia n.s. 38 (1969), pp. 97f.

Note that there is no space or double ruling between the two extracts.

No. 438 (93). Inana and her Temples: fragment of a one-column tablet, obverse and reverse; an 'e$_2$-eš$_2$-dam' text; duplicates OECT I, pl. 15 iii lines 5f., with variants in line order.

Nos. 439-463. The following fragments of undetermined content are all written in the same small script as UET 6/10+433 and many of the other fragments of Inana's Descent to the Netherworld, and are placed here in case they may be found to be part of that composition or its variant.

Nos. 439-446. Fragments previously copied by Kramer, PAPS 124 (1980), p. 302, as fragments F, G, H, I, J, K, L, M.

Nos. 447-449. Unnumbered fragments stored with UET 6/10+433 but not previously copied.

No. 450 (219). Fragment, one side only.

No. 451 (224). Fragment, one side only.

No. 452 (275). Fragment, obv. and rev.

No. 453 (299+504). Fragment, one side only.

No. 454 (300). Fragment, edge and reverse.

No. 455 (314). Fragment, one side only.

No. 456 (417). Fragment, one side only.

No. 457 (423). Fragment, one side only.

No. 458 (501). Flake.

No. 459 (553). Fragment, one side only.

No. 460 (555). Fragment, one side only.

No. 461 (558). Fragment, one side only.

No. 462 (560). Fragment, one side only.

No. 463 (562). Fragment, one side only.

Note that no. 495 below (Gilgameš? fragment) is written in a similar script.

Nos. 464-467. Dumuzi's Dream (1.4.3); see B. Alster, *Dumui's Dream* (Mesopotamia 1, Copenhagen, 1972).

No. 464 (243+480). Obverse fragment; just touches no. 465; cited as source H in Alster, op. cit., pages 45 and 49; lines 11-22.

No. 465 (114+155). Joined obverse fragments of a multi-column tablet; no. 464 is an upper fragment of this tablet but only just touches no. 465 without a secure join; cited as sources M$_1$ and M$_2$ in Alster, op. cit., pages 45 and 49; lines 25-40. Note obv. 11´, ^{d}nin-SIG$_7$.AMA (not ^{d}nin-BUL.AMA, as edition, ibid. p. 56. line 35) to be read ^{d}nin-imma$_3$^{ama}.

No. 466 (60). Reverse fragment; joins UET 6/187; cited as source e$_2$ in Alster, op. cit., pp. 46 and 49, lines 138-144a.

No. 467 (118). Fragment, one side only; lines 260-261; not used in the published edition by Alster.

Nos. 468-475. Other Dumuzi texts.

No. 468 (241). Fragment of a multi-column tablet; obverse and reverse. Duplicates Scheil, RA 8, figure opposite p. 161 and p. 162-169, an eršemma of Inana and Dumuzi, edited in M. E. Cohen, *Sumerian Hymnology*, pp. 71-84. Obv. col. i, unplaced; col. ii = lines 33?-38 and unplaced lines; rev. col. i, around line 97, col. ii uninscribed.

No. 469 (81). Fragment of a multi-column tablet; obverse and reverse; duplicates no. 470 below.

No. 470 (110). Obverse fragment, probably of a multi-column tablet; duplicates no. 469 obverse and reverse.
No. 471 (175). Fragment of a one-column tablet; obverse and reverse.
No. 472 (186). Fragment of a one-column tablet; obverse, reverse uninscribed.
No. 473 (249). Fragment of a one-column tablet; obverse, reverse badly rubbed but where preserved uninscribed with traces of some lines at right angles made with the stylus.
No. 474 (508). Fragment, one side only; mentions ᵈ$\tilde{g}$eštin-a[n-n]a in line 2´.
No. 475 (622). Flake, one side only.

Nos. 476-479. The Exploits of Ninurta (Lugal-e) (1.6.2); see J. J. van Dijk, *Lugal ud me-lám-bi nir-$\tilde{g}$ál* (Leiden, 1983), with details of these exemplars in vol. II. p. 17.
No. 476 (260+477). Joined fragments of a one-column tablet, obverse and reverse; obv., lines 6-25, rev., lines 26-53; partly cited by van Dijk as source B$_3$.
No. 477 (94). Fragment of a multi-column tablet; obv., lines 457-462, rev., lines 465-469; cited by van Dijk as source C$_3$.
No. 478 (70). Fragment of reverse; lines 527-532 (529 omitted); cited by van Dijk as source D$_3$; note variant in line 530, zadim for za-e-gim.
No. 479 (237). Fragment of a one-column tablet, obverse and reverse; obv., lines 664-665, 667-682; rev., lines 694-709; cited by van Dijk as source E$_3$.

No. 480 (20). Ninurta and the Turtle (also known as Ninurta's Pride and Punishment) (1.6.3). Fragment of a one-column tablet; cf. S. N. Kramer, Aula Orientalis 2 (1984) pp. 231f., where this fragment is transliterated in note 1. The identification of obverse and reverse is uncertain, but the "obverse" apparently duplicates the beginning of UET 6/2, while the "reverse" is unplaced.

No. 481 (221). Nin$\tilde{g}$išzida's Journey to the Netherworld (previously Nin$\tilde{g}$išzida and Damu) (1.7.3). Fragment, obverse and reverse; obv., lines 1-2; rev., lines 58(?)-59. Possibly part of the same tablet as UET 6/23.

Nos. 482-488. Gilgameš, Enkidu and the Netherworld (1.8.1.4). A new edition of this text by Alhena Gadotti (Baltimore) is in preparation. A French translation is given by A. Shaffer and R. J. Tournay, *L'épopée de Gilgamesh* (Littératures anciennes du Proche-Orient 15, Paris, 1994), pp. 248-274. For an English translation see A. R. George, *The Epic of Gilgamesh* (London, 1999), pp. 175-195, and for a partial edition (lines 172-end) with English translation see A. R. George, *The Babylonian Gilgamesh Epic* (Oxford, 2003), pp. 743-777.

No. 482 (23). Fragment of a one-column tablet; obv., lines 65-76, rev., lines 119-126; probably part of the same tablet as nos. 483 and 484.
No. 483 (30+298). Joined fragments of a one-column tablet; obv., lines 75-86 (83 omitted); rev., lines 111-120; obverse badly rubbed.
No. 484 (19). Fragment of a one-column tablet; obv., lines 85-90, rev., lines 106-107 (108); small fragments of the text as copied by Shaffer are now missing.
No. 485 (134). Fragment of a multi-column tablet; obv., lines 100-102, rev., lines 161, 155, 162-164.
No. 486 (18+192+301). Joined fragments of a one-column tablet; obv., lines 201-218, rev., lines 255-267; perhaps part of the same tablet as no. 487.
No. 487 (284+393). U.5635. Joined fragments of a one-column tablet; obv., lines 226-234 (omitting line 232), lower edge and rev., lines 238-247.
No. 488 (473). Fragment of a one-column tablet; obv., lines 219-221, 221a, 221b, rev., variant recension before and after lines 248, 249 and 253.

Nos. 489-494. Gilgameš and Huwawa A (1.8.1.5) (previously Gilgamesh and the Cedar Forest: or Gilgamesh and the Land of the Living): see the edition by D. O. Edzard, 'Gilgameš und Huwawa', in ZA 80 (1990) 165-203 and 81 (1991) 165-233. A French translation is given by A. Shaffer and R. J. Tournay, *L'épopée de Gilgamesh* (Littératures anciennes du Proche-Orient 15, Paris, 1994), pp. 292-305. For an English translation see A. R. George, *The Epic of Gilgamesh* (London, 1999), pp. 149-166.
Nos. 489-491 are parts of a tablet containing the complete text of the epic and having two columns on each side.
No. 489 (399). Flake from the upper left corner of the obverse; beginning of col. i. Cited as source UrB in D. O. Edzard, loc. cit.
No. 490 (86+154+400). Joined fragments of a four-column tablet; joins UET 6/50+51+53 (50 and 53 join "back to back"); lower part of col. i, middle of col. iii and upper part of col. iv. Cited as part of source UrA in D. O. Edzard, loc. cit. The copies of the joined fragments are not fully joined on the plate.
No. 491 (14+63). Fragment, obverse and reverse, containing the end of col. ii and the beginning of col. iii. Cited as part of source UrA in D. O. Edzard, loc. cit.
No. 492 (268). Fragment, one side only. Cited as source UrC in D. O. Edzard, loc. cit.
No. 493 (539). Fragment, one side only. Cited as source UrD in D. O. Edzard, loc. cit.
No. 494 (68+146). Joined fragments of a one-column tablet; joins UET 6/52 (recopied here); obv. and rev. Cited as source UrG in D. O. Edzard, loc. cit.

No. 495 (550). Sumerian literary: fragment, obverse and reverse; mentions Gilgameš in rev. 4´. The script of this fragment is similar to the tablets of Inana's Descent to the Netherworld; see nos. 420-463 above.

No. 496 (205).   Lugalbanda in the Mountain Cave (Lugalbanda and Hurrum) (1.8.2.1). Fragment, one side only; lines 229-237 with two additional lines after line 232.

No. 497 (40+534).   Enmerkar and the Lord of Aratta (1.8.2.3). Joined fragments of a one-column tablet; joins UET 6/47; obv. lines 178-190, 215-235. See S. Cohen, *Enmerkar and the Lord of Aratta* (University Microfilms, Ann Arbor, 1973), where this text is cited as text Q but not fully used; the complete join restores the colophon, and thereby yields the incipit (previously known only from literary catalogues) as:
   im-[gi]d$_2$-da 4-kam-ma
   uru-k[i-g]u$_4$-huš an-uraš ni$_2$-gal gur$_3$-ru
and also shows that the complete lines 235a-c of MS Q are identical to lines 181-183.

No. 498 (321).   Mythological text: fragment, one side only; joins UET 6/29 (join by Ludwig).

No. 499 (100).   Mythological text: reverse fragment of a multi-column tablet; joins UET 6/30 (join by Ludwig); duplicates UET 6/29+498.

No. 500 (39).   Mythological text with cosmogonic introduction: probably a school text; upper obverse fragment of a one-column tablet; the text on the obverse runs round to the reverse. The reverse has remains of two lines written perpendicular to the direction of writing on the obverse, one with the incipit [ud n]am-lu$_2$-l[u$_7$ ...], the second with [...] ^{d}lu$_2$-x-[...] (where x = la[l$_3$?), perhaps part of the personal name of the scribe(?).

No. 501 (161).   Epic or mythological composition: fragment of a multi-column tablet; one side only, two columns preserved.

No. 502 (182).   Epic or mythological text: reverse fragment of a multi-column tablet; mentions "the great door of Eridu". See D. R. Frayne, ZA 88, 6-19, who quotes this fragment as UET 6/3 *182 (on pp. 16-17) and suggests that it is a part of Išme-Dagan A+V (nos. 526-529 below); it is, however, certain that this is not part of the same tablet as those fragments, and there seems to be no clear evidence that it is part of the same composition.

No. 503 (506).   Mythological text: joined fragments of a one-column tablet, obverse and reverse; reverse has a colophon added lightly.

Nos. 504-564.   Historical texts, laments and royal hymns.

Nos. 504-505.   The Sumerian King List (2.1.1). See T. Jacobsen, *The Sumerian King List* (Assyriological Studies 11, Chicago, 1939).

No. 504 (263).   Fragment of a multi-column tablet, obverse, reverse and left edge. Obv. col. i has Jacobsen's col. i lines 19-24 (Larak), followed by Bad-Tibira, reversing the usual order; col. ii has Jacobsen's col. i lines 38 and 40-43 (Kish). Reverse gives summations of dynastic totals. In format the tablet, with a narrow blank left edge and archaizing script, is similar to nos. 599 and 648.

No. 505 (208b).   Fragment, one side only; col. v 34-42; cf. Jacobsen, op. cit., pp. 103-104.

Nos. 506-507.   The Curse of Agade (2.1.5).

No. 506 (176).   Fragment of a one-column tablet; obverse, reverse uninscribed; extract tablet of couplets, lines 126?-127, 173-174, 200-201, 213-214; cited as source D$_4$ in J. S. Cooper, *The Curse of Agade* (Baltimore and London, 1983), p. 70; inscribed along the long axis.

No. 507 (525).   Fragment of a multi-column tablet, obv. = lines 1-7, rev. = lines 254-257.

Nos. 508-509.   The Lament for Ur (= Lamentation over the Destruction of Ur) (2.2.2). See W. H. Ph. Römer, *Die Klage über die Zerstörung von Ur* (AOAT 309, 2004).

No. 508 (25).   Reverse fragment; joins UET 6/136; the join is to the lower right corner of the reverse, without a direct join of text; lines 111-116, plus four unplaced (variant) lines (line 111 corresponds to line 107 in Gadd's copy); cf. S.N. Kramer, *Lamentation over the Destruction of Ur* (Assyriological Studies 12, Chicago, 1940).

No. 509 (290).   Fragment, one side only; possibly part of the same tablet as UET 6/139b (U.16900N; not copied in UET 6 part 2), but does not join; lines 206-208.

Nos. 510-514.   The Lament for Sumer and Ur (= Lamentation over the Destruction of Sumer and Ur) (2.2.3). See P. Michalowski, *Lamentation over the Destruction of Sumer and Ur* (Winona Lake, 1989).

No. 510 (24+43+139+242).   Joined fragments of a four-column tablet; obv. i, lines 1-9, 12-16, 20-27, rev. iii, lines 66-69 and 1-9, rev. iv, blank; probably part of the same tablet as UET 6/126 and 6/127, forming a practice tablet where the scribe began anew three times, the first time doing lines 1-ca. 60, the second time lines 1-69, and the third time not much more than ten lines. Cited by Michalowski, op. cit., as source DD (but note that his reference on p. 32 to a join to UET 6 °434 was an error for UET 6 °43); see also the photograph on pl. 16.

No. 511 (157).   Reverse fragment; lines 309-326; joins UET 6/130. Cited by Michalowski, op. cit., as source GG.

No. 512 (21+22).   Fragment of a one-column tablet; obv., at least lines 95-98, rev., at least lines 123-130. Cited by Michalowski, op. cit., as source LL; the problem of the identification of the reverse is discussed on pp. 25-26; see also the photograph on pl. 17.

No. 513 (26). Fragment, possibly of a multi-column tablet; right edge, lower obverse (only traces of wedges and the ends of line 414-415 overflowing onto the right edge) and upper reverse, lines 418-427. Cited by Michalowski, op. cit., as source MM; see also the photograph on pl. 17.

No. 514 (272). Fragment, one side only; four unplaced lines, then lines 335-347. Cited by Michalowski, op. cit., as source NN; see also the photograph on pl. 17.

No. 515 (61+85+138). Lament over the Destruction of Nippur (Ur version) (2.2.4). Joined fragments of a one-column tablet; joins UET 6/143; not used in the published edition of the Nippur Lament by S. Tinney.

Nos. 516-517. Lament over the Destruction of Uruk (2.2.5).
No. 516 (239). Fragment, possibly of a multi-column tablet, obverse and reverse; lines 1.22-1.27 and 4.15-4.21. See M. W. Green, JAOS 104/2 (1984), p. 255; cf. UET 6/63 and 6/141.
No. 517 (409). Fragment, obverse and reverse; lines 2.16´-2.22´; cf. Green, op. cit., 253f.

No. 518 (147). Hymn to Ur-Nammu D (The Coronation of Ur-Nammu = Ur-Nammu the canal-digger), Ur recension (2.4.1.4). Fragment of a one-column tablet; joins UET 6/76; obv., lines 1´-5´, rev., lines 38´-40´. See W. W. Hallo, JCS 20 (1966), pp. 133-141, E. Flückiger-Hawker, *Urnamma of Ur in Sumerian Literary Tradition* (OBO 166), p. 228-259 and pls. 21-22 (photographs), and S. Tinney, JCS 51, 31f-49 and pl. II (photographs).

Nos. 519-520. Self Praise of Šulgi (Šulgi A) (2.4.2.1).
No. 519 (402+403). Joined fragments of a multi-column tablet; joins UET 6/78. Cited by J. Klein, *Three Šulgi Hymns* (Ramat Gan, 1981), pp. 235f.; on p. 236 line 28 read he-em-si-sa$_2$, and line 30 end, uš or du. The colophon on UET 6/78 has to be read šu-nigin$_2$ 60+50 (=110); this figure accounts for the eight extra lines of text in the Ur recension of Šulgi A, of which seven are preserved here (86 a-c and 86 g-j in Klein, op. cit., pp. 236-237); only one line is missing at col. iv. top.
No. 520 (617). U.11696; fragment, obverse, reverse uninscribed; obv., lines 1-6.

No. 521 (2+3+4+5+10a). The Execration of Shulgi's Enemies (Šulgi S) (2.4.2.19). Joined fragments of a one-column tablet, a šir$_3$ nam-erim$_2$-ma text ('hostile song') with a-mu-zu sections; against the invocation in oath by the king's enemies of the power of the divine names. Duplicates are UET 6/93 and 6/94 and ISET 1, pl. 184 Ni. 9783; compare OECT V, pp. 20f., no. 8.

The reverse has traces of a colophon: [i]m-gid$_2$!-da z[ag!?-til-la].

No. 522 (430). Šulgi text; U.7774. Fragment of a one-column tablet, obverse, reverse, lower and left edge; deeply inscribed late ductus; possibly a Kassite period copy. The tablet has a reddish slip over yellowish clay. The incipit of the composition, ur-^{d}lama-ra, is possibly found in the Ur literary catalogue, UET 6/196, rev. line 4´; see A. Shaffer in A. R. George and I. L. Finkel (eds.), *Wisdom, Gods and Literature: Studies in Assyriology in Honour of W. G. Lambert* (Eisenbrauns, 2000), p. 433; see also no. 789 below.

Nos. 523-524. Amar-Suen and Enki's Temple (2.4.3.1).
No. 523 (327). U.5307; joins UET 8/33; cf. ibid., p. 7. See also no. 524, which may be part of the same composition.
No. 524 (487). Fragment, top of a one-column tablet; possibly joins UET 8/32, and possibly part of the same composition as no. 523.

No. 525 (38). Išbi-Erra text: lower left obverse fragment of a multi-column(?) tablet concerning Nippur (line 3) and the Ekur (line 5); Išbi-Erra is mentioned in line 4´.

Nos. 526-529. Royal Hymn of Išme-Dagan, Išme-Dagan A+V (^{d}en-lil$_2$ diri-še$_3$) (2.5.4.01 + 2.5.4.22). See W. H. Ph. Romer, *Sumerische 'Königshymnen' der Isin-Zeit*, pp. 39-55 (Išme-Dagan A), M.-C. Ludwig, *Untersuchungen zu den Hymnen des Išme-Dagan von Isin* (SANTAG 2, 1990), p. 2, 161-225 (Išme-Dagan V), and D. R. Frayne, ZA 88, 6-19 (comments on the reconstruction of the present fragments). Four fragments probably from the same multi-column tablet in archaizing script. Note, however, that the intercolumnar rulings are much clearer on no. 526 than on the other fragments. Assuming that the fragments do all belong together then the tablet had at least 10 columns on each side, and the text of the fragments is described on that basis. No. 502 (182) above, which Frayne treats as a fragment of the final column of this tablet, is quite certainly not a part of this tablet, having a larger script and a blank final column. It is not at all clear that it is part of the same composition.
No. 526 (52+96). Joined fragments of a multi-column tablet; joins UET 8/95. Including that join the lines attested are now (according to the numbering in ETCSL): obv. i, lost; obv. ii, lines 33-35; obv. iii, lines 58-61; obv. iv, lines 80-87; obv. v, lines 106-114; obv. vi, lines 135-141; what remains of the reverse, three or four broken lines, is unplaceable.
No. 527 (255). Obverse fragment of a multi-column tablet; col. vi, line 140?, col. vii, lines 167-169, col. viii, lines 191-193, col. ix, 219-221.
No. 528 (109). Obverse fragment of a multi-column tablet; col. ix, lines 215-216; col. x, lines 244-248; the

subsurface clay suggests the loss of at least one more column.

No. 529 (16+145+208a). Joined reverse fragments of a multi-column tablet; col. i´, lines 316-318; col. ii´, lines 336-346; col. iii´, 366-370; col. iv´, 399-401. Cited as source C in Ludwig, op. cit., with photograph on pl. 8. There is certainly no join to no. 526 as suggested by Frayne.

Nos. 530-532. Royal Hymn, Lipit-Ištar A (2.5.5.1), see W. H. Ph. Römer, *Sumerische 'Königshymnen' der Isin-Zeit*, pp. 29f.
No. 530 (141). Fragment of a one-column tablet, upper edge of one side only; lines 30-35.
No. 531 (159). Fragment of a one-column tablet; obv. and rev., lines 97-103.
No. 532 (395). U.5621/U.5656 (apparently numbered twice); fragment of a one-column tablet; obv., lines 49-58, rev., lines 90-96, one unidentified line on the left edge.

No. 533 (8+188+289). Royal Hymn, Sin-iddinam B (2.6.6.2). Joined fragments; joins UET 6/99, restoring part of the beginning of obv. col. iii and supplementing rev. col. iv and v. Originally the six-column tablet consisted of about 230 'short-lines', being five columns of 40 lines each and a sixth column of 12 lines.

Nos. 534-537. Royal Hymns of Rim-Sin; cf. UET 6/90-92.
No. 534 (234). Fragment of a large, probably multi-column, tablet; joins UET 8/88 (note that in UET 8, pl. XXII, no. 88 is erroneously labelled '89' and vice versa).
No. 535 (258). Fragment, obverse and reverse.
No. 536 (55). Fragment, obverse and reverse, not further identified, but perhaps a Rim-Sin text .
No. 537 (166). Fragment, one side only.

Nos. 538-556. Other royal hymns or inscriptions
No. 538 (101+194+199). Royal hymn(?), Isin-Larsa style(?): joined reverse fragments; joins UET 6/88. The hymn was identified as one for Lipit-Ishtar in UET 6, part 1, p. 9. This was based on a reading of the incomplete obv. 2´ of no. 88 as dL[i-pi$_2$-it-eš$_4$-tar$_2$ ...]; one of the joined fragments shows the reading to be dingir en$_3$-tar-tar.
No. 539 (122+125). Royal hymn: joined reverse fragments of a one-column tablet.
No. 540 (232). Royal hymn: fragment of a multi-column tablet, obverse and reverse; archaizing script.
No. 541 (281). Royal hymn: fragment of a multi-column tablet, one side only.
No. 542 (527). Royal hymn: fragment, obverse and reverse.
No. 543 (544). Royal hymn: fragment, one side only.
No. 544 (585). Royal hymn: fragment, obverse, reverse uninscribed.

No. 545 (9). Royal hymn or inscription: obverse fragment of a multi-column tablet; two columns preserved.
No. 546 (325). Royal hymn or inscription: U.8806A; fragment, one side only; archaizing script.
No. 547 (13). Royal inscription, Ibbi-Sin: obverse, reverse uninscribed. Joins UET 8/36Q; cf. ibid. pp. 7f., and H. Steible, *Die neusumerischen Bau- und Weihinschriften* (Freiburger Altorientalische Studien, 9/2, 1991), pp. 279-281, Ibbi-Suen 1-2. Despite the fact that Shaffer copies only the fragment which he joined to the fragment previously identified by Sollberger, we include this copy in order to draw attention to Sollberger's suggestion that the tablet was an Old Babylonian copy, and therefore possibly part of the group of Old Babylonian copies of historical texts found at 7 Quiet Street.
No. 548 (47+153). Royal inscription(?): fragment of a multi-column tablet, obverse and reverse. The copies of the joined fragments are not fully joined on the plate.
No. 549 (112). Royal inscription: fragment of a one-column tablet; obverse and reverse; archaizing copy.
No. 550 (609). Royal inscription: fragment, one side only.
No. 551 (485). Royal inscription, Išme-Dagan: fragment, one side only.
No. 552 (486). Royal inscription, Šu-Suen: fragment, obverse and reverse.
No. 553 (27). Royal inscription(?): reverse fragment, obverse destroyed; note lugal-am$_3$, line 1´.
No. 554 (578). Sumerian text of undetermined content: school text, mentioning Samsu-iluna; reverse fragment.
No. 555 (251). Copy of an inscription on a statue of Lama: fragment of a multi-column tablet, obverse and reverse; signed by the scribe šu dInana-x; no. 556 is possibly part of the same tablet.
No. 556 (273). Fragment, one side only.

Nos. 557-564. Letters.

No. 557 (532). Letter of Aradmu to Šulgi (3.1.01): obverse fragment; joins UET 6/174, at the top of col. b, restoring lines 19-25 of the letter; see P. Michalowski, *The Royal Correspondence of Ur* (University Microfilms, Ann Arbor, 1972), pp. 135 ff.
No. 558 (264). Letter of Puzur-Šulgi to Ibbi-Sin (3.1.19): joined fragments of a poorly preserved one-column tablet, obverse and reverse; lines 1-36. See F. Ali, *Sumerian Letters* (University Microfilms, Ann Arbor, 1964), letter collection A-3, pp. 42f. Cited as source O in P. Michalowski, op. cit., pp. 253 ff.
No. 559 (225). Letter of Sin-iddinam, king of Larsa, to Ninisina (3.2.06); joined fragments of a one-column tablet; joins UET 8/70. Cited as sources C and F by W. W. Hallo in *Kramer Anniversary Volume* (AOAT 25, 1976), pp. 214f. The copy here is a composite of Edmond Sollberger's copy of the obverse from UET 8/70 (top) plus Shaffer's copy of the new fragment

(lower part); the reverse of the new fragment is lost.

No. 560 (149). Letter of Uršaga to a king (3.3.01): fragment of reverse; lines 12-14. See F. Ali, op. cit., letter B-6, p. 81.

No. 561 (187). Letter of Ur-dun, the dam-gar$_3$: obverse and reverse. This is not the known letter of Ur-dun.

No. 562 (428). Royal letter or letter prayer: duplicate to TCL 16, 57, for which see also van Dijk, *La sagesse suméro-accadienne*, p. 5. Complete excerpt tablet with glosses; landscape orientation. The tablet is marked in pencil U.17818a, but according to the excavation register U.17818 comprised two broken circular tablets found in the filling of PG/1848.

No. 563 (425). Sumerian letter or letter prayer: fragment of a one-column tablet, obverse and reverse.

No. 564 (427). Letter of Nanna-ki-aǧ to Lipit-Ištar (3.2.03): fragment, one side only; lines 7-14. Identified by P. Michalowski.

Nos. 565-610. Hymns to deities, temples and cities.

Nos. 565-566. Enlil Hymn, ^{d}en-lil$_2$ su$_3$-ra$_2$-še$_3$, "Enlil in the Ekur" (4.05.1); cf. D. Reisman, *Two Neo-Sumerian Royal Hymns* (University Microfilms, Ann Arbor, 1969), pp. 42f., and the recent edition by W. H. Ph. Römer in Bibliotheca Orientalis 47 (1990), 381ff.

No. 565 (548). Fragment, obverse and reverse; joins UET 6/65, restoring the beginnings of lines 67-69 and 108-113; note the "10" (Winkelhaken) in the left margin against lines 69 and 109, reflecting the fact that this tablet begins with line 60.

No. 566 (62). Joined fragments of a one-column tablet; probably part of the same tablet as UET 6/65+565; signs on the lower edge (glosses?) are impressed lightly (added later?); obv. and rev., lines 73-101.

No. 567 (323+398). Sumerian Literary Compendium: U.8820; joined fragments of an originally three-column tablet, obverse and reverse; 1. obverse, The Exaltation of Inana, nin-me-šar-ra (4.07.2): obv. ii, lines 50-65, obv. iii, lines 101-118, cited as source 'UrF' in A. Zgoll, *Der Rechtsfall der En-ḫedu-Ana im Lied nin-me-šara* (AOAT 246, 1997), 199; cf. nos. 568-569 below and the literature cited there; 2. reverse, the Enlil hymn, ^{d}en-lil$_2$ su$_3$-ra$_2$-še$_3$ (4.05.1): rev. iv, lines 28-45, rev. v, lines 129-133; cf. nos. 565-566 above and the literature cited there.

Nos. 568-569. Exaltation of Inana, nin-me-šar-ra (4.07.2), see W. W. Hallo and J. van Dijk, *The Exaltation of Inanna* (Yale Near Eastern Researches 3, New Haven and London, 1968), and A. Zgoll, AOAT 246 (see no. 567 above).

No. 568 (151). Fragment of a one-column tablet; obv., lines 141-146, rev., lines 147-149;

No. 569 (408). Reverse fragment; lines 103-109.

Nos. 570-571. Hymn to Inana, in-nin ša$_3$-gur$_4$-ra (4.07.3); see A. W. Sjöberg, ZA 65 (1975), pp. 161-253.

No. 570 (418). Fragment, obverse and reverse of a one-column tablet; rev., lines 132-139, obv., presumably preceding lines.

No. 571 (424). Reverse of a one-column tablet; lines 183-192 (partly filling a gap after line 187). The obverse is entirely destroyed, but the ends of some lines overlap onto the reverse.

No. 572 (34). Inana-Dumuzi song (4.08.11): fragment, probably of a multi-column tablet. With the first line compare the incipit in the tablet catalogue UET 5, no. 86, line 4, guruš lu$_2$ šir$_3$-ra-ra (see the recent edition by D. Charpin, *Le Clergé d'Ur au siècle d'Hammurabi*, pp. 453f.); probably part of the same tablet as no. 573.

No. 573 (53). Inana-Dumuzi song: large flake; probably part of the same tablet as no. 572.

No. 574 (387). The Lament of Lisin (4.10.1): U.5628; fragment of a one-column tablet; joins UET 6/144 (U.8810 B); obv., lines 1-10; rev., lines 67-77.

No. 575 (390). Hymn(?), mentioning Marduk: U.5631; fragment, one side only. Compare the texts edited by J. van Dijk, Mitteilungen des Instituts für Orientforschung XII/2 (Berlin, 1966), 57-74.

Nos. 576-577. Hymns to Nanna.

No. 576 (58). Fragment of a one-column tablet; obverse and reverse; written along the long axis of the tablet ('landscape orientation').

No. 577 (117). Fragment, one side only; rubrics sa-gid$_2$-da and [giš-gi$_4$-ga]l$_2$-bi.

No. 578 (127+256). Joined fragments of a multi-column tablet; bilingual.

Nos. 579-584. Nidaba and Enki hymn, Nidaba hymn A, nin mul-an-gim (4.16.1); see W. W. Hallo in *Actes de la XVIIe Rencontre Assyriologique* (Bruxelles, 1970), pp. 116f.

No. 579 (6+17+28+95+8/92). Bilingual version: new reverse fragments of a multi-column tablet, including one first published as UET 8/92 (recopied here), which join UET 6/388; cited by Hallo, loc. cit., as texts D and D1. Note that new material has been joined to the tablet since Hallo's edition; in total the additions to UET 6/388 add in col. b parts of lines 40, 47, 45, 46 and 48, and in col. c parts of lines 51-56.

No. 580 (288). Bilingual version: fragment, probably of a multi-column tablet, obverse and reverse; obv., 1´-4´ unplaced Akkadian, 5´-6´ = line 10, rev., lines 56-57 of the bilingual version.

No. 581 (397). Bilingual version: reverse fragment; lines 35-37 with Akkadian translation of line 35.

No. 582 (72). Fragment, obverse and reverse; joins UET 6/66 "back to back" and these join UET 6/71;

17

UET 6/66+71 were joined by Hallo in 1969 and are cited by Hallo, loc. cit., as text C (ignoring the new fragment); obv., lines 6-15, rev., line 55; note among variants, line 9, ki-im(=ni$_2$) si-ud-da for ki-GAR(=ni$_3$)-a šed$_x$-de$_3$.

No. 583 (250). Fragment of a one-column tablet, obverse and reverse; obv., lines 1-20, rev., lines 43-57; cited by Hallo, loc. cit., as text F.

No. 584 (106). Fragment of a one-column tablet; obv. lines 9-15, rev. lines 41-48.

Nos. 585-588. Hymns to Ningal.

No. 585 (77). Fragment of a one-column tablet; obverse, reverse uninscribed; joins UET 6/189.

No. 586 (144). Fragment of a one-column tablet; obverse and reverse.

No. 587 (143). Fragment of a multi-column tablet; obverse and reverse; archaizing script.

No. 588 (471). Fragment of a multi-column tablet; obverse and reverse; archaizing script; perhaps part of the same tablet as no. 587.

No. 589 (442). Hymn to Ninḡišzida: fragment of an excerpt tablet, obverse and reverse.

No. 590 (7). Hymn to Ningublaga (Ningublaga C) (4.20.3): upper left obverse fragment of a possibly multi-column tablet; for the incipit, [luga]l me-lam$_2$-zu UD [...], cf. E. Ebeling, *Keilschrifttexte aus Assur religiösen Inhalts*, 158 iii 5 lu-gal me-le-em-zu NI [...].

No. 591 (600). Hymn to Ninšubur (4.25.99): fragment, obverse and reverse; reverse uninscribed.

No. 592 (74). Adab, perhaps of Ninurta: fragment of a one-column tablet; obverse and reverse.

Nos. 593-594. Hymn to Nungal A (Nungal in the E-kur) (4.28.1); see A. Sjöberg, Archiv für Orientforschung 24 (1973) 19f.

No. 593 (172). Fragment, obv. and rev.; obv. = lines 23-24.

No. 594 (435). Fragment, one side only; lines 85-90

Nos. 595-596. Hymns to Suen.

No. 595 (90). Fragment, obverse and reverse.

No. 596 (92). Reverse fragment.

Nos. 597-601. The Collection of Sumerian Temple Hymns (4.80.1): see A. Sjöberg, TCS 3.

No. 597 (231). Fragment of a one-column tablet, obverse and reverse; obv., lines 39-45, rev., lines 54-59; cited as source F$_1$ in Sjöberg, TCS 3, pp. 14 and 19-20; archaizing script.

No. 598 (91). Joined fragments of a one-column tablet; bilingual; obv. and rev., lines 51-59; text cited as F$_2$ in Sjöberg, TCS 3, pp. 14 and 19-20, but the Akkadian text was not used.

No. 599 (322). U.7782; fragment of a multi-column tablet; obv. i´, lines 196-200, obv. ii´, lines 211-215, rev. iii´, lines 246-254, rev. iv´, lines 273-278; cf. Sjöberg, TCS 3, pp. 29-33; archaizing script. In format the tablet, with a narrow blank right edge, is similar to nos. 504 and 648.

No. 600 (158). Fragment, probably of a multi-column tablet; obv. and rev., lines 246-248; cf. Sjöberg, TCS 3, 31.

No. 601 (481). Fragment, one side only; around lines 263-265; cf. Sjöberg, TCS 3, p. 32.

Nos. 602-605. The Keš Hymn (4.80.2); see G. B. Gragg, in TCS 3, pp. 155-188.

No. 602 (11). Fragment of a one-column tablet; obverse and reverse; lines 112-119 and 122-127; cf. Gragg, TCS 3, pp. 174-175; joins UET 6/116.

No. 603 (49). Upper half of a one-column tablet containing, according to the colophon at rev. 6´, the fifth stanza of the hymn; obv., very faint traces, lines 74f. (not copied); rev., lines 83-86; cf. Gragg, TCS 3, p. 172.

No. 604 (103). Obverse fragment; lines 38-42; cf. Gragg, TCS 3, p. 169.

No. 605 (164). Obverse fragment; lines 20-32; cf. Gragg, TCS 3, p. 174f.

Nos. 606-610. Hymns to Ur.

No. 606 (226). Hymn to Ur: fragment of a multi-column tablet, obverse, lower edge, reverse and left edge.

No. 607 (229). Hymn, mentioning the Ekišnugal temple: fragment, obverse and reverse.

No. 608 (230). Hymn, mentioning the Ekišnugal temple: fragment of a multi-column tablet, obverse and reverse.

No. 609 (257). Hymn, mentioning the Ekišnugal temple: fragment, obverse, lower edge and reverse.

No. 610 (244). Hymn to the priestess Enanedu and Ur: fragment of a one-column tablet, obverse and reverse. For an inscription of Enanedu, en priestess of Nanna and daughter of Kudur-mabuk, presumably from Ur, see C. J. Gadd, Iraq 13 (1951), pp. 27-39 (and the recent edition by D. Frayne, RIME 4.2.14.20).

Nos. 611-618. Other hymns.

No. 611 (259). Hymn, bilingual: reverse fragment of a multi-column tablet, one side only; cf. no. 528 and UET 6/389.

No. 612 (64+142). Hymn: joined obverse fragments of a large, possibly multi-column, tablet; flake from the right edge.

No. 613 (173). Hymn: fragment, one side only; mentions Eridu.

No. 614 (201). Hymn: fragment, one side only; cf. line 4´, bar-sud$_3$-am$_3$.

No. 615 (479). Hymn, to a deity: fragment; obverse, reverse uninscribed.

No. 616 (440). Hymn, to a deity; fragment, one side only.

No. 617 (614). Hymn: fragment, one side only.

No. 618 (174). Hymn, to a city: mentions Larsa; fragment of a one-column tablet; glosses on edge and reverse; the gloss on the reverse is recopied on a larger scale by M.-C. Ludwig.

Nos. 619-620. School texts, E-dub-ba.

No. 619 (57+282+283). Dialogue between a Father and his Disobedient Son (Edubba B; 5.1.2). Joined fragments of a four-column tablet; joins UET 6/161+164 which are cited as Ur2 and Ur3 in the edition by A. Sjöberg in JCS 25 (1973), pp. 105-169; obv. i, lines 31-40, obv. ii, lines 73-89, rev. iii, lines 90-112, rev. iv, lines 139-145.

No. 620 (240). Edubba Regulations (Edubba R; 5.1.6). Fragment, obverse and reverse of a large, possibly multi-column, tablet; cf. UET 6/168 (same tablet?); duplicates PBS 1/2 98.

Nos. 621-624. Personal wisdom.

Nos. 621-622. Man and his God (5.2.4): cf. S. N. Kramer, Vetus Testamentum, Supplement 3 (Leiden, 1955), pp. 170f.; a new edition by Jacob Klein is in preparation.

No. 621 (262+497). Fragment of a multi-column tablet, obverse and reverse; obv. col. ii = lines 67-81, rev. col. iii unplaced. The two pieces join back to back, but the join has not been made as the inner surfaces give interesting evidence of how the tablet was made. Possibly part of the same tablet as no. 622.

No. 622 (197). Reverse fragment of a multi-column tablet; right col. = lines 110-122; possibly part of the same tablet as no. 621.

No. 623 (261). Ritual for a sick man: fragment, possibly of a multi-column tablet, obverse and reverse.

No. 624 (177). Personal lament: fragment of a one-column tablet.

Nos. 625-642. Contests and Dialogues.

Nos. 625-626. Contest between Hoe and Plough (5.3.1).

No. 625 (10b). Fragment of a one-column tablet; lines 80-87 and 108-113; joins UET 6/43; part of the same tablet as no. 626, but no direct join.

No. 626 (82+307). Joined fragments of a one-column tablet; obv., lines 68-77 (variant order, line 72 omitted), rev., lines 117-125 (variant order, line 118 omitted).

Nos. 627-628. Contest between Bird and Fish (5.3.5).

No. 627 (394). U.5641; fragment, obverse, lower edge, reverse; joins UET 6/40; lines 90-101.

No. 628 (472). Fragment, obv., lines 84-86, 123, 91-91; rev., lines 126-128, 130?, 137; one line runs over from reverse to obverse.

Nos. 629-631. Dialogue between Two Scribes (5.4.1).

No. 629 (130). Fragment of a one column tablet; obv., lines 44-50; rev. unplaced.

No. 630 (238). Fragment of a one-column tablet; obv., lines 53-60, rev., lines 71-80.

No. 631 (83+185+276). Joined fragments of a one-column tablet; joins UET 6/156; obv. and rev., lines 116-132.

Nos. 632-635. Dialogue between Enkihegal and Enkitalu (5.4.2).

No. 632 (105). Obverse fragment; lines 80-89 plus four unplaceable lines.

No. 633 (35+189). Joined fragments of a multi-column tablet, one side only; lines 128-151; probably part of the same tablet as no. 632 and almost certainly part of UET 6/64, just touching col. i without a secure join.

No. 634 (248). One-column tablet, obverse (faint traces, not copied) and reverse; lines 111-134.

No. 635 (426). Fragment of a one-column tablet, obverse, reverse uninscribed; lines 156-163 (omitting line 159).

Nos. 636-642. Dialogue between Two Women, B (5.4.5).

No. 636 (54). Left edge fragment of a one-column tablet; bilingual version; lower left obverse, lines 8-9, upper left reverse, lines 11-13.

No. 637 (88). Fragment of a one-column tablet; obv., lines 1-6; reverse uninscribed.

No. 638 (309). Fragment, one side only; probably reverse; lines 59-63.

No. 639 (220+278+292). Joined fragments of a one-column tablet; obv., lines 123-131 (124-125 omitted); rev., lines 168-174.

No. 640 (295). Fragment, obverse and reverse; joins UET 6/157; obv., lines 125-133; rev., lines 152-158.

No. 641 (303). Fragment of a one-column tablet, obverse and reverse; obv., lines 168-174; rev., lines 218-221.

No. 642 (37). Centre reverse fragment of a one-column tablet, line numbering uncertain, but around line 220.

Nos. 643-645. Song of the Hoe (5.5.4).

No. 643 (168). Fragment, one side only; lines 1-5; probably from the same tablet as no. 645.

No. 644 (206). Reverse fragment of a multi-column tablet; lines 79-83.

No. 645 (152). Reverse fragment of a multi-column tablet; left column, lines 105-109; right column, traces only, unplaced.

Nos. 646-648. Instructions of Šuruppak (5.6.1); see B. Alster, *Instructions of Suruppak*, Mesopotamia 2 (Copenhagen, 1974).

No. 646 (59). Fragment of a one-column tablet; obv., lines 202-208 (now 197-203); rev., lines 209-217 (now 204-212); cited as 'Ur 5' in Alster, op. cit., p. 26.

No. 647 (227). Joined fragments of a one-column tablet; obv., lines 151-164 (line 155 after line 157) (now 146-159); rev., lines 177-196? (now 172-191); partially used in Alster, op. cit., p. 26, where it is cited as 'Ur 4'.

No. 648 (429). U.7827y. Fragment of a multi-column tablet, obverse and reverse; identified by B. Alster in NABU 1999, no. 88 A. Obv. col. i, lines 12-18, col. ii, lines 30?, 31-32; rev. col. i´, unplaced, col. ii´, lines 259-269. In format the tablet, with a narrow blank left edge and archaizing script, is similar to nos. 504 and 599.

Nos. 649-654. Proverbs (6.2.3). See B. Alster, *Proverbs of Ancient Sumer* (CDL Press, 1997), and see also nos. 863-887 below.

No. 649 (235). Proverbs: fragment of a multi-column tablet, one side only; joins UET 6/339. See Alster, *Proverbs of Ancient Sumer*, I, pp. 321-322. No. 302 below is possibly part of the same tablet.

No. 650 (302). Proverbs: fragment of a multi-column tablet, one side only. See Alster, *Proverbs of Ancient Sumer*, I, p. 327.

No. 651 (404). Proverbs: fragment of a multi-column tablet, one side only; written in a very similar script to nos. 649 and 650, but slightly smaller; cf. W. G. Lambert, *Babylonian Wisdom Literature* (Oxford, 1960), p. 255.

No. 652 (31). Proverbs: fragment of a one-column tablet, obverse and reverse. Rev. 3´ and 4´ duplicate lines 195/200 and 199/204, respectively, of the Instructions of Šuruppak (cf. Alster, *The Instructions of Suruppak*, Mesopotamia 2, Copenhagen 1974, p. 44). These lines are also duplicated in Proverbs Collection 22. See Alster, *Proverbs of Ancient Sumer*, I, p. 326

No. 653 (80). Proverbs: fragment of a one-column tablet; obverse, edge and reverse; obv. 5-6 duplicates Proverb Collection 6 nos. 32-34; see Alster, *Proverbs of Ancient Sumer*, pp. 150-151 and 327.

No. 654 (271). Proverbs: fragment, obverse and reverse; possibly bilingual, with interlinear rulings.

No. 655 (484). Riddles?: fragment, one side only; note line 5´, ki-bur₂-bi, and cf. Civil, Aula Orientalis 5 (1987) 17-37.

Nos. 656-660. Laments.

No. 656 (167). Lament, for a king or deity; reverse fragment.

No. 657 (407). Lament: reverse fragment of a multi-column tablet.

No. 658 (415). Lament, mentioning Inana: obverse fragment, traces of reverse on edge.

No. 659 (603). Lament: fragment, obverse and reverse.

No. 660 (137). Lament(?): fragment, obverse and reverse, right-hand side.

Nos. 661-664. Cultic texts.

No. 661 (107). Description of Emblems: joined fragments of a multi-column tablet; obverse and reverse; reverse, so far as preserved, blank except for traces in the left column. The copies of the joined fragments are not fully joined on the plate. Cf. T. Fish, *Catalogue of the Sumerian Tablets in the John Rylands Library* (Manchester, 1932), no. 551; perhaps part of the same tablet as nos. 662 and 663.

No. 662 (420). Description of Emblems: fragment, one side only.

No. 663 (475). Description of Emblems: fragment, one side only.

No. 664 (573). Sacrifices for the Gods: fragment, obverse and reverse.

Nos. 665-666. Incantations.

No. 665 (183). Incantations: fragment of a one-column tablet; obverse and reverse; incantations for purifying the uri₃-gal and for the a-gub₃-ba.

No. 666 (524). Incantation: fragment, one side only; [ini]m-inim-ma a-ba-ra-k[am]

Nos. 667-668. Balags.

No. 667 (36). Balag lamentation: fragment of a one-column tablet, obverse and reverse; OB fore-runner of uru₂-am₃-i-ra or a-še-er-gi₆-ta or the like; cf. M. E. Cohen, *The Canonical Lamentations of Ancient Mesopotamia* (1988), pp. 541f. and 711 respectively; rev. 8f, are quoted in the extract tablet no. 668, rev. lines 1f.

No. 668 (401). Balag, extract tablet: fragment of a one-column tablet, obverse and reverse

Nos. 669-674. Bilingual texts.

No. 669 (245). Bilingual text, concerning Eridu: fragment of a multi-column tablet, one side only.

No. 670 (247). Bilingual: fragment of a one-column tablet, obverse and reverse.

No. 671 (254). Bilingual: fragment of a large, probably multi-column, tablet; obverse, reverse uninscribed.

No. 672 (308). Bilingual: fragment of a multi-column tablet, one side only; parts of two columns preserved; archaizing script.

No. 673 (618). U.30643. Bilingual grammatical text: fragment of a multi-column tablet; obverse (parts of two columns preserved) and reverse (uninscribed).

No. 674 (529). Bilingual lexical list: fragment, one side only. See also no. 836.

Nos. 675-682. Lexical and grammatical texts. See N. Veldhuis, *Elementary education at Nippur* (Groningen, 1997)

No. 675 (526). Lexical: fragment, obverse, reverse uninscribed; lú.

No. 676 (538). Lexical: fragment of a multi-column tablet, obverse and reverse; geographical list.

No. 677 (396+549). Lexical: joined fragments of a multi-column tablet, one side only; ĝiš. Perhaps part of the same tablet as no. 678; cf. also UET 7/87. Quoted as Ur-I-01 by Veldhuis, pp. 270-273 and 331-332.

No. 678 (545). Lexical: fragment of a multi-column tablet, one side only; ĝiš. Perhaps part of the same tablet as no. 677.

No. 679 (297). Grammatical or lexical: reverse fragment.

No. 680 (431+537). List of personal names: joined fragments of a six-column tablet, obverse and reverse; mentions en-me-te-na; colophon.

No. 681 (207). Lexical: reverse fragment; possibly from a lenticular tablet; two columns.

No. 682 (621). U.30497. Lexical: fragment of a multi-column tablet, one side only. OB copy of ED Lu A i´ 92-94 and ii´ 115-121, with glosses. Duplicates UET 7/86. See M. Civil, Oriens Antiquus 22 (1983), 1 n. 2 (transliteration).

Nos. 683-686. Miscellaneous texts.

No. 683 (277). Date list of Sumu-El of Larsa: fragment, one side only; years 12-22; cf. RlA 2, pp. 149f., and UET 8, p. 12f., no. 66.

No. 684 (165). Model contracts(?): fragment of a one-column tablet; obverse, reverse uninscribed.

No. 685 (193). Mathematical problem text: fragment, one side only.

No. 686 (217). Mathematical problem text; fragment, one side only.

Nos. 687-788. Sumerian texts of undetermined content.

No. 687 (45). Upper left obverse corner of a multi-column tablet; narrow columns; reverse ruled for columns but uninscribed.

No. 688 (51). Obverse fragment of a one-column tablet, reverse uninscribed; note in line 5´ the eme-sal form du_5-mu; cf. in line 4´, mu du-lum-ma, 'year of misfortune', and in line 5´, du_5-mu du-lum-ma, 'misfortune's child'.

No. 689 (65). Fragment of a one-column tablet. Possibly Gilgameš, Enkidu and the Netherworld (1.8.1.4); cf. obv. 4´, dingir-re-e-[ne], obv. 5´, igi-b[i_2-duh-am_3?], and obv. 7´, ki-ná ding[ir-r]e-e-[ne].

No. 690 (71). Fragment, possibly of a multi-column tablet; obverse and reverse.

No. 691 (75). Fragment of a one-column tablet; obverse and reverse.

No. 692 (84). Flake.

No. 693 (97). Fragment, obverse and reverse.

No. 694 (102). Fragment, lower right corner of one side only; probably reverse.

No. 695 (104). Reverse fragment.

No. 696 (115). Fragment, ends of lines on right edge of obverse, and reverse.

No. 697 (123). Fragment, one side and left edge; the Ekur is mentioned three times.

No. 698 (124). Fragment of a multi-column tablet; one side only.

No. 699 (126). Reverse fragment of a multi-column tablet.

No. 700 (129). Reverse fragment.

No. 701 (136). Fragment, obverse and reverse, right-hand side; with Akkadian glosses.

No. 702 (140). Fragment, obverse and reverse; surface very worn; possibly part of same tablet as no. 703.

No. 703 (150). Fragment, obverse and reverse; surface of reverse very worn.

No. 704 (162). Fragment, obverse and reverse; perhaps lexical.

No. 705 (191). Fragment, one side only.

No. 706 (195). Fragment, one side only.

No. 707 (196). Fragment, one side only.

No. 708 (198). Fragment, one side only.

No. 709 (200). Fragment, one side only.

No. 710 (202). Fragment of a multi-column tablet, one side only.

No. 711 (203). Flake, possibly from a lenticular tablet.

No. 712 (209). Fragment, one side only.

No. 713 (211). Fragment, one side only.

No. 714 (212). Fragment, one side only, with signs overlapping from the other side.

No. 715 (216). Fragment, obverse and reverse.

No. 716 (218). Fragment, obverse and reverse.

No. 717 (222). Fragment, one side only; possibly compare Inana and Ebih (1.3.2), line 134.

No. 718 (223). Fragment, one side only.

No. 719 (228). Fragment of a large, possibly multi-column, tablet, obverse and reverse.

No. 720 (233). Fragment, one side only.

No. 721 (236). Fragment, possibly of a multi-column tablet, obverse and reverse.

No. 722 (246). Fragment of a multi-column tablet, obverse and reverse.

No. 723 (252). Fragment of a multi-column tablet, obverse and reverse.

No. 724 (253). Cylinder fragment; legal?; parts of four columns preserved. In form the fragment is reminiscent of the larger cylinder published by E. Sollberger in G. van Driel et al. (eds.), *Zikir Šumim: Assyriological Studies Presented to F. R. Kraus* (Leiden, 1982), 346-350, which could have come from Ur.

No. 725 (266). Fragment, one side only.

No. 726 (270). Fragment, obverse and reverse; obv., similar to lines at the end of the Song of the Hoe; rev., unplaceable traces only.

No. 727 (279). Fragment, one side only.

No. 728 (280). Fragment, one side only.

No. 729 (286). Fragment, one side only.

No. 730 (287). Fragment, one side only.

No. 731 (293). Fragment, one side and lower edge.

No. 732 (294). Fragment, one side only.

No. 733 (304). Fragment, obverse and reverse.

No. 734 (305). Fragment, one side only.

No. 735 (310). Fragment, one side only.

No. 736 (312). Fragment, one side only.

No. 737 (313). Fragment, one side only.

No. 738 (315). Fragment, one side only.

No. 739 (316). Fragment, one side only.

No. 740 (317). Fragment, one side only.

No. 741 (433). Fragment of a multi-column tablet, one side only.

No. 742 (474). Fragment, obverse and reverse.

No. 743 (482). Fragment, obverse, reverse and edge.

No. 744 (489). Fragment, one side only.

No. 745 (493). Flake, one side only.

No. 746 (494). Fragment, one side only.

No. 747 (496). Fragment, obverse, reverse uninscribed.

No. 748 (499). Fragment, obverse and reverse; reverse has very light 'trial' wedges'.

No. 749 (503). Fragment, one side only.

No. 750 (509). Fragment, one side only.

No. 751 (510). Fragment, one side only.

No. 752 (511). Fragment, obverse and reverse.

No. 753 (513). Fragment, one side only.

No. 754 (516). Fragment, one side only.

No. 755 (517). Fragment, obverse, reverse and upper edge.

No. 756 (518). Fragment, one side and edge.

No. 757 (519). Fragment of a multi-column tablet, one side only.

No. 758 (520). Fragment, one side only.

No. 759 (521). Fragment, obverse and reverse; reverse (not copied) has random practice entries.

No. 760 (522). Fragment, one side only.

No. 761 (530). Fragment, one side only; archaizing script.

No. 762 (531). Fragment, one side only.

No. 763 (536). Fragment, obverse, reverse uninscribed.

No. 764 (546). Fragment, one side only; archaizing script.

No. 765 (554). Fragment, one side and edge; catalogue?

No. 766 (556). Fragment, obverse and reverse.

No. 767 (557). Fragment, one side only.

No. 768 (561). Fragment of a multi-column tablet, one side only.

No. 769 (563). Fragment, one side only.

No. 770 (564). Fragment, one side only.

No. 771 (565). Fragment, one side only.

No. 772 (566). Fragment, one side only.

No. 773 (567). Fragment, obverse, reverse uninscribed.

No. 774 (569). Fragment of a multi-column tablet, one side only; parts of two columns preserved..

No. 775 (570). Reverse fragment of a multi-column tablet; left column uninscribed.

No. 776 (571). Fragment, obverse and reverse; reverse (not copied) has a few traces (of a colophon?).

No. 777 (572). Fragment, obverse, reverse and upper edge.

No. 778 (574). Fragment, one side only.

No. 779 (575). Fragment, obverse, reverse and edge.

No. 780 (576). Fragment, one side and edge; signs overlapping from the other side.

No. 781 (579). Fragment, obverse and reverse. Some signs on the lower part of the reverse have been lost since copied by Shaffer.

No. 782 (581). Fragment, one side only.

No. 783 (584). Fragment, one side only.

No. 784 (587). Reverse fragment of a multi-column tablet, final column.

No. 785 (590). Fragment, one side and signs overlapping from the other side.

No. 786 (601). Flake.

No. 787 (605). Fragment, obverse and reverse.

No. 788 (607). Reverse fragment of a multi-column tablet; left column uninscribed.

Nos. 789-888 Lenticular school texts, inscribed with exercises in names, lexical citations, short literary extracts and proverbs.

No. 789 (359). Personal names; a-a-; obverse and reverse; "book turning".

No. 790 (340). Personal names; a-ba-; obverse, reverse ruled but uninscribed.

No. 791 (355). Personal names; lugal-; obverse, reverse ruled but uninscribed.

No. 792 (361). Personal names; lugal-; obverse and reverse.

No. 793 (364). Personal names; lugal-; obverse and reverse.

No. 794 (382). Personal names; lugal-; obverse, reverse uninscribed.

No. 795 (625). Personal names; lugal-; obverse, reverse uninscribed. The tablet is wrongly marked U.7790; that number certainly belongs to UET 6/172.

No. 796 (133). Personal names; ^{d}nanna-; fragment; one side only.

No. 797 (459). Personal names; ^{d}nanna-; obverse and reverse.

No. 798 (365). Personal names; NI(.NI)-; obverse, reverse uninscribed.

No. 799 (339). Personal names; ur-^{d}lama; compare no. 522, of which this is the incipit; obverse, reverse uninscribed.

No. 800 (330). Personal names; ur-; obverse, reverse uninscribed.

No. 801 (334). Personal names; ur-; obverse, reverse uninscribed.

No. 802 (341). Personal names; ur-; obverse, reverse uninscribed.

No. 803 (344). Personal names; ur-; obverse, reverse uninscribed.

No. 804 (346). Personal names; [ur]-; obverse and reverse.

No. 805 (350). Personal names; ur-; obverse and reverse.

No. 806 (348). Personal names; ur-; obverse, reverse uninscribed.

No. 807 (368). Personal names; ur-; obverse, reverse ruled but uninscribed.

No. 808 (366). Personal names; ur-; obverse and reverse.

No. 809 (460). Personal names; ur-; obverse, reverse uninscribed.

No. 810 (333). Personal names; ur-; obverse, reverse uninscribed.

No. 811 (377). Personal names; ur-; obverse, reverse uninscribed.

No. 812 (446). Personal names; ur-; obverse, reverse uninscribed.

No. 813 (335). Personal names; geme$_2$-; obverse and reverse.

No. 814 (376). Personal names; geme$_2$-; obverse, reverse uninscribed.

No. 815 (352). Lexical, nin-, or personal names; obverse, reverse mathematical (traces of erased numerals, not copied)

No. 816 (345). Lexical, nin-, or personal names; obverse and reverse.

No. 817 (353). Lexical, nin-, or personal names; obverse and reverse; "book turning".

No. 818 (354). Lexical, nin-, or personal names; obverse and reverse.

No. 819 (358). Lexical, nin-, or personal names; obverse and reverse, "book turning".

No. 820 (369). Personal names; Akkadian; a-hu-; obverse and reverse.

No. 821 (454). Personal names; Akkadian; [^{d}we-er]-illat-; obverse and reverse.

No. 822 (383). Personal names; Akkadian; ^{d}we-er-illat-; obverse, reverse uninscribed.

No. 823 (450). City names; obverse and reverse.

No. 824 (336). Divine names; ^{d}nin-; signed by the scribe, Apil-erṣetim, followed by one erased line; obverse, reverse uninscribed.

No. 825 (379). Lexical; Akkadian; obverse, reverse uninscribed.

No. 826 (367). Lexical; anše; MSL IX, 199; obverse and reverse.

No. 827 (370). Lexical; gi- (reed); obverse and reverse.

No. 828 (342). Lexical; ĝiš-; quoted as Ur-IV-03 by N. Veldhuis, *Elementary education at Nippur* (Groningen, 1997), pp. 273 and 332; obverse and reverse.

No. 829 (338). Lexical; ĝiš-; quoted as Ur-IV-04 by Veldhuis, op. cit., pp. 273 and 332; obverse, reverse uninscribed.

No. 830 (347). Lexical; ĝiš-; cf. Veldhuis, op. cit., pp. 166 and 272, Ni. 666-8; obverse, reverse uninscribed.

No. 831 (351). Lexical; ĝiš-; cf. Veldhuis, op. cit., p. 153, Ni. 86-8; obverse and reverse.

No. 832 (360). Lexical; ĝiš-; cf. Veldhuis, op. cit., pp. 156 and 172, Ni. 210, 203? and one extra line, ĝiš-úr-gu-za; obverse, reverse uninscribed.

No. 833 (371). Lexical; ĝiš-; bilingual lexical exercises; obverse, reverse uninscribed.

No. 834 (373). Lexical; ĝiš-; quoted as Ur-IV-05 by N. Veldhuis, op. cit., pp. 273 and 332; obverse and reverse.

No. 835 (384). Lexical; ĝiš-; cf. Veldhuis, op. cit., p. 287, NP IV-16; obverse and reverse.

No. 836 (375). Lexical; igi-; obverse and reverse.

No. 837 (453). Lexical; lú-; obverse and reverse.

No. 838 (356). Lexical; na$_4$-; obverse and reverse.

No. 839 (349). Lexical; utul-; obverse and reverse.

No. 840 (362). Lexical; zabar; MSL VII; obverse and reverse.

No. 841 (465). Lexical; še-; obverse and reverse.

No. 842 (363). Lexical; muš-; Hh. XIV 506; MSL VIII/2, 7.obverse, reverse uninscribed.

No. 843 (343). Lexical; syllabary; obverse, reverse ruled but mostly defaced.

No. 844 (331). Lexical; obverse and reverse.

No. 845 (332). Lexical; obverse, reverse uninscribed.

No. 846 (337). Lexical; obverse, reverse uninscribed.

No. 847 (449). Lexical; with name of scribe(?); obverse, reverse destroyed.

No. 848 (451). Lexical or proverbs; obverse, reverse blank except for a ruling.

No. 849 (372). Lexical; obverse and reverse.

No. 850 (381). Lexical; obverse, reverse uninscribed.

No. 851 (386). Lexical; obverse, reverse uninscribed.

No. 852 (448). Lexical; obverse and reverse.

No. 853 (457). Lexical; obverse, reverse ruled but uninscribed.

No. 854 (131). Lexical(?): fragment; obverse, reverse destroyed.

No. 855 (623). U.30. Lexical; obverse and reverse.

No. 856 (627). U.8830. Lexical; obverse, reverse uninscribed.

No. 857 (629). U.11644. Lexical, forerunner to Hh. XXIII-XXIV, cf. Nippur forerunner, section 11; obverse and reverse.

No. 858 (630). U.11663. Lexical; obverse and reverse.

No. 859 (631). U.13630. Lexical; obverse, reverse uninscribed.

No. 860 (632). U.13631. Lexical, ĝiš-; cf. Veldhuis, op. cit., p. 158 Ni. 326-8; obverse, reverse uninscribed.

No. 861 (633). U.15027. Lexical; obverse, reverse uninscribed.

No. 862 (635). U.17653 b. Lexical; obverse, reverse uninscribed.

No. 863 (50). Proverbs. Sumerian Proverbs Collection 5, 80. See Alster, *Proverbs of Ancient Sumer*, I, p. 136. Obverse, reverse uninscribed.

No. 864 (378). Proverbs on obv. (6.2.3 Proverbs Collection from Ur = Alster, op. cit., p. 328); rev. mathematical (E. Robson, OECT XIV, 263, and Friberg, RA 94, pp. 136-137).

No. 865 (452). Proverbs on obv. (6.2.3 Proverbs Collection from Ur = Alster, op. cit., p. 328); rev. mathematical (E. Robson, OECT XIV, 258, and Friberg, RA 94, pp. 130).

No. 866 (455). Proverbs (6.2.3 Proverbs Collection from Ur = Alster, op. cit., p. 328). Obverse, reverse blank except for traces of stray wedges and lines.

No. 867 (458). Proverbs (6.2.3 Proverbs Collection from Ur = Alster, op. cit., I, p. 328). Obverse, reverse destroyed.

No. 868 (462). Proverbs (6.2.3 Proverbs Collection from Ur = Alster, op. cit., p. 328). Obverse and reverse.

No. 869 (463). Proverbs (6.2.3 Proverbs Collection from Ur = Alster, op. cit., p. 328). Obverse, reverse destroyed.

No. 870 (464). Proverbs (6.2.3 Proverbs Collection from Ur = Alster, op. cit., p. 328). Obverse, reverse uninscribed.

No. 871 (634). U.15084. Proverbs (6.2.3 Proverbs Collection from Ur = Alster, op. cit., p. 328). Obverse, reverse uninscribed.

No. 872 (636). U.8814 B. Proverbs (6.2.3 Proverbs Collection from Ur = Alster, op. cit., p. 328). Obverse and reverse.

No. 873 (120). Proverbs on obv., rev, mathematical (Robson, OECT XIV, p. 263, and Friberg, RA 94, p. 136).

No. 874 (374). Proverbs on obv.; rev., mathematical (E. Robson, OECT XIV, 257, and Friberg, RA 94, p. 131).

No. 875 (385). Proverbs on obv.; rev., mathematical (E. Robson, OECT XIV, p. 26).

No. 876 (466). Proverbs on obv.; rev., mathematical (E. Robson, OECT XIV, p. 257).

No. 877 (628). U.10144. Proverbs on obv.; rev., remains of a calculation.

No. 878 (214). Proverbs(?); obverse and reverse.

No. 879 (357). Proverbs(?); obverse, reverse destroyed.

No. 880 (380). Proverbs; obverse and reverse.

No. 881 (444). Proverbs; obverse, reverse blank except for practice wedges.

No. 882 (447). Proverbs(?); obverse, reverse uninscribed.

No. 883 (456). Proverbs(?); obverse, reverse uninscribed.

No. 884 (56). Proverbs or wisdom text; obverse and reverse.

No. 885 (411). Proverbs or literary extract; flake from reverse.

No. 886 (445). Proverbs or literary extract; dated ud-3-kam; obverse and reverse.

No. 887 (626). U.7827 z. Proverbs or literary extract; obverse, reverse uninscribed.

No. 888 (624). U.7703; unidentified; Kassite period?; obverse, reverse uninscribed. From Larsa according to the field catalogue.

Nos. 889-908. Akkadian texts.

No. 889 (421). Akkadian hymn to Nanaya: fragment of a multi-column tablet, obverse and reverse; the reverse has faint traces of one line and is otherwise ruled for columns but uninscribed; probably part of the same tablet as UET 6/404.

No. 890 (432). Akkadian hymn to Sin: fragment of a multi-column tablet, obverse and reverse; reverse uninscribed except for end ruling and sign trace.

No. 891 (500). Akkadian hymn: joined fragments of a multi-column tablet, obverse and reverse; obv. iii and reverse ruled but uninscribed.

No. 892 (591). Akkadan text, possibly a practice letter: fragment, obverse, reverse uninscribed.

No. 893 (441). U.16523. Akkadian letter, to or from an official of Rim-Sin; obverse and reverse.

No. 894 (422). Akkadian lexical text: fragment of a four-column tablet; obverse and reverse; begins with divine names and continues with epithets; key-word šarrum.

No. 895 (108). Akkadian medical text: fragment of a multi-column tablet; describes the preparation of a mustard-seed concoction; note that the obverse, contrary to the usual practice, is convex while the reverse is flat.

No. 896 (437). U.16856. Akkadian medical prescription; one-column tablet, obverse and reverse.

No. 897 (619). U.30654. Akkadian medical commentary: fragment, obverse, reverse and edge.

No. 898 (620). U.30655. Akkadian medical text, with incantation to Gula and ritual, probably against dog-bite; scribe EŠx4-taq-bi-S[I.SÁ], ...-taqbi-līšir: fragment, obverse, reverse and edge. See I. L. Finkel in *Ancient Magic and Divination* I, pp. 221-223 and 244.

No. 899 (498). Akkadian musical instructions for tuning a stringed instrument: fragment of a multi-column tablet, obverse and reverse; obverse col. ii and reverse uninscribed. On the place of music in the school curriculum see A. Sjöberg in *Assyriological Studies* 20 (Chicago, 1976), 168-170.

No. 900 (12). Akkadian literary: right corner fragment of a multi-columned tablet, lower obverse and upper reverse.

No. 901 (148). Akkadian text of undetermined content: obverse and reverse.

No. 902 (169). Akkadian text of undetermined content: school text; obverse and reverse.

No. 903 (318). Akkadian text of undetermined content: fragment, obverse, reverse uninscribed.

No. 904 (324). Akkadian text of undetermined content: U.8810; fragment, obverse, reverse uninscribed.

No. 905 (388). Akkadan text of undetermined content: U.5629; fragment, one side only.

No. 906 (540). Akkadian text of undetermined content: fragment, obverse and reverse.

No. 907 (541). Akkadian text of undetermined content: fragment, obverse and reverse.

No. 908 (542). Akkadian text of undetermined content: fragment, one side only; mentions ᵈnin-ĝiš-[zi-da] in line 6´.

Nos. 909-928. Late Babylonian texts.

No. 909 (406). Sumerian hymn to Meslamtaea, emesal: joined fragments of a one-column tablet; obverse, reverse and right edge.

No. 910 (412). Sumerian litany, eme-sal: fragment of a one-column tablet, obverse and reverse.

No. 911 (419). Sumerian litany, excerpts: one-column tablet, obverse and reverse.

No. 912 (163). Sumerian lament: fragment of a one-column tablet, obverse and reverse.

No. 913 (436). Sumerian lament, excerpts: one-column tablet, obverse and reverse; landscape orientation.

No. 914 (469). Sumerian lament, listing gods and temples: fragment, probably of a one-column tablet, obverse and reverse.

No. 915 (588). Sumerian(?) proverb(?): complete, reverse uninscribed. See Alster, *Proverbs of Ancient Sumer*, I, p. 328 (omitting part of line 1).

No. 916 (583). Bilingual incantation: fragment, one side only; mentions Asalluḫi.

No. 917 (438). Bilingual incantation: fragment, obverse and reverse, probably of a multi-column tablet.

No. 918 (615). Bilingual literary and lexical extracts; fragment, obverse and reverse; the beginning of the obverse is left blank; cf. UET 6/406.

No. 919 (434). Akkadian monologue of Šulgi: one-column tablet, obverse and reverse; landscape orientation.

No. 920 (470). Akkadian medical text; stone list and prescriptions: fragment, obverse and reverse.

No. 921 (551). Akkadian omens(?): fragment, obverse and reverse.

No. 922 (568). Akkadian text of undetermined content: fragment, one side only.

No. 923 (589). Akkadian literary text of undetermined content: fragment, obverse and reverse.

No. 924 (490). List of stars: fragment of a multi-column tablet; the right column is a partial duplicate to the list of ziqpu-stars in AO 6478 (J. Schaumberger, ZA 50 (1952), 228-229). The two surviving columns of text appear to be continuous from obverse to reverse over the lower edge.

No. 925 (533). Lexical(?): fragment, obverse and reverse.

No. 926 (389). U.5630. Unidentified: fragment, one side only.

No. 927 (391). U.5633. Unidentified: fragment, one side and edge with signs overlapping from the other side.

No. 928 (392). U.5634. Unidentified: fragment, one side and last line on the lower edge.

For other Late Babylonian literary texts see nos. 200-207, 391-393, 398, 401, 405-410 and 413 in the preceding volume.

Other published texts

In addition to the texts published in UET VI, literary, religious and scholastic texts and copies of historical inscriptions have been published in UET I (relevant texts listed below in the range U.7725-7757), V (no. 86, U.16876 B, found at 1 Broad Street, now in the Iraq Museum), VII (see p. 10 for provenances) and VIII (VIII/1 nos. 12-14, 32-34, 36q, 37, 58-62, 65-66, 70-71, 79, 86, 88, 92-95, 103 and VIII/2 no. 39a, mostly having no provenance). One should also note the following texts from the excavations at Ur, published in other contexts, which are relevant to reconstructing the full picture of scholarly activity at Ur. Other fragments from Woolley's excavations, particularly of lexical texts, remain to be published. In addition there remain unpublished texts from the excavations of Taylor (BM 1859-10-14 collection) and Hall (BM 1919-10-11 collection), and probaby from other official or unofficial excavations at Ur.

U.2815. Late Babylonian school text, literary and lexical extracts: P. D. Gesche, *Schulunterricht in Babylonien* (AOAT 275, 2000), pp. 666 (copy), 781, 788. The tablet, which comes from room ES. 3 (previously numbered ES. 7) of the Neo-Babylonian E-gig-par, is described in the field register as follows, "Clay tablet. Fragment - New Babylonian Syllabary; List of signs gish. Colophon: é ban-da, house of the boys - Probably material of the school. ES. 7" It is also referred to in UE IX p. 17, as "a part of a syllabary endorsed 'the property of the boys' school'". See also Woolley in Antiquaries Journal V (1925), p. 383. Thus the misreading of the text is responsible for Woolley's designation of this room as a school.

U.2816. Late Babylonian school text, literary and lexical extracts; P. D. Gesche, op. cit., pp. 667 (copy), 781, 788. Same provenance as U.2815.

U.7739(+)U.7740. Old Babylonian, Law code of Ur-Nammu (3.41). O. R. Gurney and S. N. Kramer in *Assyriological Studies* 16 (Chicago, 1965), 13-19; J. J. Finkelstein, JCS 22, 66-82. Part of a hoard found in burnt level over upper (2nd period) floor of rooms 5-6, no. 7, Quiet Street (UE VII 228 and field catalogue)

U.7752+U.7759 (443). Old Babylonian, Akkadian liver omens: joined fragments of a one-column tablet; omens concerning the ṣibtum. Published in U. Jeyes,

Old Babylonian Extispicy, pp. 3 and 137f. and pls. 10-11, as no. 9 (under the number "U 443 (7752)+ U.7759"). Same provenance as U.7739.

U.18122. Late Babylonian, Akkadian. Fifth tablet of the Era Epic, written on a tablet shaped in the form of an amulet. W. G. Lambert, Iraq 24 (1962) 119-125. Found in surface soil in the area NNCF, north-west of the Temenos wall.

U.30495. Late Babylonian, Akkadian. Names of Marduk on the seven stages of the journey to the Akītu-house. W. G. Lambert, RA 91 (1997), 78-80; duplicates E. Ebeling, Keilschrifttexte aus Assur religiosen Inhalts, no. 142. No povenance.

U.30503. Old Babylonian Akkadian incantation. I. L. Finkel, in *Ancient Magic and Divination* I, pp. 235-236 and 247, under wrong number U.30501. No provenance.

TABLET DIMENSIONS

This list gives the dimensions in centimetres of all tablets and fragments published in this volume except for those fragments joined to fragments already published in UET 6 parts 1 and 2.
Dimensions are given in the order: length, width, thickness. Complete dimensions are marked with an asterix * The number in the second column is Shaffer's provisional number.

415	066	9.0 x 5.7 x 2.4	457	423	5.1 x 4.2 x 2.5
416	156	6.0 x 5.8 x 2.5	458	501	4.9 x 3.3 x 1.5
417	015	9.6 x 9.2 x 3.7	459	553	2.0 x 2.1 x 1.3
418	129a	5.6 x 4.5 x 2.0	460	555	2.1 x 3.1 x 1.9
419	079	2.4 x 5.0 x 2.5	461	558	2.6 x 2.9 x 1.4
420	495	2.2 x 2.0 x 0.7	462	560	3.1 x 2.0 x 1.7
421	559	2.8 x 3.7 x 2.6	463	562	2.5 x 1.7 x 1.7
422	502	2.8 x 2.1 x 1.7	464	243	9.1 x 6.8 x 2.2
423	414	5.0 x 4.6 x 2.1	465	114	9.3 x 7.1 x 2.6
424	580	4.6 x 6.9 x 3.0	467	118	5.0 x 2.9 x 1.4
425	320	2.8 x 3.4 x 2.2	468	241	7.2 x 6.7 x 3.8
426	269	2.1 x 3.4 x 1.6	469	081	4.8 x 6.1 x 2.6
427	483	3.7 x 4.8 x 1.9	470	110	6.1 x 4.8 x 1.7
428	416	3.7 x 3.8 x 1.0	471	175	4.1 x 6.8 x 2.4
429	267	2.3 x 2.5 x 0.8	472	186	4.4 x 3.0 x 2.3
430	291	2.6 x 2.0 x 1.0	473	249	12.0 x 7.3 x 3.2
431	306	1.7 x 2.6 x 1.2	474	508	1.8 x 4.7 x 1.6
432	488	2.8 x 4.1 x 2.4	475	622	2.8 x 3.1 x 0.4
434	A	1.4 x 1.9 x 1.1	476	260	12.6 x 7.6 x 2.8
435	Ca	1.6 x 1.5 x 1.0	477	094	3.3 x 4.4 x 2.5
436	Ba	1.3 x 7.8 x 2.5	478	070	7.0 x 4.5 x 2.7
437	029	11.2 x 5.8 x 3.2	479	237	8.6 x 6.6 x 3.1
438	093	5.0 x 4.2 x 2.5	480	020	3.5 x 3.0 x 2.5
439	F	4.0 x 3.0 x 2.5	481	221	2.4 x 5.0 x 1.9
440	G	1.9 x 1.6 x 0.8	482	023	5.5 x 4.0 x 3.3
441	H	2.4 x 1.4 x 0.4	483	030	6.6 x 3.8 x 2.6
442	I	1.6 x 1.1 x 0.5	484	019	4.1 x 4.5 x 2.5
443	J	1.3 x 1.0 x 0.3	485	134	4.2 x 7.1 x 3.1
444	K	0.9 x 1.1 x 0.2	486	018	6.1 x 6.1 x 3.1
445	L	2.2 x 1.5 x 0.8	487	284	4.5 x 6.8 x 2.8
446	M	1.5 x 1.2 x 0.3	488	473	4.1 x 4.3 x 3.3
447	X	1.3 x 1.8 x 1.0	489	399	8.4 x 6.5 x 2.3
448	Y	2.1 x 2.9 x 0.9	491	014	5.1 x 8.7 x 3.3
449	Z	2.0 x 1.3 x 1.9	492	268	3.4 x 2.9 x 1.3
450	219	3.2 x 3.0 x 1.9	493	539	3.7 x 4.1 x 1.7
451	224	3.4 x 1.8 x 2.3	495	550	2.5 x 2.9 x 1.9
452	275	3.0 x 3.1 x 2.5	496	205	5.0 x 3.6 x 1.8
453	299	4.7 x 2.6 x 1.1	498	321	3.8 x 2.8 x 0.8
454	300	2.7 x 2.3 x 1.5	500	039	3.4 x 6.3* x 2.3
455	314	1.7 x 3.7 x 1.8	501	161	6.3 x 4.5 x 1.9
456	417	3.8 x 3.8 x 1.6	502	182	7.0 x 6.8 x 2.6
			503	506	2.5 x 7.4 x 2.8
			504	263	8.6 x 8.1 x 3.3
			505	208b	4.2 x 4.0 x 1.9
			506	176	6.1 x 7.8 x 2.4
			507	525	6.3 x 10.1 x 3.1
			509	290	2.4 x 2.7 x 1.2
			510	024	11.4 x 11.0 x 3.3
			512	021	6.8 x 5.7 x 3.5
			513	026	5.5 x 6.0 x 2.4

514	272	6.4 x 4.2 x 1.7	583	250	12.2 x 6.6* x 3.7
516	239	7.2 x 6.6 x 4.0	584	106	4.5 x 2.7 x 2.1
517	409	4.0 x 5.3 x 2.6	586	144	4.4 x 3.4 x 2.3
520	617	4.0 x 4.4 x 2.0	587	143	4.1 x 8.0 x 3.0
521	002	12.5 x 7.1 x 3.0	588	471	6.7 x 5.7 x 3.0
522	430	7.6 x 7.9 x 2.8	589	442	5.6 x 7.1 x 2.3
523	327	not measured	590	007	5.4 x 6.6 x 3.2
524	487	1.9 x 6.0* x 2.1	591	600	4.3 x 7.5 x 2.3
525	038	8.0 x 4.4 x 3.2	592	074	4.6 x 3.4 x 2.5
526	052	11.2 x 11.9 x 3.6	593	172	2.1 x 5.1 x 1.8
527	255	4.6 x 8.6 x 2.8	594	435	3.8 x 5.1 x 2.3
528	109	7.1 x 5.4 x 2.3	595	090	3.8 x 4.5 x 2.5
529	016	13.5 x 9.5 x 3.1	596	092	6.2 x 3.8 x 3.0
530	141	3.8 x 3.1 x 1.8	597	231	9.7* x 5.8* x 3.2
531	159	2.3 x 5.3 x 2.0	598	091	5.9 x 5.2 x 3.0
532	395	5.4 x 5.6 x 3.0	599	322	9.4 x 6.8 x 3.8
534	234	14.7 x 6.8 x 4.9;	600	158	3.2 x 3.7 x 2.5
535	258	6.9 x 6.0 x 3.9	601	481	6.4 x 3.7 x 2.7
536	055	4.2 x 2.8 x 2.7	603	049	6.6 x 6.0* x 2.5
537	166	5.3 x 4.0 x 2.2	604	103	4.0 x 4.8 x 2.0
539	122	3.6 x 7.4 x 2.0	605	164	6.5 x 5.0 x 2.3
540	232	4.2 x 8.2 x 3.1	606	226	5.7 x 5.8 x 2.7
541	281	6.1 x 5.6 x 2.2	607	229	7.0 x 3.8 x 3.5
542	527	3.7 x 3.3 x 2.5	608	230	7.2 x 6.9 x 3.2
543	544	3.7 x 3.0 x 2.4	609	257	7.7 x 6.8 x 3.5
544	585	1.5 x 4.1 x 1.5	610	244	10.9 x 8.3 x 4.0
545	009	6.4 x 4.5 x 1.5	611	259	10.0 x 8.5 x 4.0
546	325	7.4 x 6.4 x 3.2	612	064	8.2 x 4.5 x 3.0
547	013	not measured	613	173	6.1 x 6.0 x 2.5
548	047	3.2 x 8.6 x 3.3	614	201	3.6 x 2.5 x 1.5
549	112	4.4 x 4.5 x 2.6	615	479	4.7 x 3.4 x 3.2
550	609	2.7 x 3.2 x 2.1	616	440	4.6 x 3.6 x 1.7
551	485	4.0 x 3.7 x 1.2	617	614	5.5 x 4.1 x 1.5
552	486	1.7 x 4.4 x 2.2	618	174	7.9 x 6.6 x 2.7
553	027	7.4 x 4.3 x 2.6	620	240	10.6 x 3.7 x 4.0
554	578	4.0 x 4.5 x 2.0	621	262	8.9 x 6.7 x 3.5
555	251	13.6 x 8.0 x 4.0	622	197	5.3 x 4.3 x 2.7
556	273	5.0 x 5.4 x 1.3	623	261	6.0 x 5.5 x 2.4
558	264	11.3 x 6.1* x 2.8	624	177	3.4 x 3.9 x 2.6
559	225	12.1* x 9.1* x 3.8*	626	082	4.3 x 6.8* x 3.0
560	149	5.9 x 4.1 x 2.0	628	472	4.9 x 2.4 x 2.8
561	187	3.4 x 4.5 x 2.8	629	130	3.5 x 6.8 x 2.5
562	428	3.9 x 5.3 x 1.9	630	238	5.9 x 6.3 x 3.3
563	425	7.3 x 6.8 x 3.2	632	105	8.7 x 7.0 x 2.0
564	427	5.2 x 3.5 x 1.3	633	035	10.3 x 6.0 x 2.5
566	062	7.7 x 7.1 x 2.7	634	248	9.7 x 6.1* x 3.0
567	323	11.4 x 8.2 x 4.0	635	426	3.7 x 7.8* x 2.4
568	151	3.0 x 5.6 x 2.3	636	054	6.2 x 4.1 x 3.0
569	408	3.8 x 4.0 x 1.7	637	088	2.6 x 7.5* x 2.4
570	418	4.2 x 5.3 x 2.6	638	309	4.0 x 3.1 x 1.3
571	424	5.4 x 8.3* x 2.5	639	220	4.3 x 5.2 x 2.7
572	034	4.6 x 6.1 x 2.3	641	303	5.5 x 5.6 x 2.5
573	053	4.1 x 5.3 x 1.2	642	037	6.2 x 5.8 x 2.2
575	390	3.7 x 2.5 x 1.4	643	168	3.9 x 4.0 x 1.8
576	058	6.2* x 8.9 x 2.9	644	206	3.1 x 5.7 x 1.5
577	117	5.1 x 5.4 x 2.1	645	152	6.9 x 5.0 x 2.5
578	127	7.4 x 10.9 x 5.1	646	059	5.8 x 5.2 x 3.1
580	288	4.9 x 4.8 x 3.1	647	227	10.5 x 7.8* x 3.2
581	397	3.7 x 5.8 x 3.0	648	429	12.0 x 7.7 x 3.4

650	302	5.0 x 5.6 x 1.2	709	200	4.1 x 4.2 x 1.3
651	404	8.2 x 7.8 x 2.8	710	202	4.5 x 3.8 x 2.0
652	031	2.6 x 6.0 x 2.2	711	203	5.0 x 4.1 x 1.2
653	080	6.4 x 5.8 x 2.8	712	209	3.5 x 2.7 x 1.8
654	271	3.0 x 2.0 x 2.2	713	211	4.0 x 3.8 x 1.7
655	484	4.5 x 3.9 x 2.5	714	212	2.9 x 3.2 x 2.6
656	167	6.5 x 7.1 x 1.8	715	216	2.7 x 4.2 x 2.3
657	407	5.4 x 7.3 x 1.8	716	218	4.1 x 3.4 x 2.8
658	415	3.7 x 2.9 x 1.9	717	222	2.3 x 4.4 x 1.9
659	603	3.0 x 4.8 x 2.5	718	223	3.3 x 4.2 x 1.7
660	137	5.4 x 3.8 x 2.4	719	228	6.7 x 3.7 x 4.7
661	107	12.0 x 7.5 x 2.9	720	233	8.7 x 7.0 x 3.7
662	420	3.8 x 4.2 x 3.6	721	236	6.0 x 6.2 x 3.7
663	475	5.9 x 4.3 x 2.2	722	246	7.2 x 7.2 x 4.4
664	573	3.1 x 4.5 x 2.0	723	252	5.6 x 7.0 x 3.5
665	183	7.4 x 5.3* x 2.4	724	253	11.2 x 7.0* diam.
666	524	3.6 x 3.9 x 0.7	725	266	4.3 x 4.2 x 2.2
667	036	6.0 x 5.0 x 2.8	726	270	4.5 x 3.8 x 2.9
668	401	3.8 x 5.4 x 1.6	727	279	3.5 x 3.4 x 1.9
669	245	10.0 x 8.2 x 3.2	728	280	2.6 x 3.2 x 2.0
670	247	10.3 x 6.0 x 3.0	729	286	5.0 x 4.8 x 2.4
671	254	9.4 x 6.7 x 4.1	730	287	2.7 x 4.3 x 1.8
672	308	3.9 x 2,4 x 1.2	731	293	1.7 x 3.7 x 1.5
673	618	5.4 x 6.2 x 3.0	732	294	2.7 x 2.8 x 1.6
674	529	4.5 x 4.2 x 2.1	733	304	1.7 x 3.2 x 1.8
675	526	3.9 x 4.4 x 2.1	734	305	3.9 x 2.6 x 1.8
676	538	5.9 x 5.9 x 2.9	735	310	4.4 x 3.3 x 1.6
677	396	10.7 x 15.8 x 4.1	736	312	4.2 x 2.9 x 2.2
678	545	4.0 x 3.9 x 2.8	737	313	3.9 x 2.8 x 1.5
679	297	4.1 x 2.4 x 0.7	738	315	3.5 x 2.6 x 1.3
680	431	5.7 x 11.9* x 3.1	739	316	4.5 x 3.6 x 1.6
681	207	4.9 x 3.7 x 1.9	740	317	3.3 x 2.4 x 1.4
682	621	6.0 x 4.9 x 2.1	741	433	7.6 x 5.9 x 1.7
683	277	5.3 x 3.8 x 1.6	742	474	3.5 x 2.4 x 2.6
684	165	3.6 x 5.3 x 2.6	743	482	3.5 x 3.8 x 2.6
685	193	4.9 x 3.7 x 2.3	744	489	4.0 x 3.8 x 2.1
686	217	4.5 x 2.9 x 1.6	745	493	2.8 x 1.9 x 0.6
687	045	4.4 x 4.0 x 2.2	746	494	2.7 x 3.1 x 1.7
688	051	7.3 x 5.5 x 2.5	747	496	5.3 x 5.7* x 2.7
689	065	4.2 x 5.0 x 2.5	748	499	4.9 x 4.2 x 3.0
690	071	5.9 x 3.2 x 2.4	749	503	3.9 x 2.0 x 1.9
691	075	4.2 x 5.4 x 3.0	750	509	4.5 x 2.5 x 2.3
692	084	5.1 x 4.5 x 1.9	751	510	2.6 x 2.7 x 1.7
693	097	2.6 x 5.3 x 2.3	752	511	3.1 x 2.6 x 3.2
694	102	4.7 x 6.1 x 2.8	753	513	2.7 x 2.6 x 1.4
695	104	3.7 x 3.9 x 1.9	754	516	2.5 x 3.3 x 1.7
696	115	5.7 x 4.1 x 2.7	755	517	1.7 x 4.2 x 11.8
697	123	6.2 x 5.5 x 2.0	756	518	1.9 x 2.7 x 1.7
698	124	2.9 x 5.6 x 2.1	757	519	3.0 x 4.1 x 1.2
699	126	3.1 x 4.6 x 1.6	758	520	2.9 x 2.0 x 1.1
700	129	5.2 x 4.0 x 3.0	759	521	4.5 x 3.7 x 2.8
701	136	6.0 x 2.6 x 2.6	760	522	1.8 x 2.6 x 1.6
702	140	5.3 x 5.7 x 3.0	761	530	2.5 x 3.8 x 1.3
703	150	7.1 x 3.0 x 2.9	762	531	2.4 x 2.3 x 1.6
704	162	4.5 x 4.8 x 2.3	763	536	6.8 x 3.9 x 3.7
705	191	4.1 x 5.7 x 2.3	764	546	3.0 x 3.6 x 1.3
706	195	4.5 x 5.2 x 1.4	765	554	5.2 x 3.9 x 1.2
707	196	4.1 x 4.4 x 2.3	766	556	3.8 x 3.2 x 2.5
708	198	4.5 x 4.5 x 1.3	767	557	2.6 x 2.4 x 1.8

768	561	2.3 x 3.0 x 0.8	827	370	8.0* diam x 2.5*
769	563	1.8 x 2.4 x 1.7	828	342	8.0* diam x 2.5*
770	564	3.6 x 3.6 x 2.2	829	338	7.6 diam x 2.2
771	565	2.6 x 2.3 x 1.5	830	347	6.9* diam x 2.3*
772	566	2.6 x 2.2 x 1.2	831	351	8.1* diam x 2.6*
773	567	2.8 x 4.4 x 2.5	832	360	8.5* diam x 2.7*
774	569	4.4 x 3.1 x 1.8	833	371	10.4* diam x 2.9*
775	570	3.1 x 4.9 x 1.6	834	373	7.9* diam x 2.6*
776	571	3.4 x 4.5 x 2.8	835	384	7.7 diam x 2.7*
777	572	1.8 x 4.0 x 2.3	836	375	9.5* diam x 2.5*
778	574	5.0 x 3.5 x 2.5	837	453	9.5* diam x 2.7*
779	575	5.0 x 4.2 x 3.0	838	356	7.2* diam x 2.5*
780	576	1.9 x 2.0 x 2.1	839	349	8.1* diam x 2.5*
781	579	6.1 x 7.4 x 2.7	840	362	9.2* diam x 3.0*
782	581	2.7 x 2.8 x 1.2	841	465	9.0 diam x 2.7*
783	584	3.4 x 4.2 x 1.7	842	363	8.7* diam x 2.7*
784	587	5.2 6.1 x 2.3	843	343	6.8* diam x 2.3*
785	590	5.2 x 3.5 x 2.2	844	331	7.3 diam x 2.5*
786	601	4.1 x 4.5 x 1.4	845	332	6.5* diam x 2.3*
787	605	2.5 x 2.4 x 2.7	846	337	6.2* diam x 2.3*
788	607	4.6 x 7.2 x 2.5	847	449	7.2* diam x 2.4*
789	359	7.1* diam x 2.7*	848	451	9.3 diam x 2.5
790	340	7.4* diam x 2.2*	849	372	7.2 diam x 2.5*
791	355	7.4* diam x 2.7*	850	381	8.5* diam x 3.6*
792	361	9.4* diam x 2.3*	851	386	6.9* diam x 2.4*
793	364	8.1* diam x 3.2	852	448	4.4 diam x 1.8
794	382	8.5* diam x 2.7*	853	457	7.1* diam x 1.9*
795	625	7.1* diam x 2.4*	854	131	7.8 diam x 2.5
796	133	5.8 diam x 1.6	855	623	7.5 diam x 2.2
797	459	7.7* diam x 2.4*	856	627	7.5* diam x 2.7*
798	365	7.9* diam x 2.5*	857	629	6.4* diam x 2.0*
799	339	7.3* diam x 2.6*	858	630	8.0 diam x 2.0
800	330	6.1* diam x 1.8*	859	631	7.4* diam x 2.4*
801	334	6.9* diam x 2.2*	860	632	6.7* diam x 2.0*
802	341	7.6* diam x 2.6*	861	633	6.3* diam x 2.1*
803	344	8.2* diam x 2.5*	862	635	7.7* diam x 3.1*
804	346	7.5 diam x 2.5*	863	050	7.0 diam x 2.8
805	350	7.4* diam x 2.4*	864	378	9.5* diam x 2.4*
806	348	6.4* diam x 2.3*	865	452	9.0* diam x 2.5*
807	368	8.7* diam x 2.3*	866	455	7.7 diam x 2.6*
808	366	7.7* diam x 2.3*	867	458	8.8 diam x 2.9*
809	460	5.8* diam x 2.2*	868	462	8.1* diam x 2.1*
810	333	6.2 diam x 2.1	869	463	6.3 diam x 2.8
811	377	7.9* diam x 2.2*	870	464	7.8 diam x 3.0
812	446	7.9* diam x 2.3*	871	634	9.1 diam x 2.8
813	335	6.9* diam x 2.5*	872	636	7.5 diam x 1.6
814	376	6.5* diam x 1.8*	873	120	9.4 diam x 2.2
815	352	8.1* diam x 2.1*	874	374	8.1 diam x 2.6*
816	345	7.9* diam x 2.9*	875	385	9.8* diam x 2.6*
817	353	7.4* diam x 2.5*	876	466	7.9 diam x 2.9
818	354	8.2* diam x 2.3	877	628	8.5* diam x 2.4*
819	358	8.2* diam x 3.0*	878	214	8.0 diam x 2.6*
820	369	8.3* diam x 2.0*	879	357	9.1 diam x 2.5
821	454	6.2 diam x 2.4	880	380	8.1 diam x 2.5
822	383	8.4* diam x 2.7*	881	444	7.5 diam x 2.3
823	450	7.2 diam x 2.4*	882	447	5.9 diam x 2.3
824	336	8.2* diam x 1.8*	883	456	7.3 diam x 2.3*
825	379	7.8 diam x 1.7*	884	056	9.1 diam x 2.7
826	367	7.5* diam x 2.3*	885	411	7.3 diam x 1.7

886	445	7.4* diam x 2.0*
887	626	8.5* diam x 2.6*
888	624	4.3* diam x 1.3
889	421	9.0 x 9.7 x 4.4
890	432	8.5 x 4.1 x 3.4
891	500	6.1 x 13.9* x 3.9
892	591	5.5 x 3.7 x 2.5
893	441	9.6 x 6.5* x 3.0
894	422	8.1 x 10.0 x 3.9
895	108	6.9 x 4.6 x 3.0
896	437	11.7* x 5.3* x 2.8
897	619	5.8 x 6.7* x 2.6
898	620	3.8* x 5.4 x 1.9
899	498	9.0 x 6.4 x 4.2
900	012	4.7 x 6.5 x 3.3
901	148	5.4 x 3.7 x 2.2
902	169	4.7 x 3.6 x 2.5
903	318	2.5 x 3.1 x 2.3
904	324	5.2 x 2.4 x 2.5
905	388	4.8 x 2.8 x 1.2
906	540	2.2 x 5.1 x 2.7
907	541	4.7 x 2.4 x 2.3

908	542	5.2 x 4.7 x 1.4
909	406	4.8 x 6.0* x 2.3
910	412	3.2 x 5.4* x 2.5
911	419	4.5* x 6.3* x 2.0*
912	163	2.1 x 6.4 x 2.0
913	436	5.9* x 8.0* x 2.6
914	469	7.8 x 3.7 x 2.2
915	588	3.4* x 7.1* x 1.5
916	583	2.3 x 3.3 x 1.5
917	438	5.2 x 5.2 x 2.4
918	615	6.1 x 5.9* x 2.3
919	434	5.6* x 7.8* x 2.3
920	470	3.8 x 5.7 x 2.7
921	551	5.1 x 3.0 x 2.5
922	568	4.3 x 1.8 x 1.9
923	589	4.5 x 3.7 x 2.6
924	490	3.1 x 3.8 x 2.3
925	533	3.0 x 2.5 x 2.0
926	389	4.3 x 2.7 x 1.7
927	391	4.3 x 2.7 x 2.0
928	392	2.4 x 2.7 x 1.6

U. NUMBERS AND PROVENANCES

The provenances of many tablets published in UET 6/1 and 6/2 were already listed in UE VII 214-254 under the relevant U. number. The initials ILF, ORG, PG, WGL and UJ refer to the publications listed on p. 15 above.

U.	UET 6	Provenance
00030	855	TTA at 3.00 level (field catalogue)
02815	PG	Room ES. 3 (previously numbered ES. 7) of the Neo-Babylonian E-gig-par
02816	PG	Same as U.2815
05307	523	Provenance unknown; no field catalogue; 1924-25 season
05621	532	Same as U.5307
05656	532	Same as U.5307
05628	574+	Same as U.5307
05629	905	Same as U.5307
05630	926	Same as U.5307
05631	575	Same as U.5307
05633	927	Same as U.5307
05634	928	Same as U.5307
05635	487	Same as U.5307
05641	627+	Same as U.5307
06320	200	KPS, B2. Box against NW outer wall of Room B.4
06321	203	KPS, Room B.4
07703	888	Senkereh (=Larsa) (field catalogue)
07707	182	EM, loose in soil
07716	351	EM, "... temple courtyard"
07725	1/274	Hoard found in burnt level over upper (2nd period) floor of rooms 5-6, no. 7, Quiet Street (IM 85460)
07728	1/294	Same as U.7725 (IM 85467)
07730	101a	Same as U.7725
07732	1/301	Same as U.7725 (IM 85471)
07733	1/299	Same as U.7725 (IM 85468)
07734	103	Same as U.7725
07736	1/276	Same as U.7725 (IM 85457)
07737	1/289	Same as U.7725 (IM -)
07738	101b	Same as U.7725
07739	ORG	Same as U.7725
07740	ORG	Same as U.7725
07741	173	Same as U.7725
07743	1/300	Same as U.7725 (IM 85469)
07744	118	Same as U.7725
07745	102	Same as U.7725
07746	1/285	Same as U.7725 (IM 85462)
07747	105	Same as U.7725
07748	8/1,86	Same as U.7725
07749	67	Same as U.7725
07750	107a	Same as U.7725
07751	104	Same as U.7725
07752	UJ	Same as U.7725
07754	1	Same as U.7725
07755	1/292	Same as U.7725 (IM 85465)
07756	1/275	Same as U.7725 (IM 85461)
07757	1/293	Same as U.7725 (IM 85466)
07758	69	Same as U.7725
07759	UJ	Same as U.7725
07760	106	Same as U.7725
07774	522	TTD (field catalogue)
07782	599	EM loose in soil (field catalogue)
07786 A	54	5, Quiet Street, Room 6 (UE VII 229); or room 4? (field catalogue)
07786 D	170	Same as U.7786 A
07795 A	170	Same as U.7786 A
07790	172	7, Quiet Street, upper level
07793	414	7, Quiet Street, upper level
07802 A	114	7, Quiet Street (UE VII 229, q.v.); room 11 (field catalogue)
07804 +07804 C	26b	7, Quiet Street, rooms 5-6 (UE VII 230); Lower floor level No. 7 Quiet St. (field catalogue)
07805 (3)	262	Same as U.7804
07827 y	648	7, Quiet Street (or EM or Quiet St. 5 Room no 4)
07827 z	887	Same as U.7827 y
07828	411	Same as U.7827 y
07836	117	7, Quiet Street (UE VII 230); room 11 (field catalogue)
07839 A	266	SM, SE face of long mud brick wall
08806	273	SM or EM
08806 a	546	SM or EM
08810	353	EM
08810	904	EM
08810 B	144+	EM
08814 B	872	SM Destruction dump
08820	567	SM Destruction dump
08830	856	TTE at east end 1 m. below surface (field catalogue)
08840	135	Part of a group of unbaked tablets left over at the end of

		the 1926-27 season, from various loci; see field catalogue for details
09364 a	56	Possibly SM (UE VII 214 and 232); not in field catalogue
10144	877	"House site, new dig" (field catalogue)
11644	857	PG (field catalogue)
11663	858	PG (field catalogue)
11696	520	PG (field catalogue)
13622	401	CLW, NE city wall, central section
13630	859	Larsa rubbish filing over PG (field catalogue)
13631	860	Larsa rubbish filing over PG (field catalogue)
15027	861	PG. Surface. (field catalogue)
15084	871	CLW (field catalogue)
16272 (?)	175	Provenance unknown (UE VII 237, duplicate number; U.16272 is a marble mace-head = UET 8/1, 35)
16342 (?)	85	Provenance unknown (UE VII 238, duplicate number; U.16342 ia a mace-head)
16523	893	7 Church Lane
16829	111	1 Broad Street (also known as A.H. School House)
16830	14	1 Broad Street
16831	73	1 Broad Street
16834	70	1 Broad Street
16835	8/2,39	1 Broad Street (IM 85470)
16836	8/1,94	1 Broad Street (IM 85685)
16838	151	1 Broad Street
16841	390	1 Broad Street
16843	412	1 Broad Street
16846	145	1 Broad Street
16847	82	1 Broad Street
16848	81	1 Broad Street
16849	177	1 Broad Street
16850	80	1 Broad Street
16852	11	1 Broad Street
16853	174	1 Broad Street
16854	86	1 Broad Street
16855	95	1 Broad Street
16856	896	1 Broad Street
16857	178	Provenance unknown
16857 A	152	1 Broad Street
16858	134	1 Broad Street
16859	8/1,60	1 Broad Street (IM 85678)
16860	77	1 Broad Street
16861	140	1 Broad Street
16862	92	1 Broad Street
16863	120	1 Broad Street
16864	75	1 Broad Street
16865	380	1 Broad Street
16867	153	1 Broad Street
16868	72	1 Broad Street
16869	98	1 Broad Street
16873	9	1 Broad Street
16874	57	Provenance unknown
16876 A	122	1 Broad Street
16876 B	5/86	1 Broad Street
16877	4	1 Broad Street
16878	58	1 Broad Street
16879 A	19	1 Broad Street
16879 B	96	1 Broad Street
16879 C	167	1 Broad Street
16879 D	39	1 Broad Street
16879 E	46	1 Broad Street
16879 F	109	1 Broad Street
16879 G	79	1 Broad Street
16879 H	198	1 Broad Street
16879 I	171	1 Broad Street
16879 K	44	1 Broad Street
16879 L	146	1 Broad Street
16879 M	3	1 Broad Street
16880	68	1 Broad Street
16882	115	1 Broad Street
16884	6	1 Broad Street
16885	183	1 Broad Street
16886	41	1 Broad Street
16888	336	1 Broad Street
16889	395	1 Broad Street
16890	396	1 Broad Street
16891	49	1 Broad Street
16892 A	28	1 Broad Street
16892 B	166	1 Broad Street;
16892 C	337	1 Broad Street
16892 D	399	1 Broad Street
16893	27	1 Broad Street
16894 A	176	1 Broad Street
16894 B	179	1 Broad Street
16894 C	154	1 Broad Street
16895	76	1 Broad Street
16896	22	1 Broad Street
16897	47	1 Broad Street
16900 A	107b	1 Broad Street
16900 B	131	1 Broad Street
16900 C	2	1 Broad Street
16900 D	26a	1 Broad Street
16900 E	124	1 Broad Street
16900 F	402	1 Broad Street
16900 G	180	1 Broad Street
16900 H	132	1 Broad Street
16900 J	136	1 Broad Street
16900 K	137	1 Broad Street
16900 L	138	1 Broad Street
16900 M	139a	1 Broad Street
16900 N	139b	1 Broad Street
16900 O	8/1,61	1 Broad Street (IM 85679)
17207, 002	260	1 Broad Street
17207, 003	274	1 Broad Street
17207, 003a	275	1 Broad Street
17207, 005	276	1 Broad Street
17207, 006	222	1 Broad Street
17207, 007	256	1 Broad Street
17207, 008	354	1 Broad Street

17207, 009	257	1 Broad Street		17207, 068	349	1 Broad Street
17207, 010	261	1 Broad Street		17207, 069	368	1 Broad Street
17207, 011	386	1 Broad Street		17207, 070	215	1 Broad Street
17207, 012	355	1 Broad Street		17207, 071	297	1 Broad Street
17207, 013	277	1 Broad Street		17207, 071a	369	1 Broad Street
17207, 014	244	1 Broad Street		17207, 072	249	1 Broad Street
17207, 015	223	1 Broad Street		17207, 073	340	1 Broad Street
17207, 016	241	1 Broad Street		17207, 074	298	1 Broad Street
17207, 017	278	1 Broad Street		17207, 075	370	1 Broad Street
17207, 018	279	1 Broad Street		17207, 076	371	1 Broad Street
17207, 019	356	1 Broad Street		17207, 077	225	1 Broad Street
17207, 020	357	1 Broad Street		17207, 079	270	1 Broad Street
17207, 021	267	1 Broad Street		17207, 080	226	1 Broad Street
17207, 022	237	1 Broad Street		17207, 081	299	1 Broad Street
17207, 023	359	1 Broad Street		17207, 082	208	1 Broad Street
17207, 024	280	1 Broad Street		17207, 083	300	1 Broad Street
17207, 025	281	1 Broad Street		17207, 084	216	1 Broad Street
17207, 025b	360	1 Broad Street		17207, 085	301	1 Broad Street
17207, 026	245	1 Broad Street		17207, 086	242	1 Broad Street
17207, 026b	282	1 Broad Street		17207, 087	302	1 Broad Street
17207, 027	258	1 Broad Street		17207, 088	268	1 Broad Street
17207, 028	263	1 Broad Street		17207, 090	303	1 Broad Street
17207, 029	264	1 Broad Street		17207, 091	238	1 Broad Street
17207, 030	250	1 Broad Street		17207, 092	217	1 Broad Street
17207, 031	361	1 Broad Street		17207, 093	343	1 Broad Street
17207, 032	362	1 Broad Street		17207, 094	304	1 Broad Street
17207, 033	283	1 Broad Street		17207, 095	305	1 Broad Street
17207, 034	233	1 Broad Street		17207, 096	332	1 Broad Street
17207, 036	363	1 Broad Street		17207, 097	306	1 Broad Street
17207, 037	284	1 Broad Street		17207, 098	239	1 Broad Street
17207, 038	210	1 Broad Street		17207, 099	240	1 Broad Street
17207, 039	246	1 Broad Street		17207, 100	387	1 Broad Street
17207, 040	342	1 Broad Street		17207, 101	335	1 Broad Street
17207, 041	364	1 Broad Street		17207, 102	251	1 Broad Street
17207, 042	285	1 Broad Street		17207, 103	220	1 Broad Street
17207, 043	286	1 Broad Street		17207, 104	252	1 Broad Street
17207, 045	358	1 Broad Street		17207, 105	307	1 Broad Street
17207, 046	365	1 Broad Street		17207, 109	372	1 Broad Street
17207, 047	287	1 Broad Street		17207, 110	373	1 Broad Street
17207, 048	213	1 Broad Street		17207, 111	308	1 Broad Street
17207, 049	224	1 Broad Street		17207, 112	211	1 Broad Street
17207, 050	288	1 Broad Street		17207, 113	236	1 Broad Street
17207, 051	289	1 Broad Street		17207, 114	309	1 Broad Street
17207, 052	247	1 Broad Street		17207, 115	271	1 Broad Street
17207, 053	366	1 Broad Street		17207, 116	334	1 Broad Street
17207, 054	367	1 Broad Street		17207, 117	310	1 Broad Street
17207, 055	290	1 Broad Street		17207, 118	333	1 Broad Street
17207, 056	331	1 Broad Street		17207, 119	311	1 Broad Street
17207, 057	214	1 Broad Street		17207, 120	344	1 Broad Street
17207, 058	291	1 Broad Street		17207, 121	374	1 Broad Street
17207, 059	292	1 Broad Street		17207, 123	341	1 Broad Street
17207, 060	381	1 Broad Street		17207, 124	312	1 Broad Street
17207, 061	293	1 Broad Street		17207, 125	385	1 Broad Street
17207, 062	294	1 Broad Street		17207, 126	375	1 Broad Street
17207, 063	248	1 Broad Street		17207, 128	313	1 Broad Street
17207, 064	234	1 Broad Street		17207, 129	314	1 Broad Street
17207, 065	235	1 Broad Street		17207, 130	350	1 Broad Street
17207, 066	232	1 Broad Street		17207, 131	376	1 Broad Street
17207, 067	296	1 Broad Street		17207, 132	315	1 Broad Street

17207, 133	316	1 Broad Street
17207, 134	377	1 Broad Street
17207, 135	317	1 Broad Street
17207, 136	221	1 Broad Street
17207, 137	345	1 Broad Street
17207, 137b	212	1 Broad Street
17207, 138	227	1 Broad Street
17207, 139	347	1 Broad Street
17207, 140	378	1 Broad Street
17207, 141	379	1 Broad Street
17207, 142	209	1 Broad Street
17207, 143	318	1 Broad Street
17207, 144	319	1 Broad Street
17207, 145	265	1 Broad Street
17207, 146	253	1 Broad Street
17222 A	89	AH site
17222 B	83	AH site
17653 A	352	PG/1931. Found low in the rubbish lying on the second floor of mud brick which extends over the shaft of PG/1847
17653 B	862	Same as U.17653 A
17900 A	403	Provenance unknown; 1931-32 season
17900 D	155	Same as U.17900 A

17900 Q	32	Same as U.17900 A
17900 F	199	Same as U.17900 A
17900 H	123	Same as U.17900 A
17900 I	165	Same as U.17900 A
17900 J	150	Same as U.17900 A
17900 K	188	Same as U.17900 A
17900 L	60	Same as U.17900 A
17900 R	91	Same as U.17900 A
17900 S	147	Same as U.17900 A
17900 V	181	Same as U.17900 A
17900 X	189	Same as U.17900 A
18122	WGL	In surface soil in the area NNCF, north-west of the Temenos wall
30495	WGL	Provenance unknown
30497	682	Provenance unknown
30503	ILF	Provenance unknown
30643	673	Provenance unknown
30654	897	Provenance unknown
30655	898	Provenance unknown
(erased)	394	Provenance unknown
ga	534+	Provenance unknown
ia	579+	Provenance unknown
k	547+	Provenance unknown
z	559+	Provenance unknown

JOINED TABLETS

Since the publication of UET 6/1, UET 6/2 and UET 8 the following joins have been made to fragments there published:

6/10	+433
6/29	+498
6/30	+499
6/40	+627
6/43	+625
6/47	+497
6/50+51+53	+490
6/52	+494
6/65	+565
6/66+71	+582
6/76	+518
6/78	+519
6/88	+538
6/99	+533
6/116	+602
6/126+127	

6/130	+511
6/136	+508
6/143	+515
6/144	+574
6/156	+631
6/157	+640
6/161+164	+619
6/174	+557
6/187	+466
6/189	+585
6/339	+649
6/388	+UET 8/92
6/388	+579
8/33	+UET 6/523
8/36Q	+UET 6/547
8/70	+UET 6/559
8/88	+UET 6/534
8/92	+UET 6/388
8/95	+UET 6/526

UET 6/10 + 433 obv.

Plate C

UET 6/10 + 433 obv. edges

Plate D

UET 6/10 + 433 rev. edges

Plate 1

415

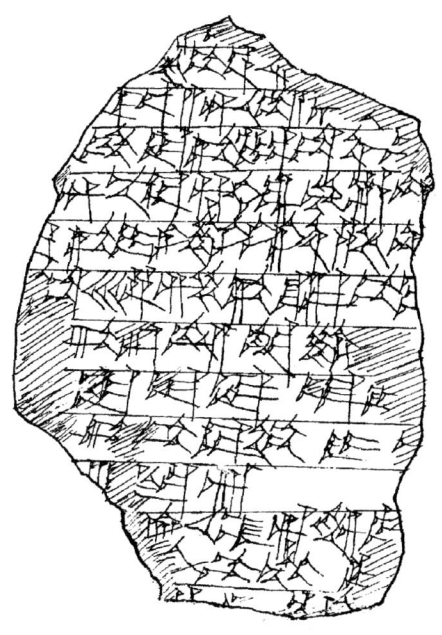

417 obv.

416

417 rev.

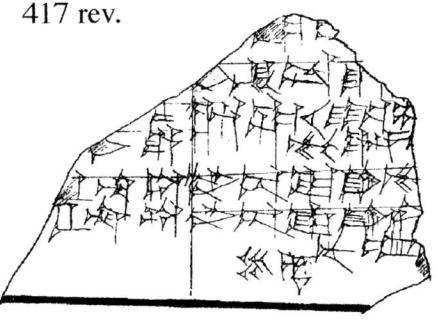

419 obv.

418

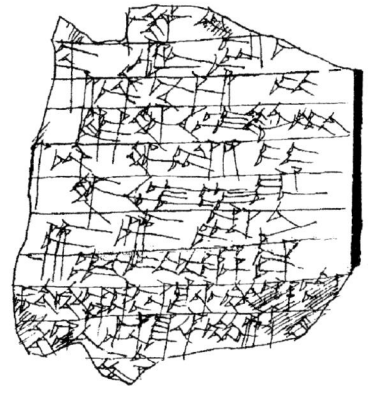

419 rev.

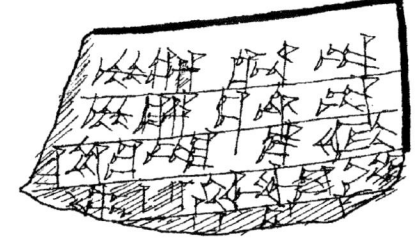

Plate 2

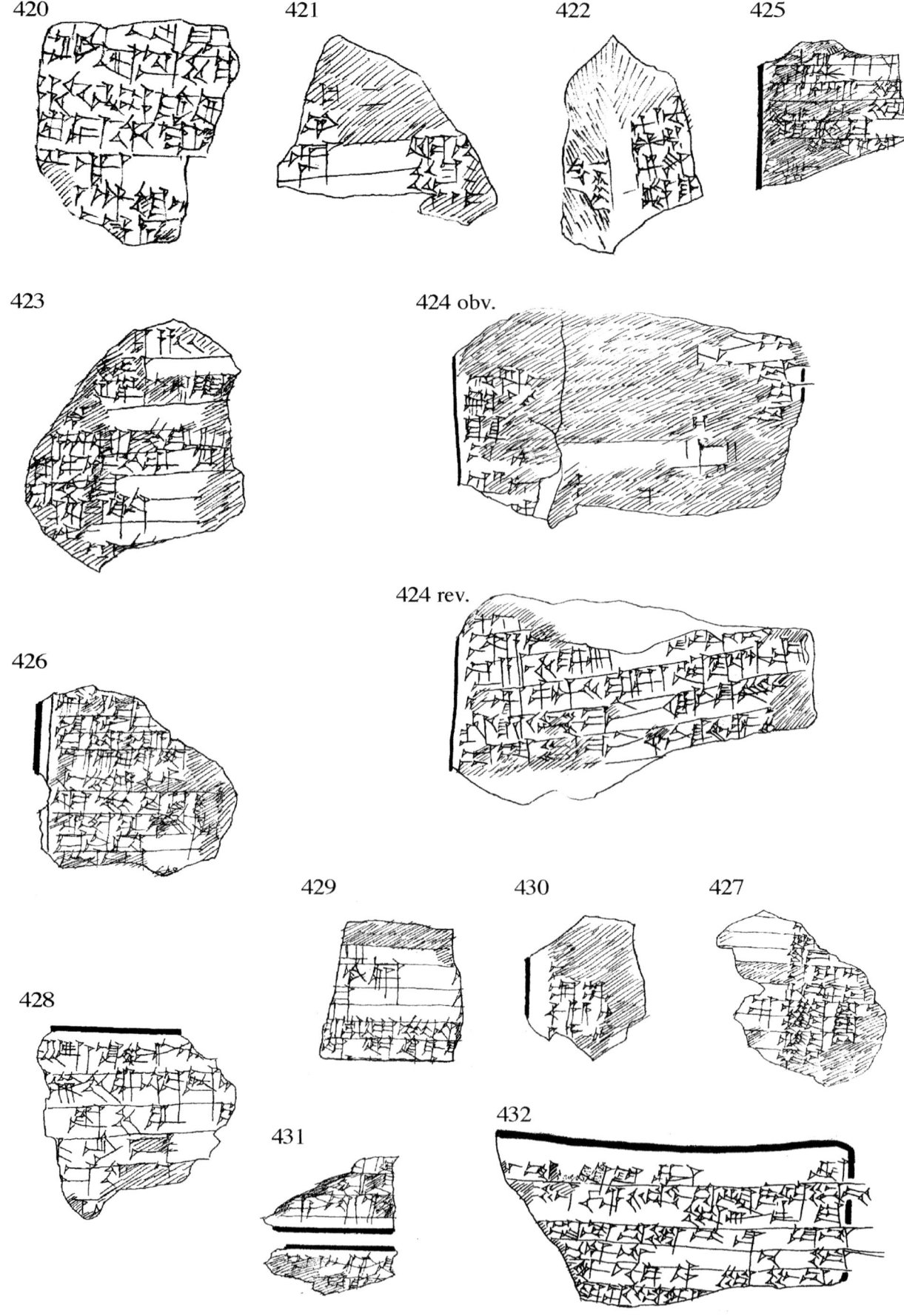

420

421

422

425

423

424 obv.

424 rev.

426

429

430

427

428

431

432

Plate 3

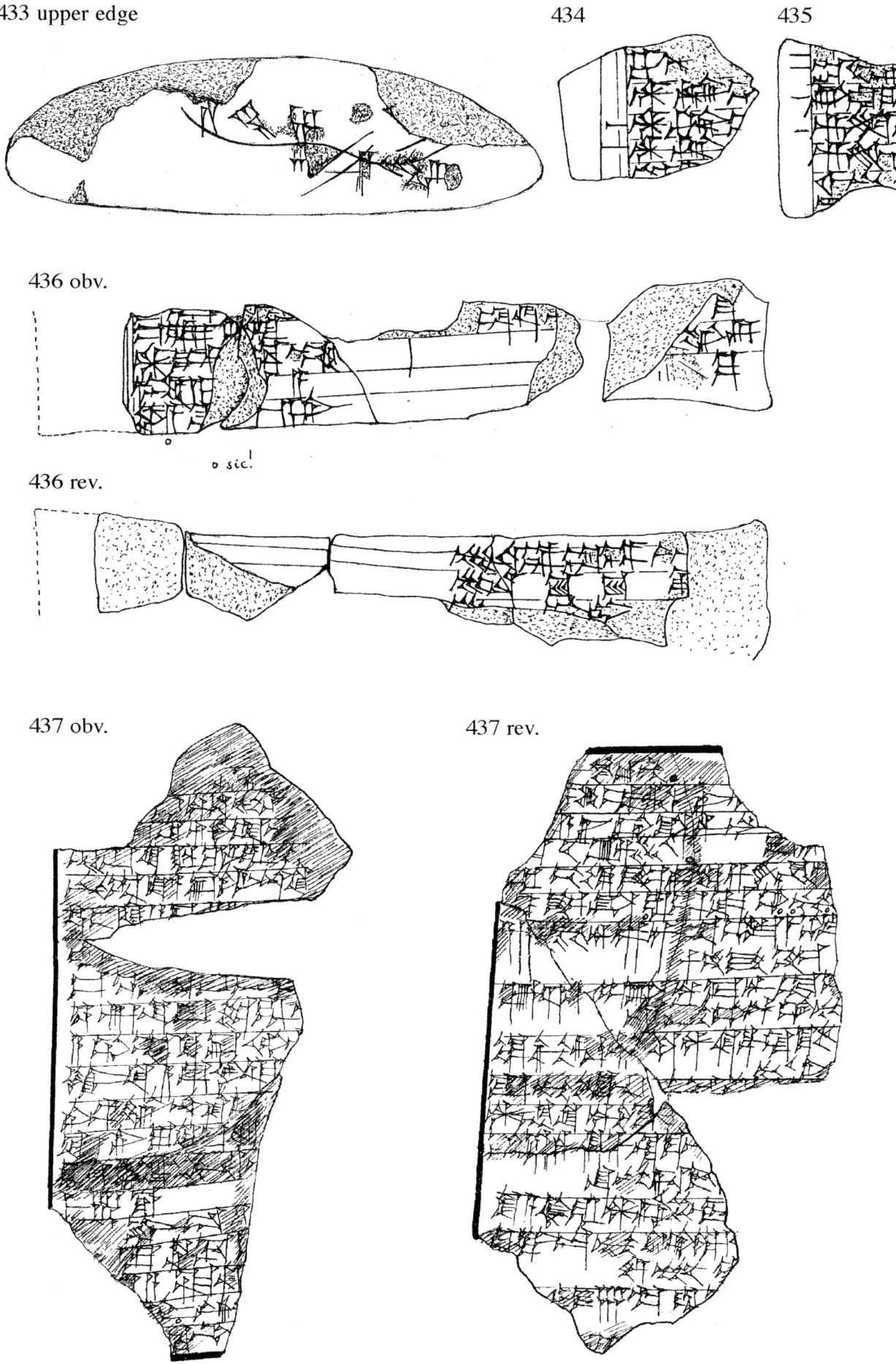

433 upper edge

434

435

436 obv.

o sic!

436 rev.

437 obv.

437 rev.

Plate 4

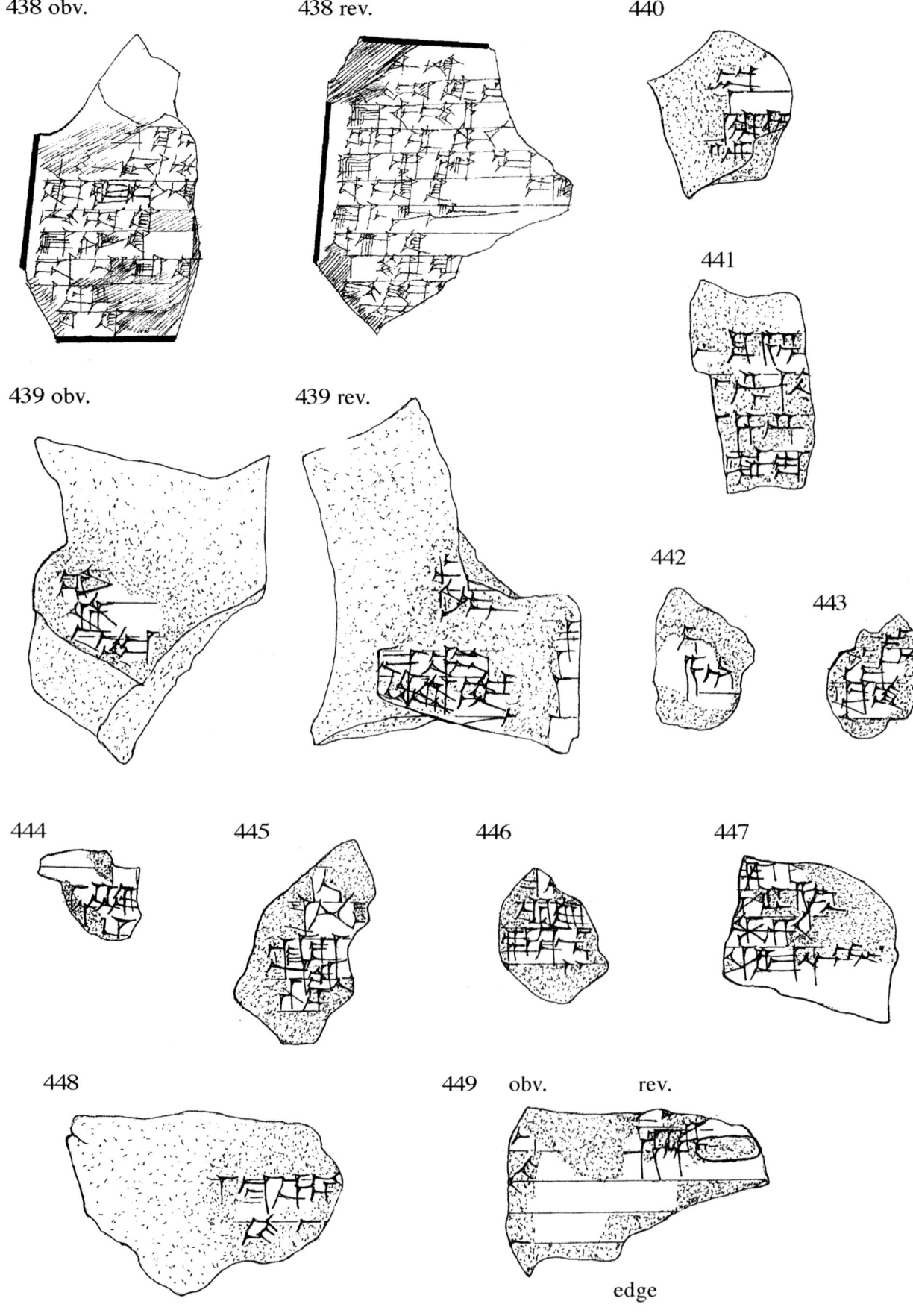

438 obv.

438 rev.

440

441

439 obv.

439 rev.

442

443

444

445

446

447

448

449 obv.   rev.

edge

Plate 5

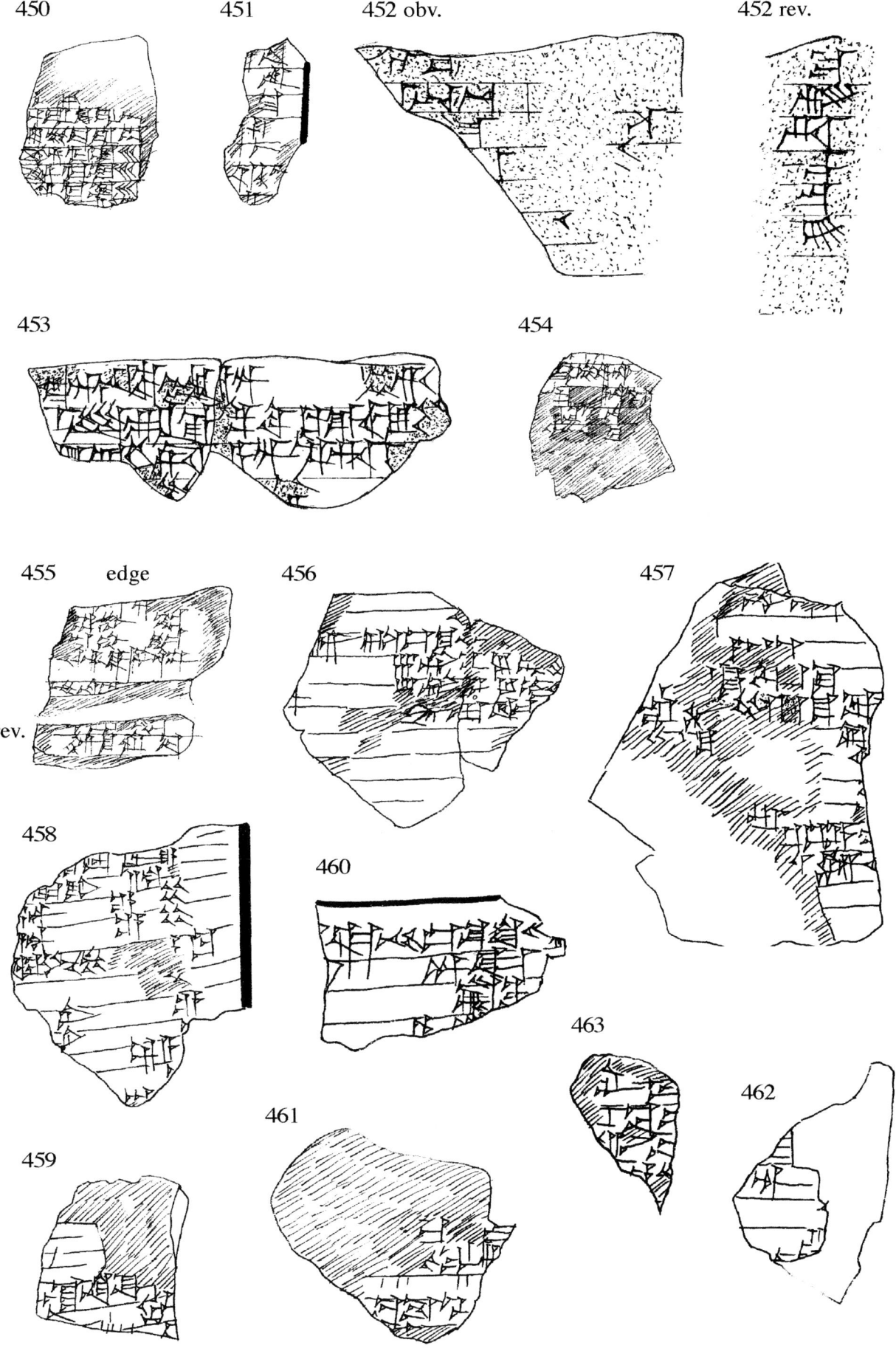

450

451

452 obv.

452 rev.

453

454

455　edge

rev.

456

457

458

460

463

462

461

459

Plate 6

464

465

466

UET 6, 187 rev.

467

468 obv.

468 rev.

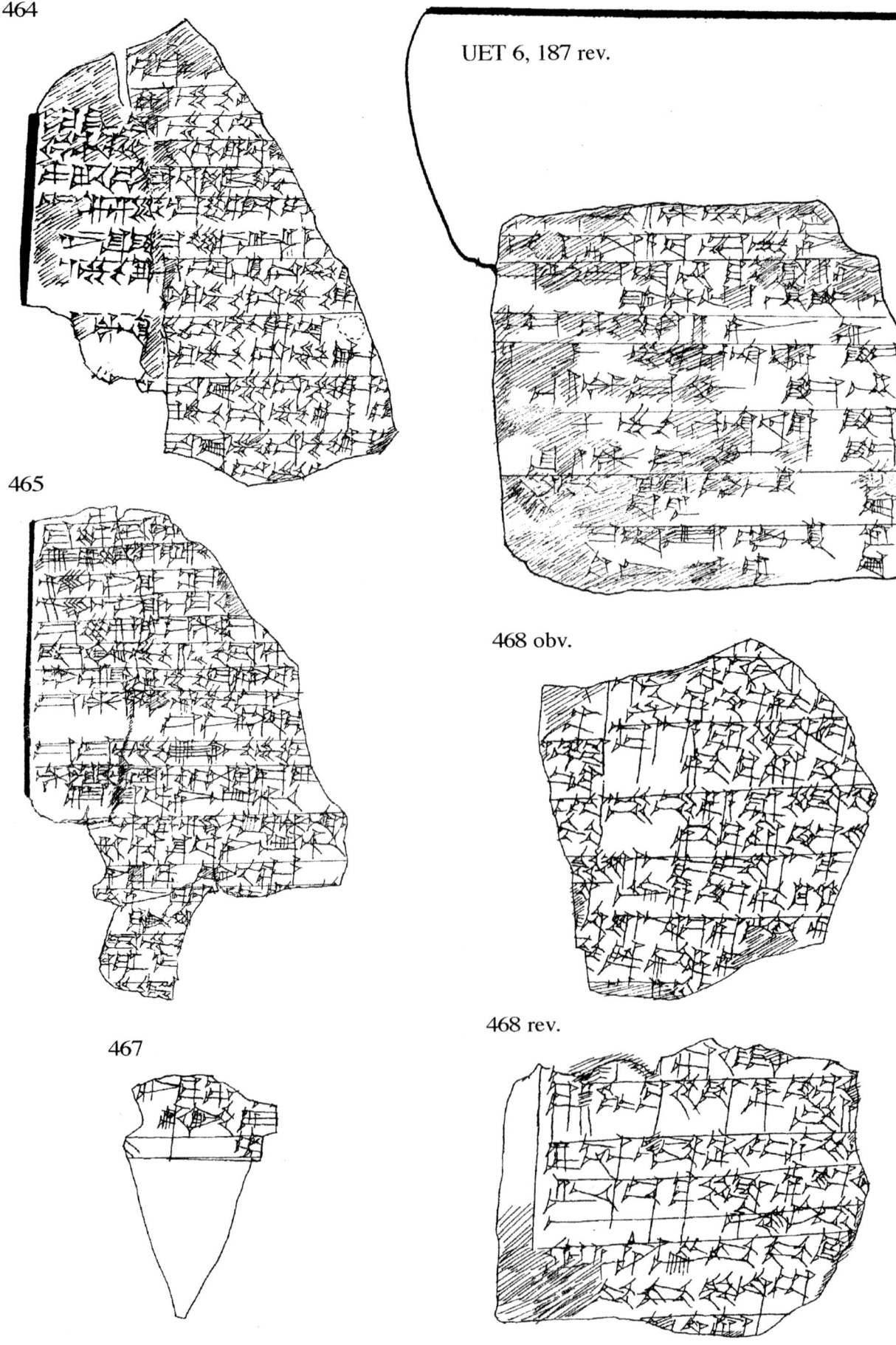

Plate 7

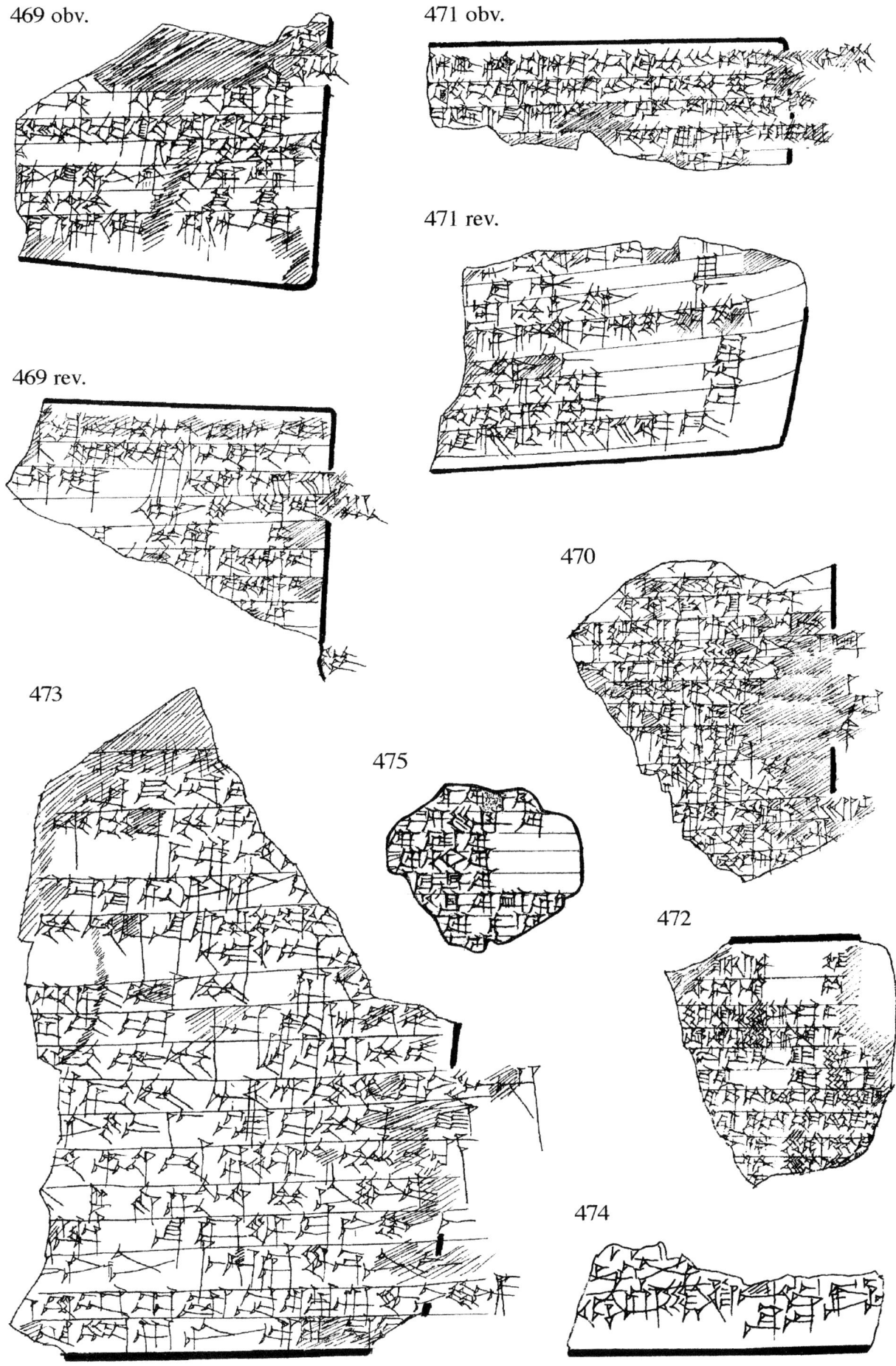

469 obv.

471 obv.

471 rev.

469 rev.

470

473

475

472

474

Plate 8

476 obv.

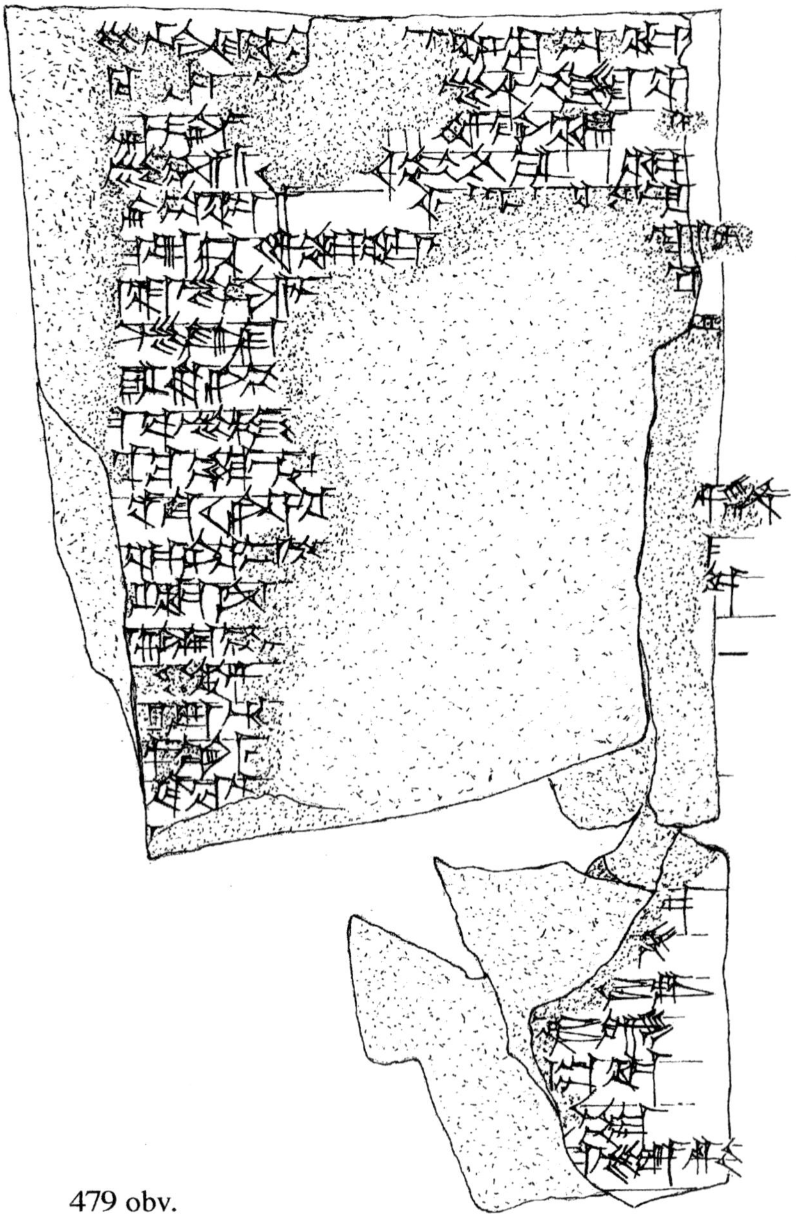

477 obv.

477 rev.

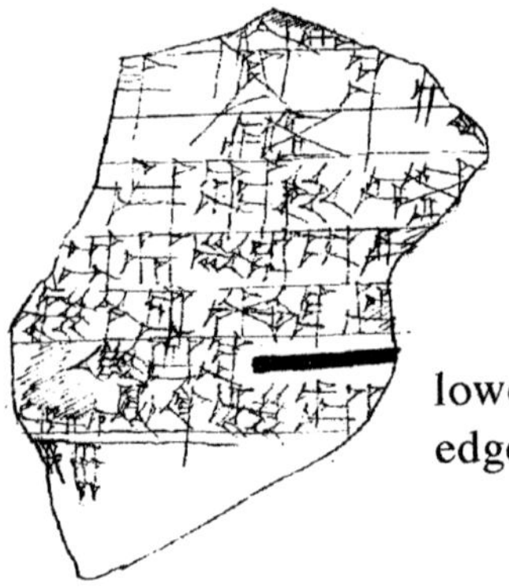

lower
edge

478

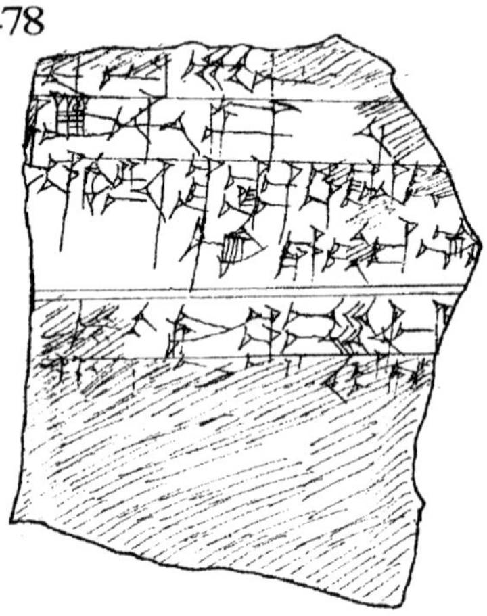

479 obv.

479 rev.

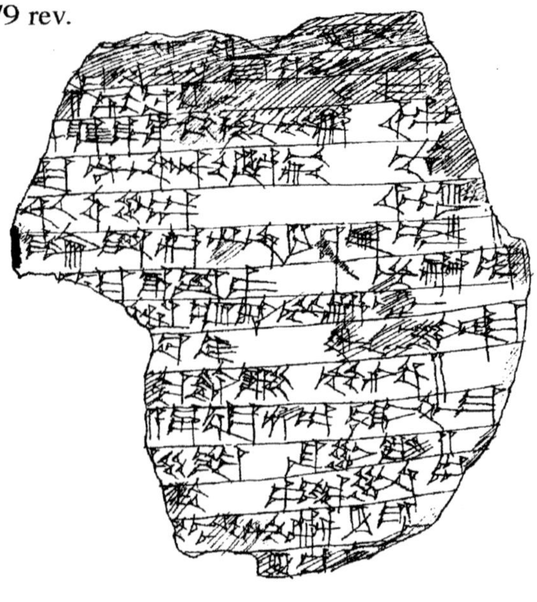

Plate 9

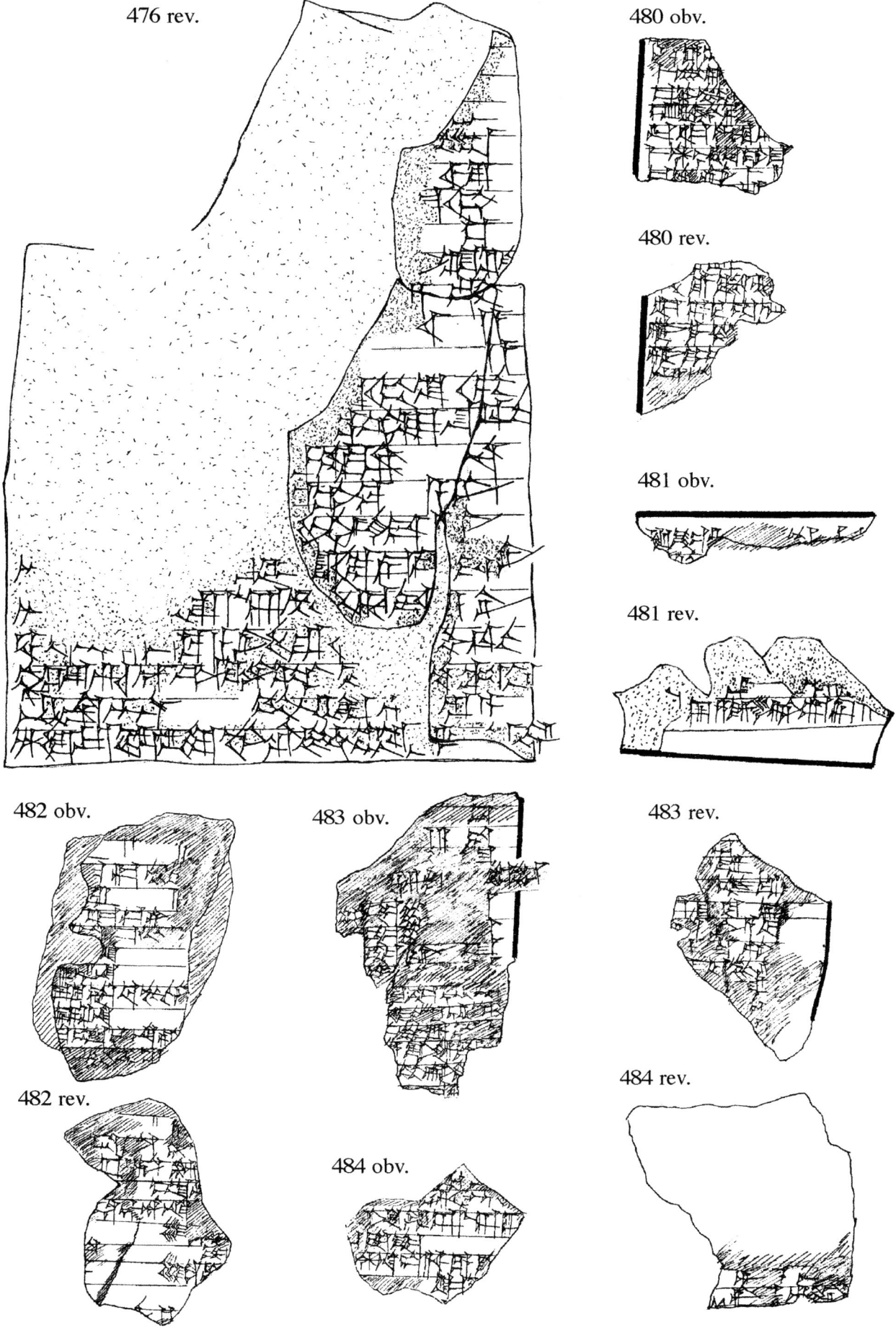

476 rev.

480 obv.

480 rev.

481 obv.

481 rev.

482 obv.

483 obv.

483 rev.

482 rev.

484 obv.

484 rev.

Plate 10

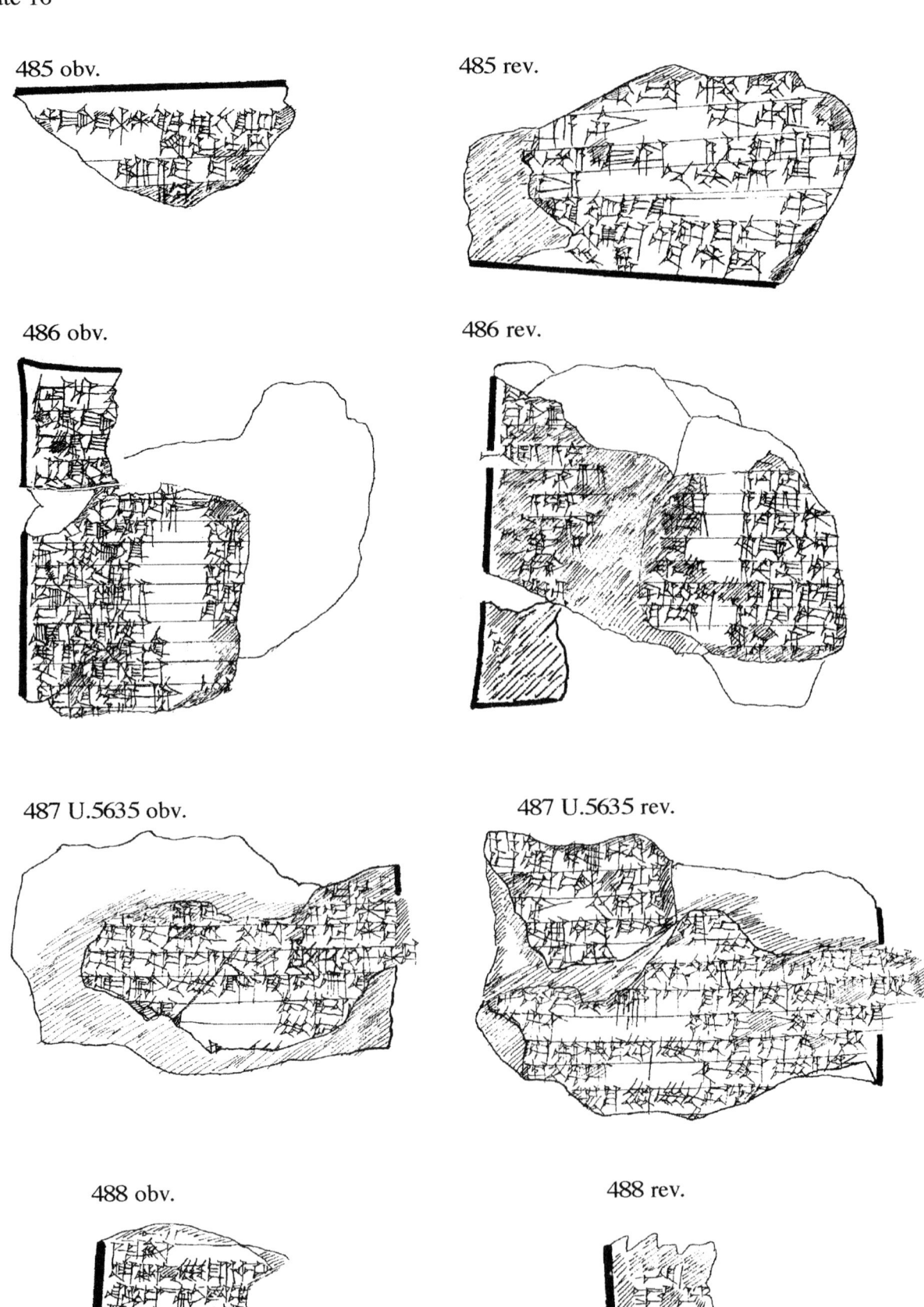

485 obv.

485 rev.

486 obv.

486 rev.

487 U.5635 obv.

487 U.5635 rev.

488 obv.

488 rev.

Plate 11

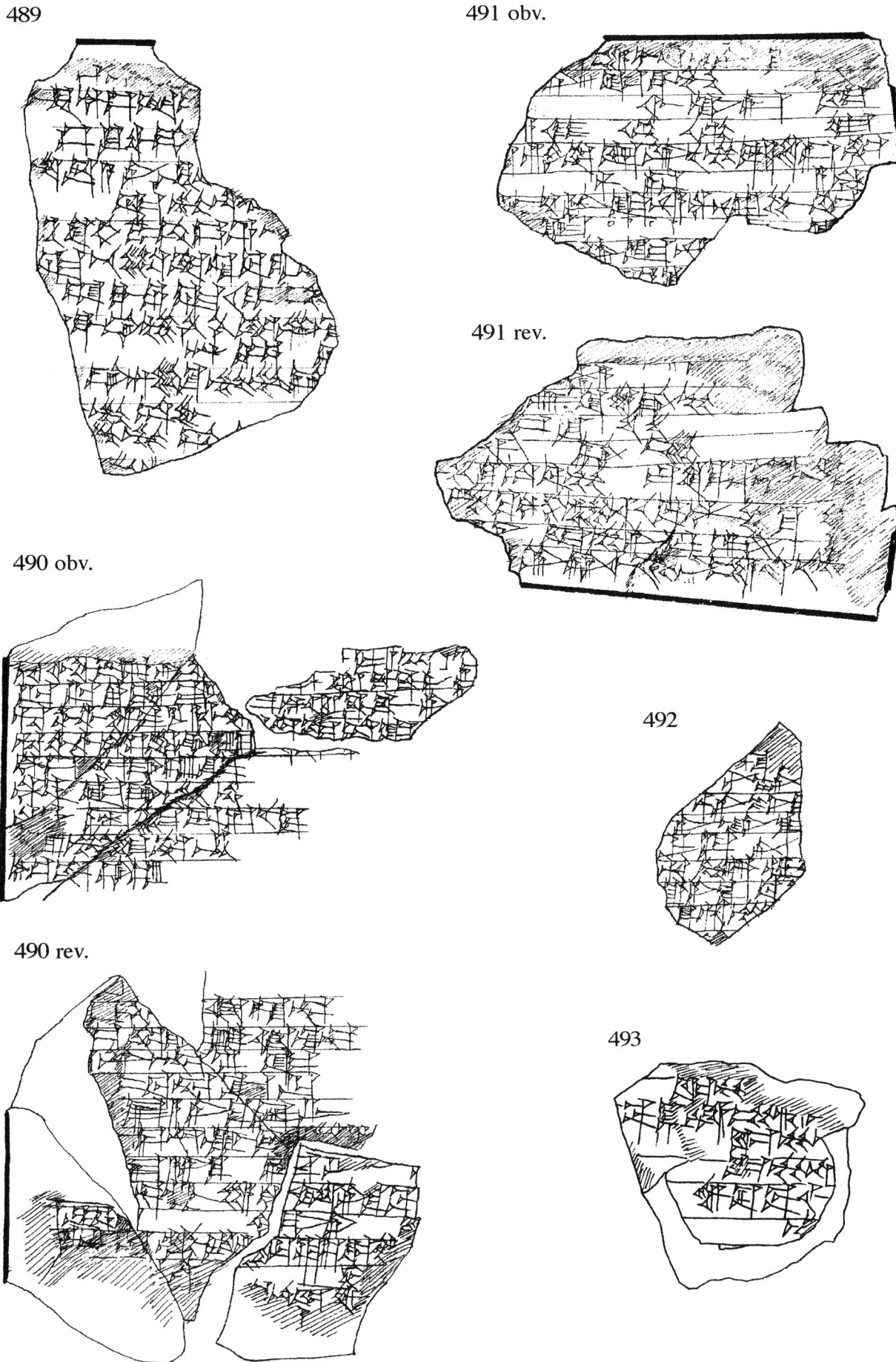

489

491 obv.

491 rev.

490 obv.

492

490 rev.

493

Plate 12

494 obv.

495 obv.

495 rev.

494 rev.

497 obv.

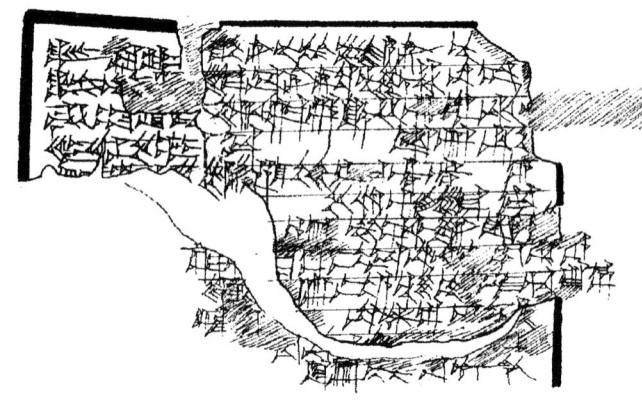

(UET 6/47)

496

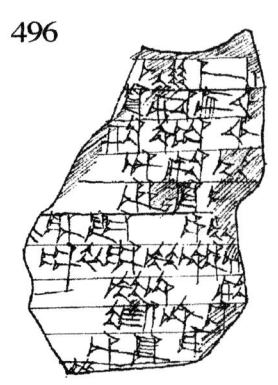

497 rev.   (UET 6/47)

Plate 13

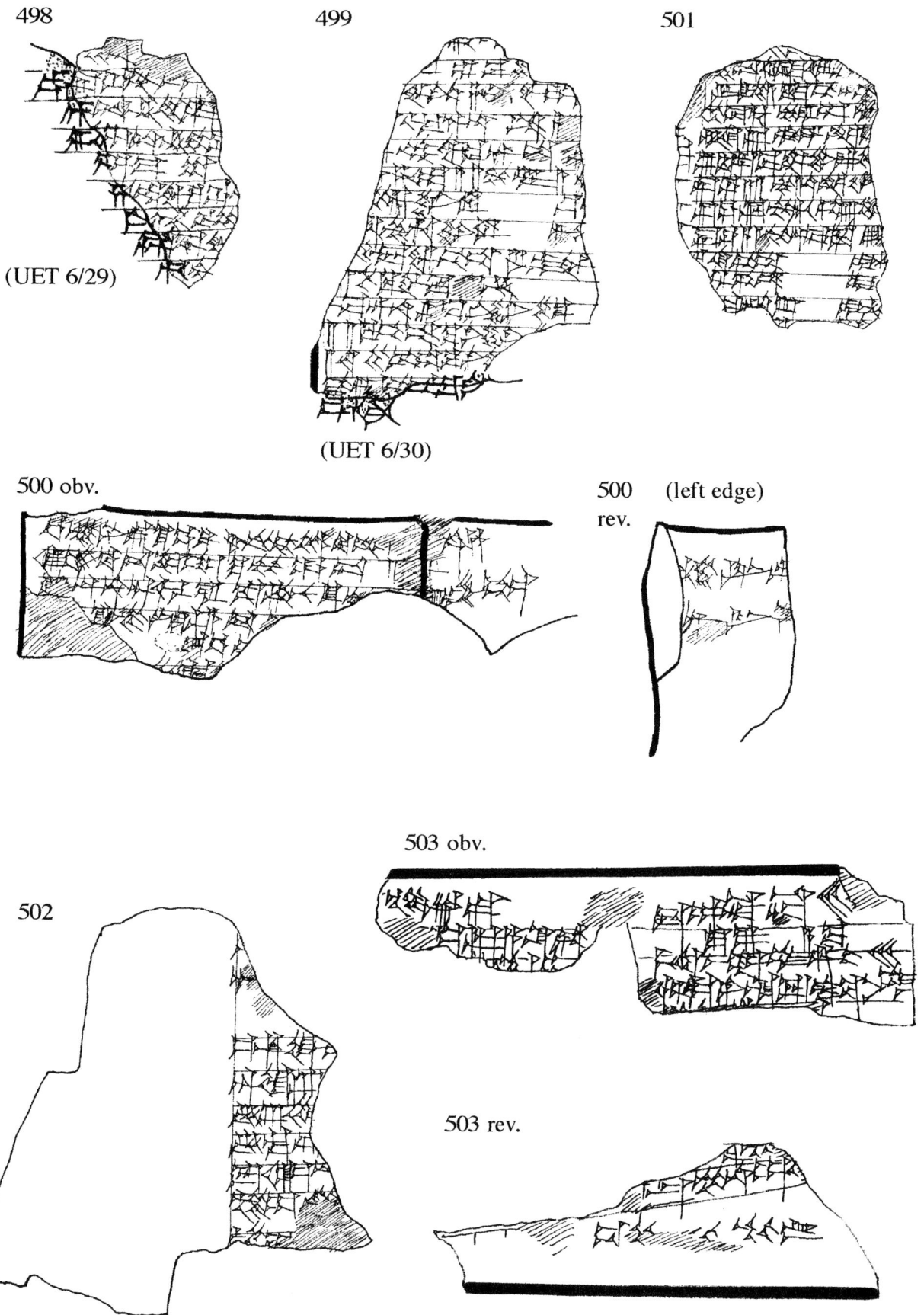

498

(UET 6/29)

499

(UET 6/30)

501

500 obv.

500
rev.

(left edge)

503 obv.

502

503 rev.

Plate 14

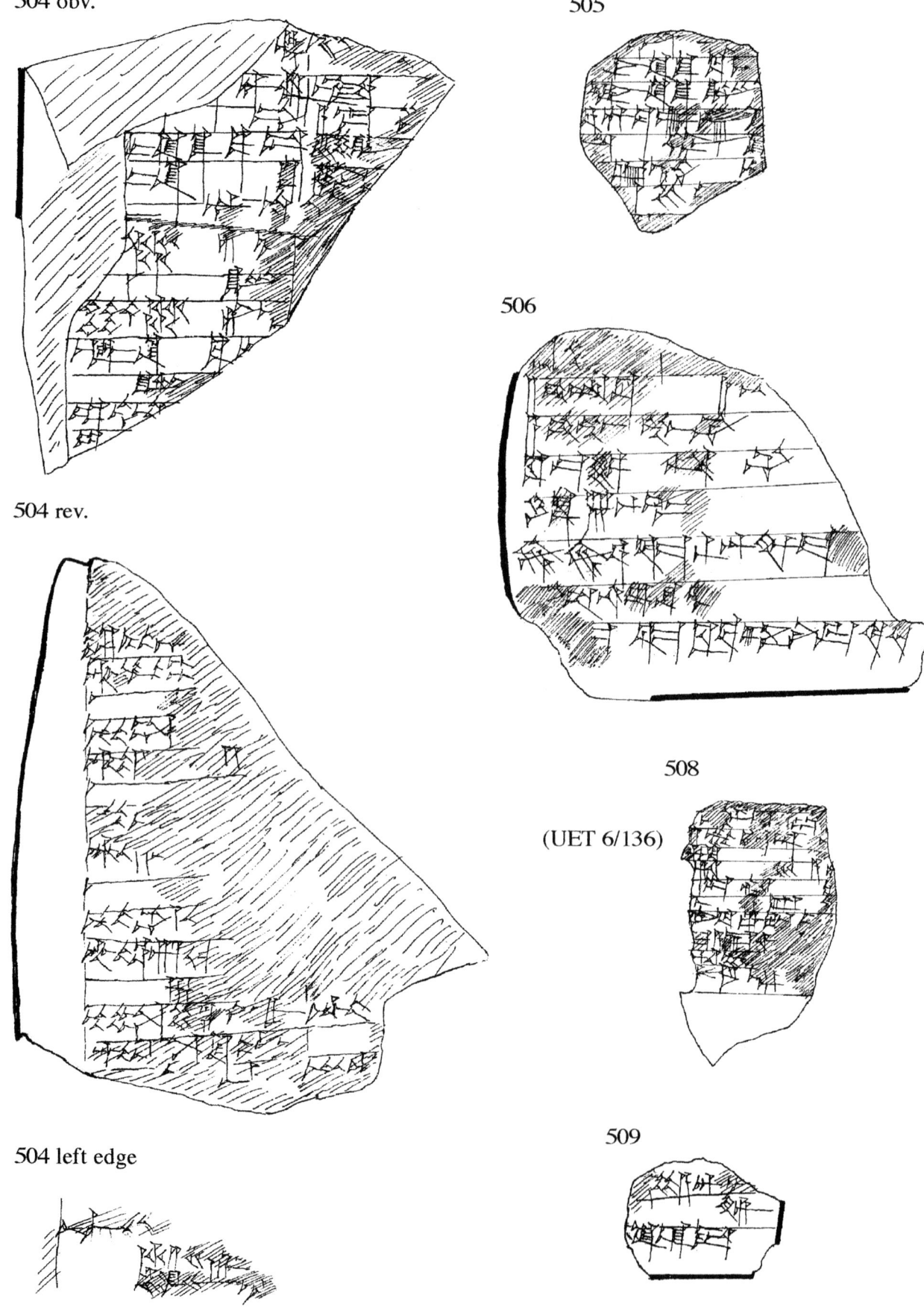

504 obv.

505

506

504 rev.

508

(UET 6/136)

509

504 left edge

Plate 15

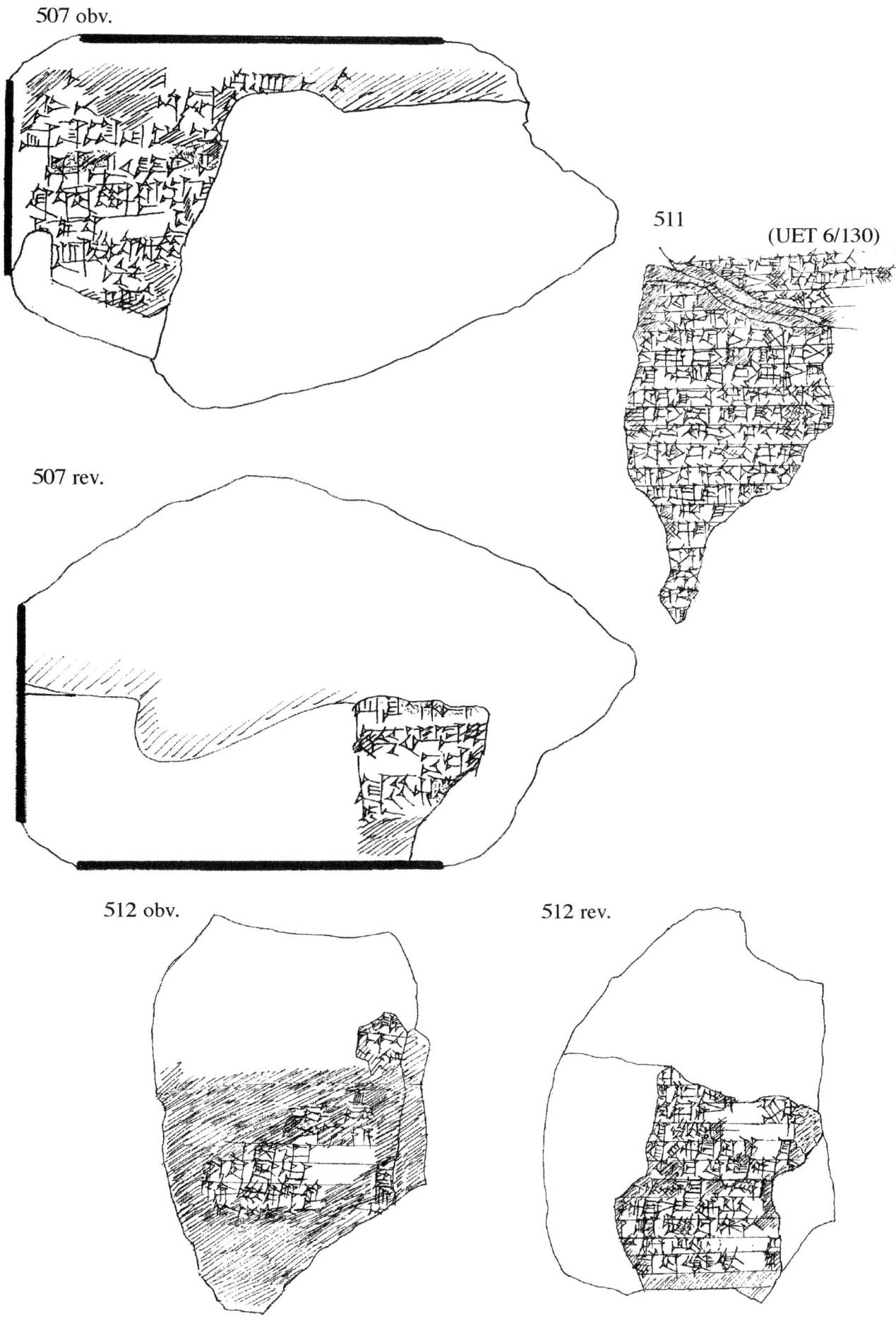

507 obv.

507 rev.

511

(UET 6/130)

512 obv.

512 rev.

Plate 16

510 obv.

513 obv. edge

513 rev.

510 rev.

514

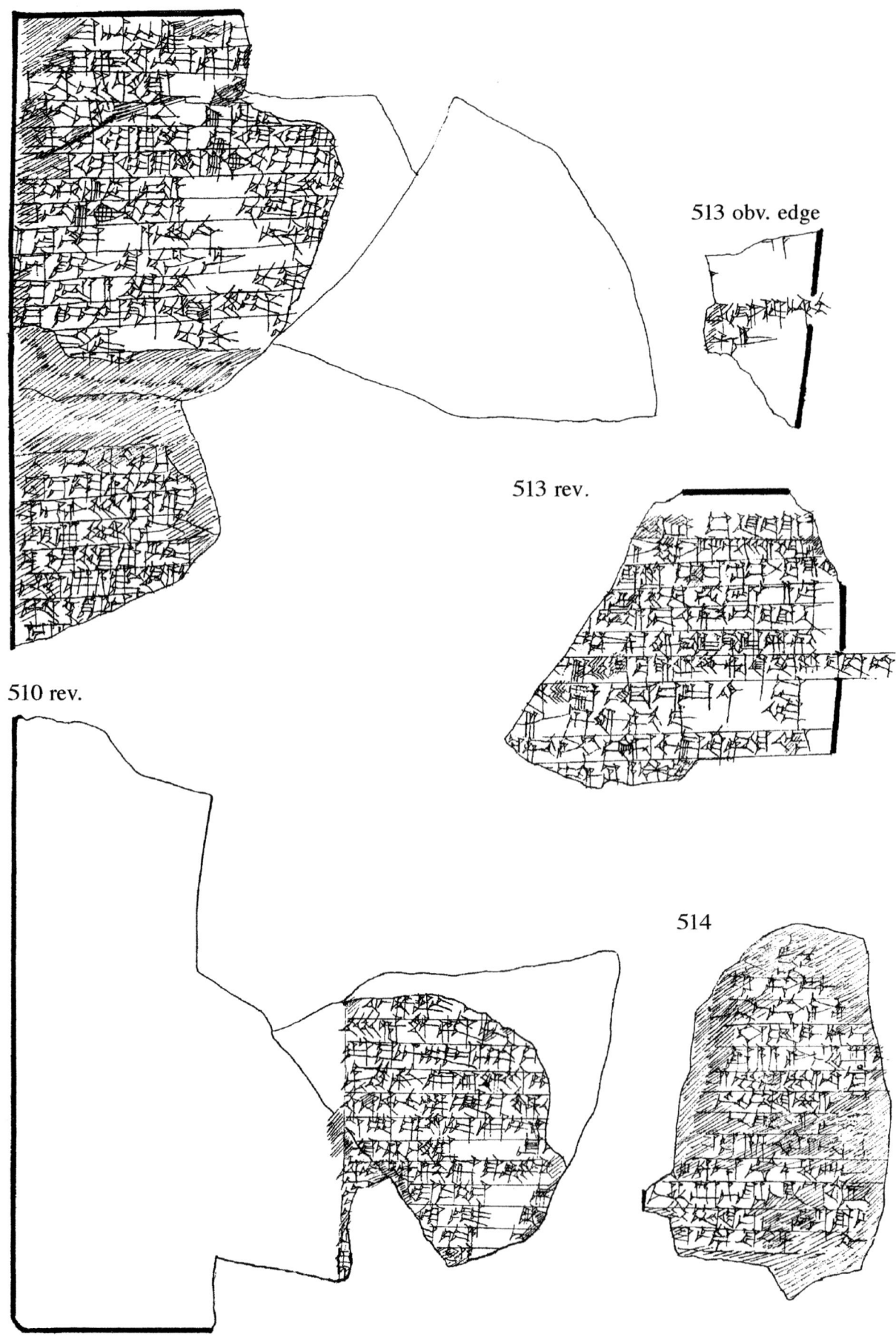

Plate 17

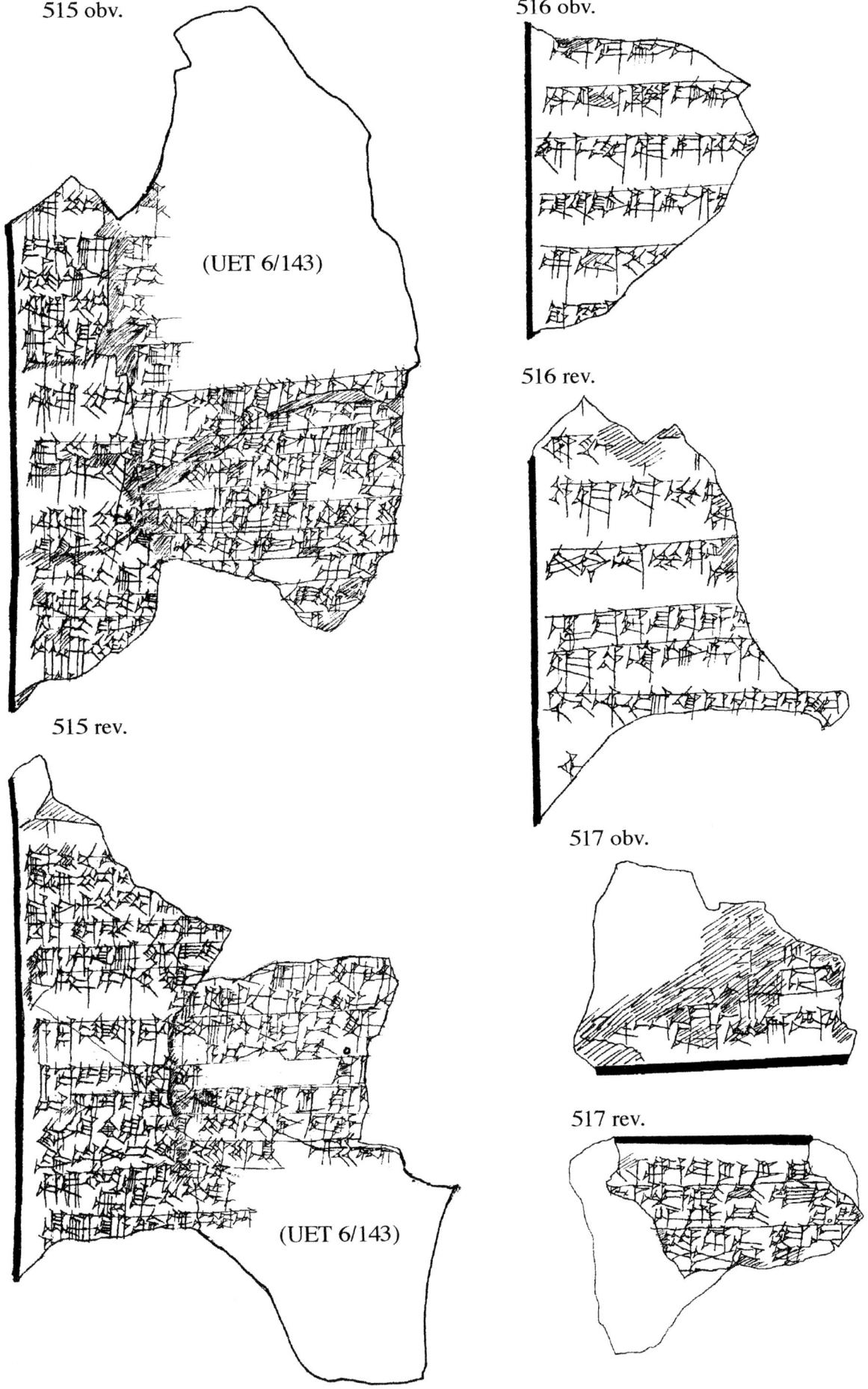

515 obv.

(UET 6/143)

515 rev.

(UET 6/143)

516 obv.

516 rev.

517 obv.

517 rev.

Plate 18

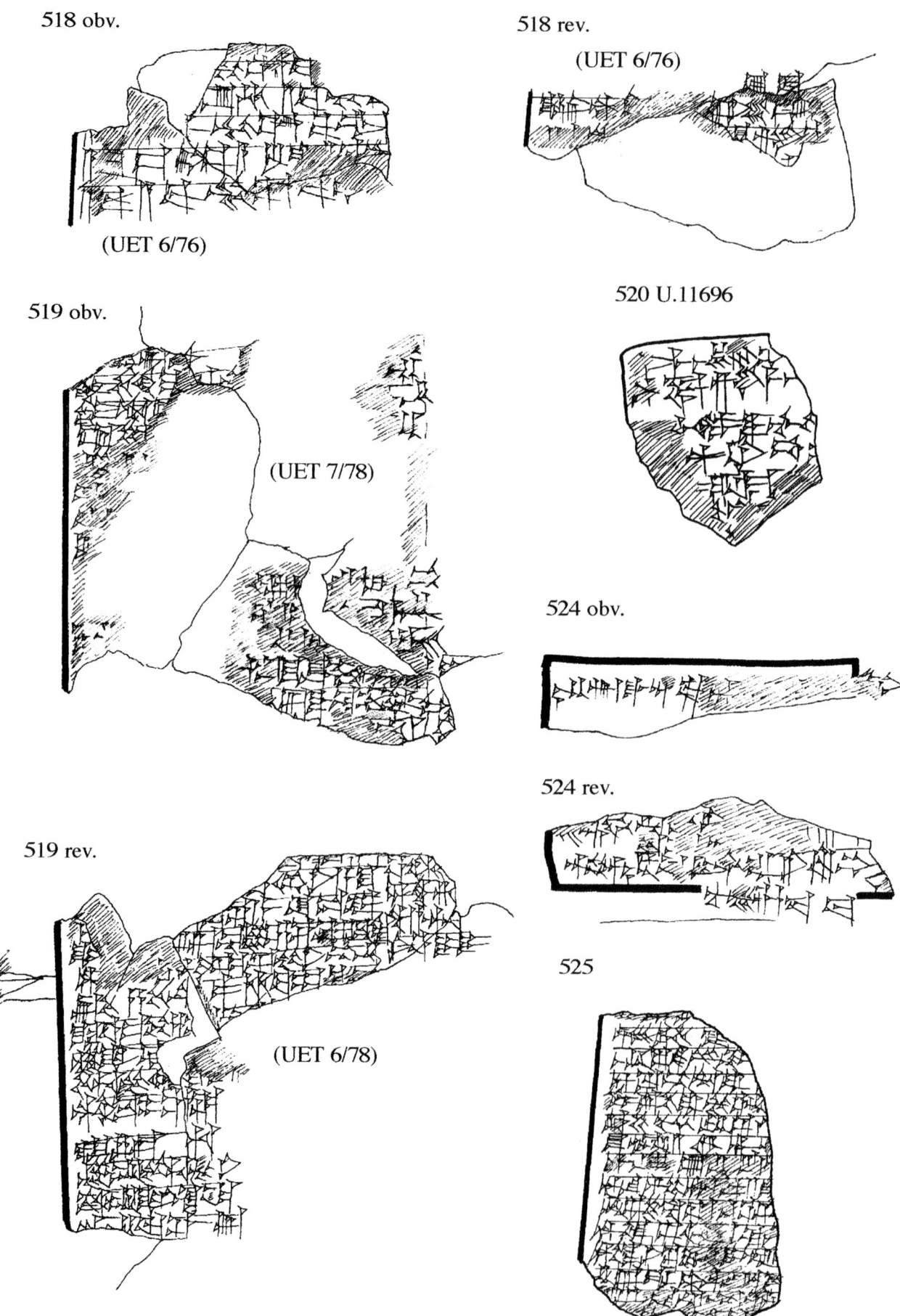

518 obv.

(UET 6/76)

518 rev.

(UET 6/76)

519 obv.

(UET 7/78)

520 U.11696

524 obv.

524 rev.

519 rev.

(UET 6/78)

525

Plate 19

521 obv.

521 rev.

523 U.5307 obv.

523 U.5307 rev.

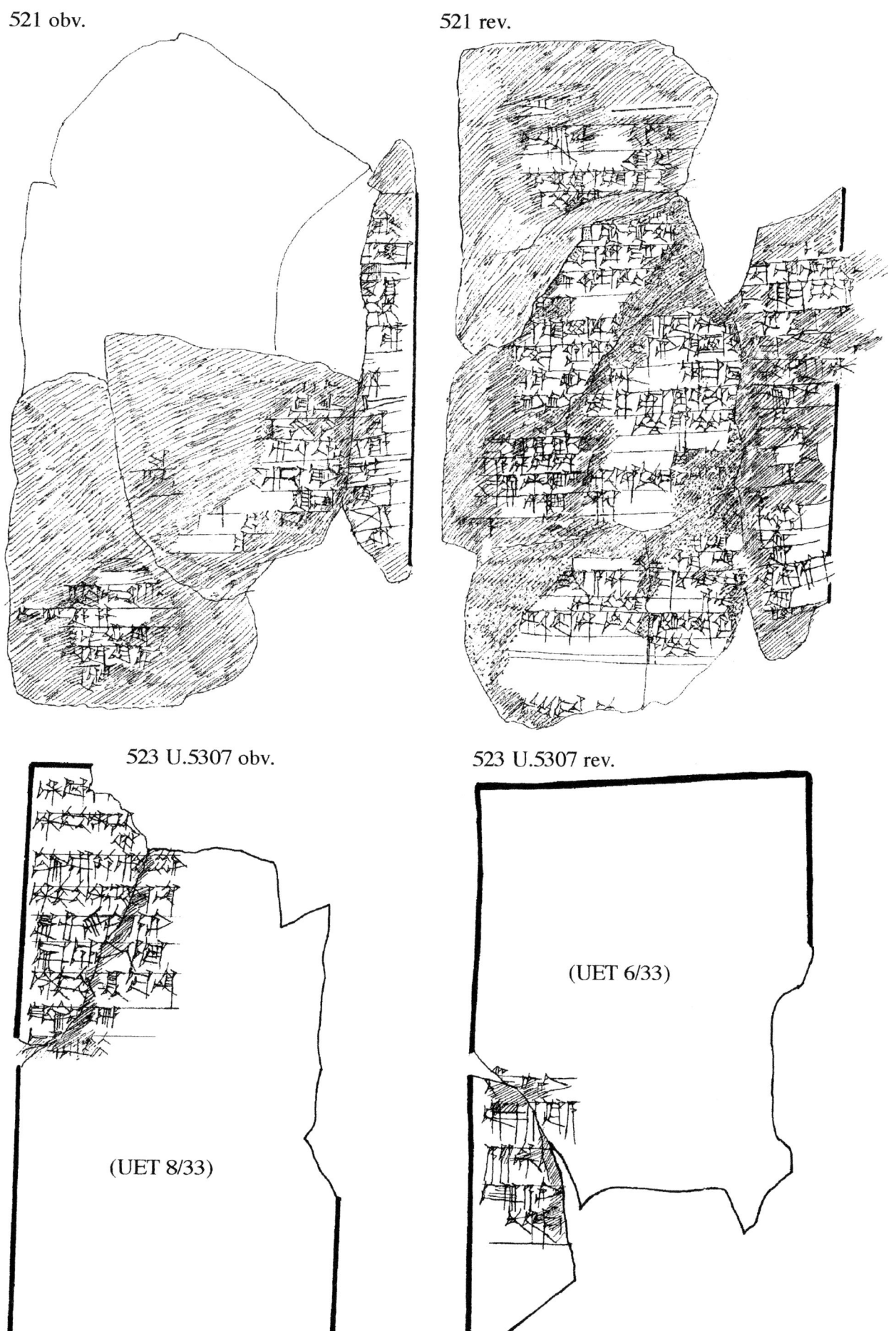

(UET 8/33)

(UET 6/33)

Plate 20

522 obv.
U.7774

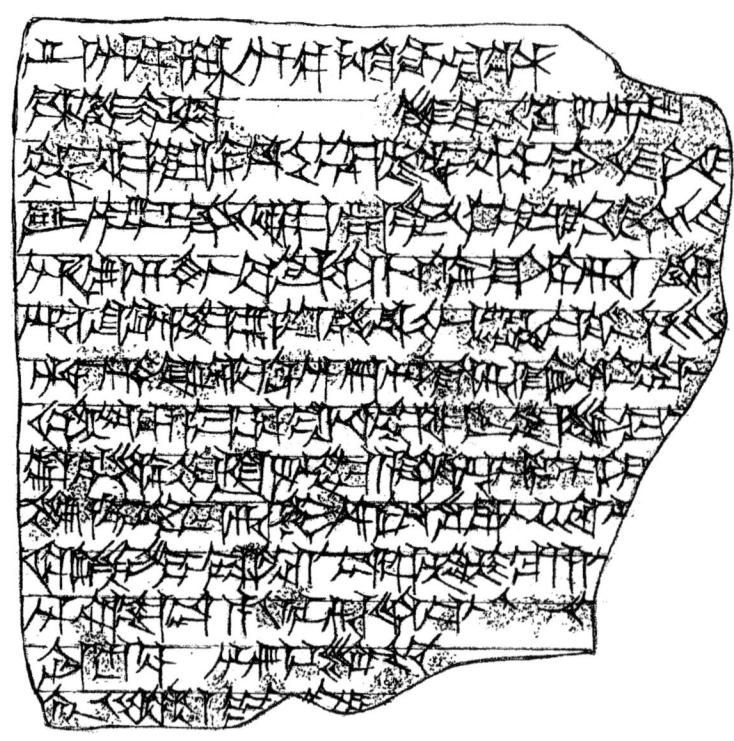

522 rev.
U.7774

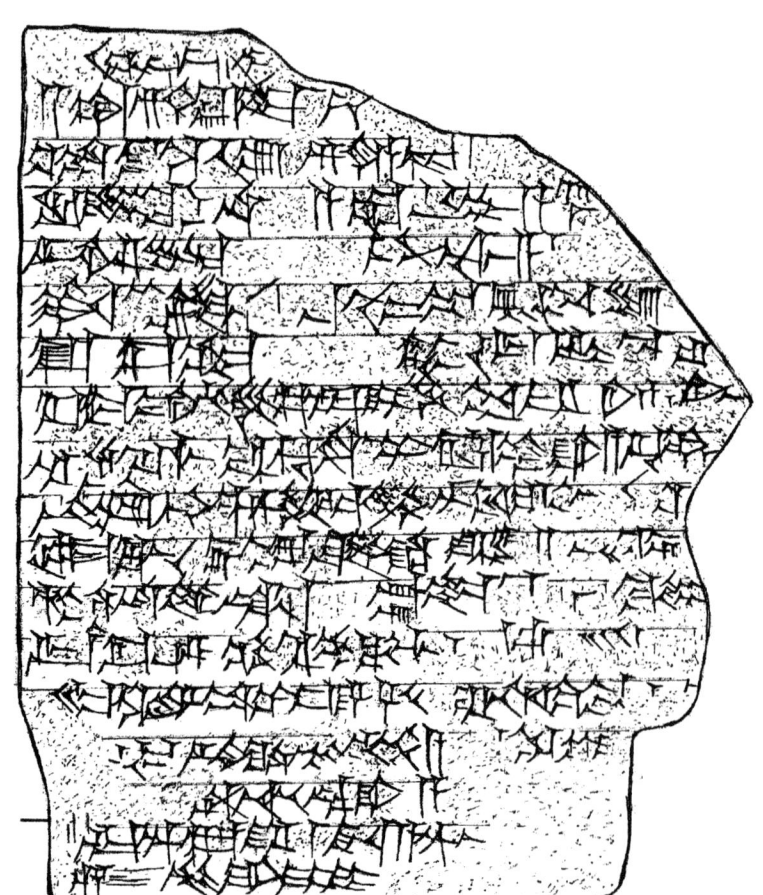

lower edge

left edge

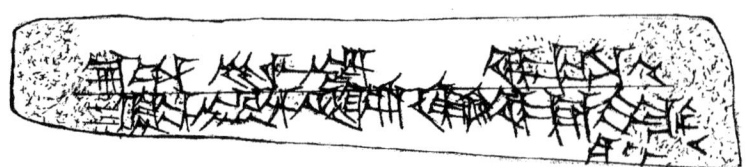

Plate 21

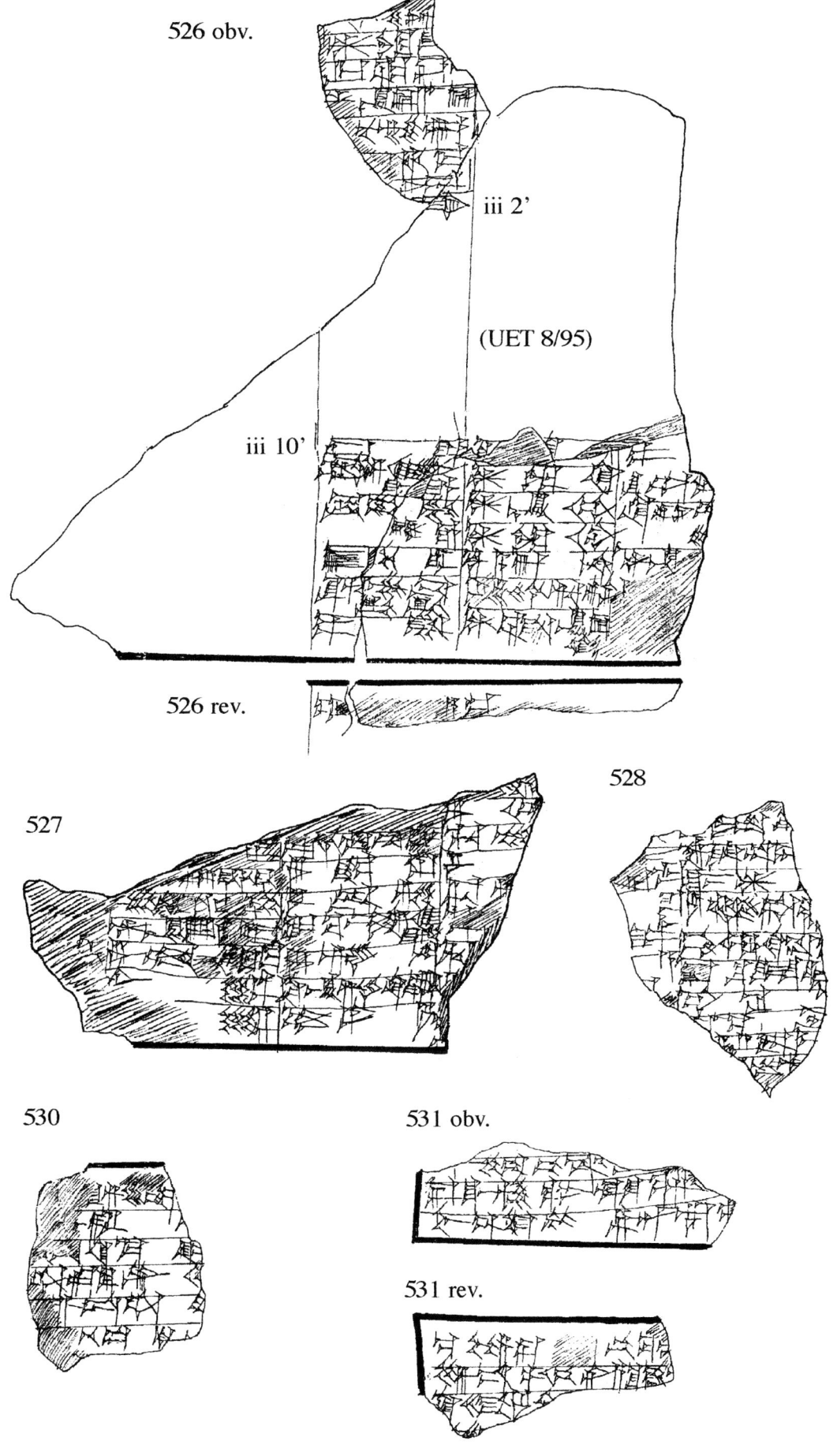

526 obv.

iii 2'

(UET 8/95)

iii 10'

526 rev.

527

528

530

531 obv.

531 rev.

Plate 22

529

532 U.5621 obv.

532 U.5621 rev.

533 obv.

533 rev.

(UET 6/99)

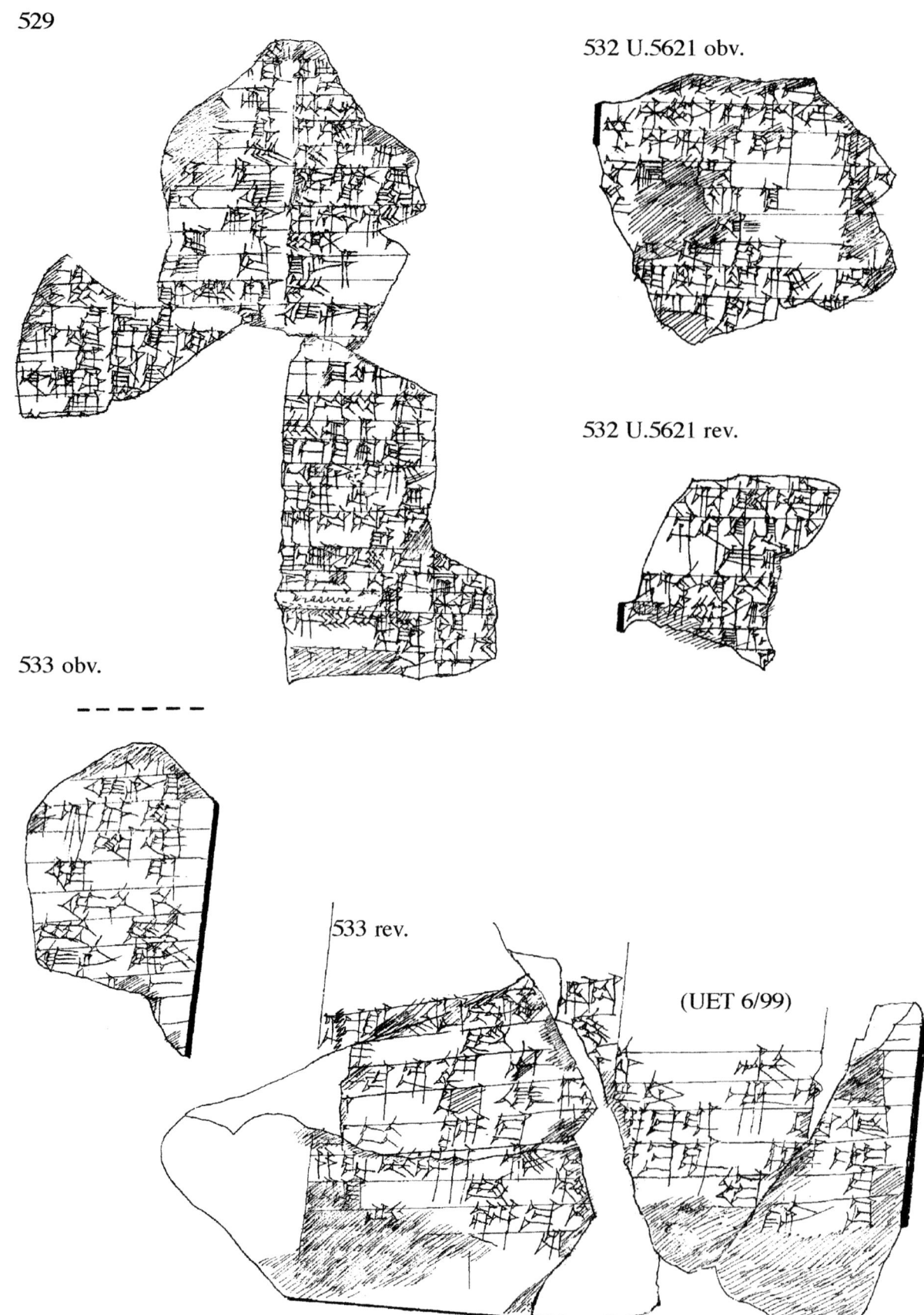

Plate 23

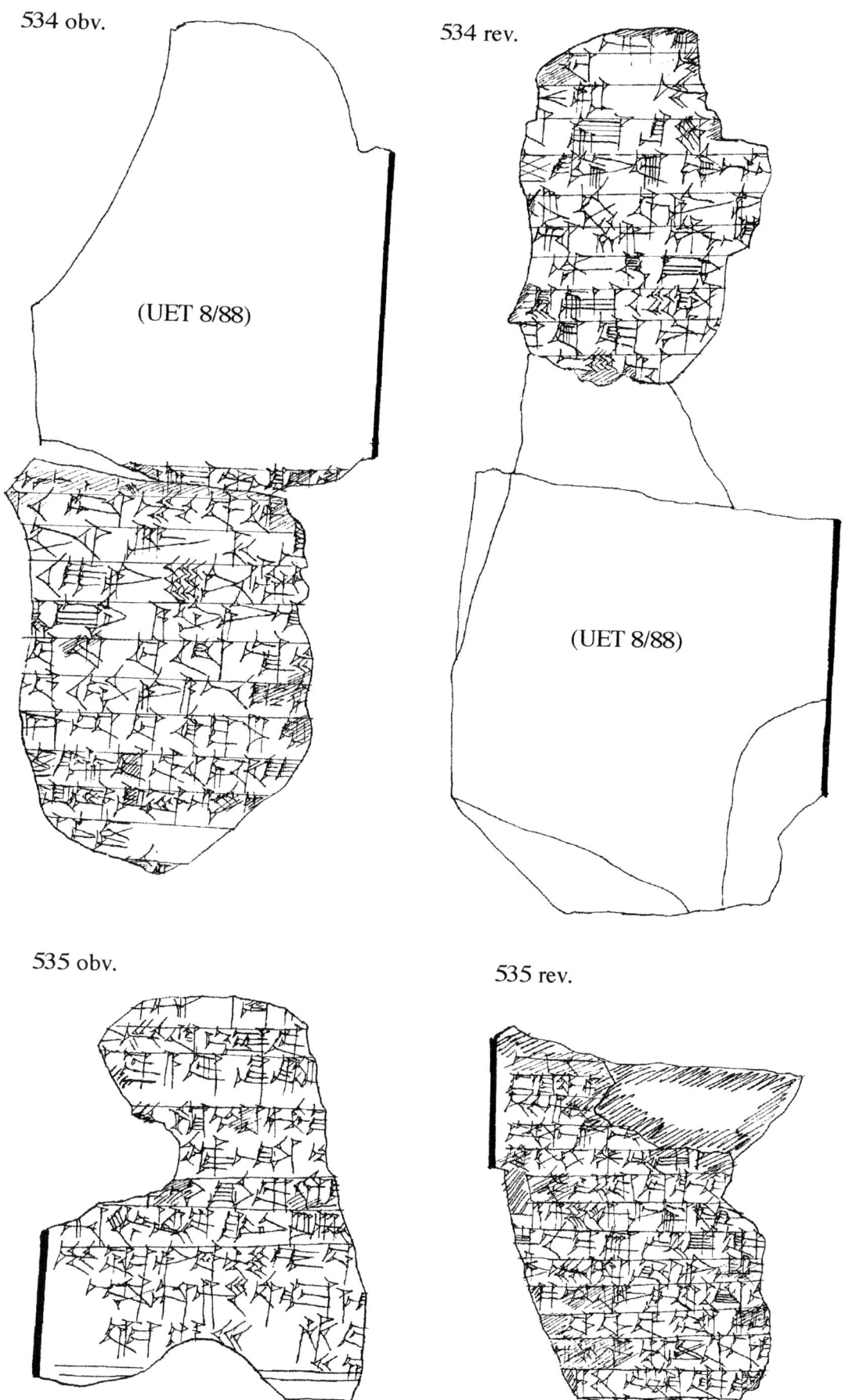

534 obv.

(UET 8/88)

534 rev.

(UET 8/88)

535 obv.

535 rev.

Plate 24

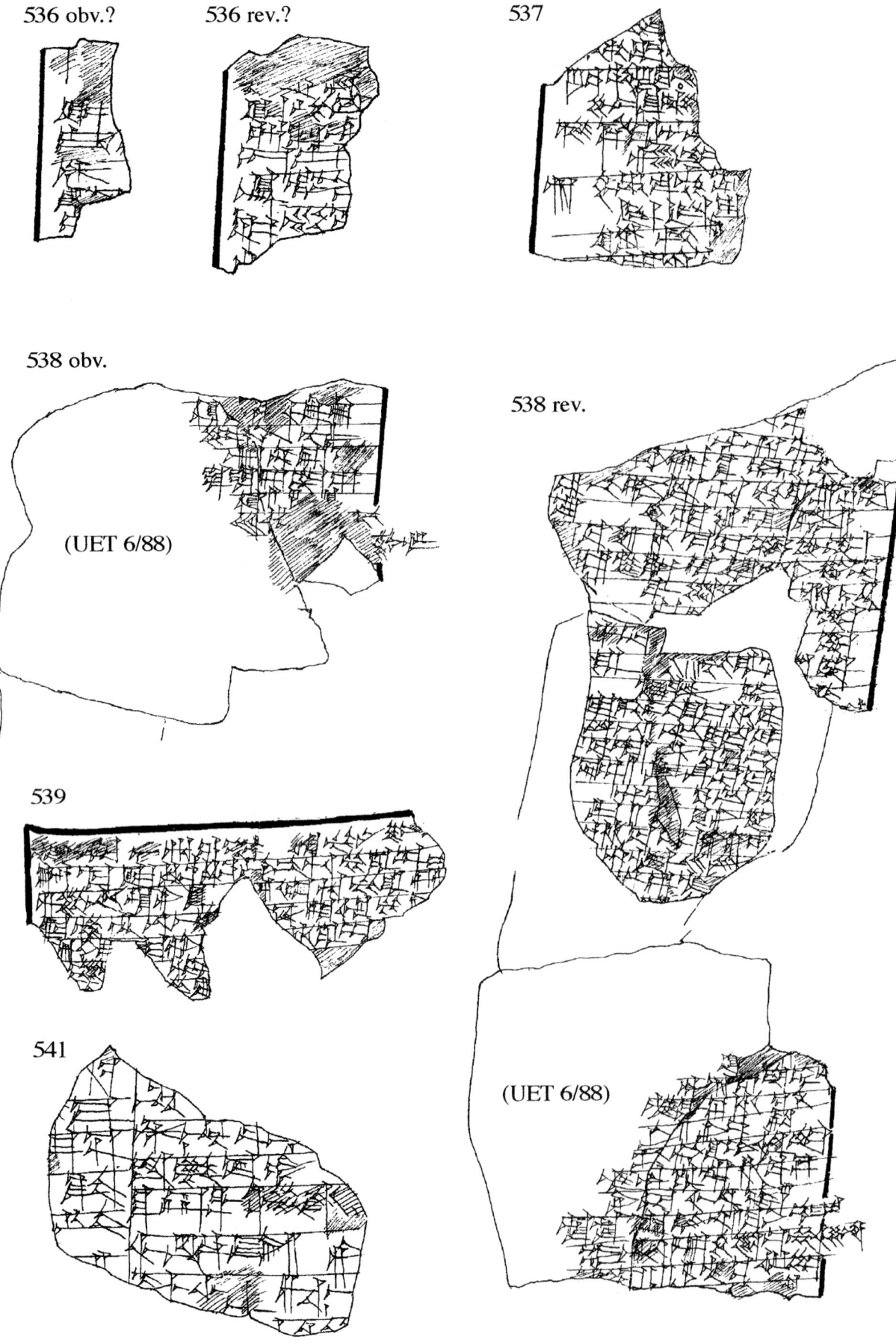

536 obv.?

536 rev.?

537

538 obv.

(UET 6/88)

538 rev.

539

541

(UET 6/88)

Plate 25

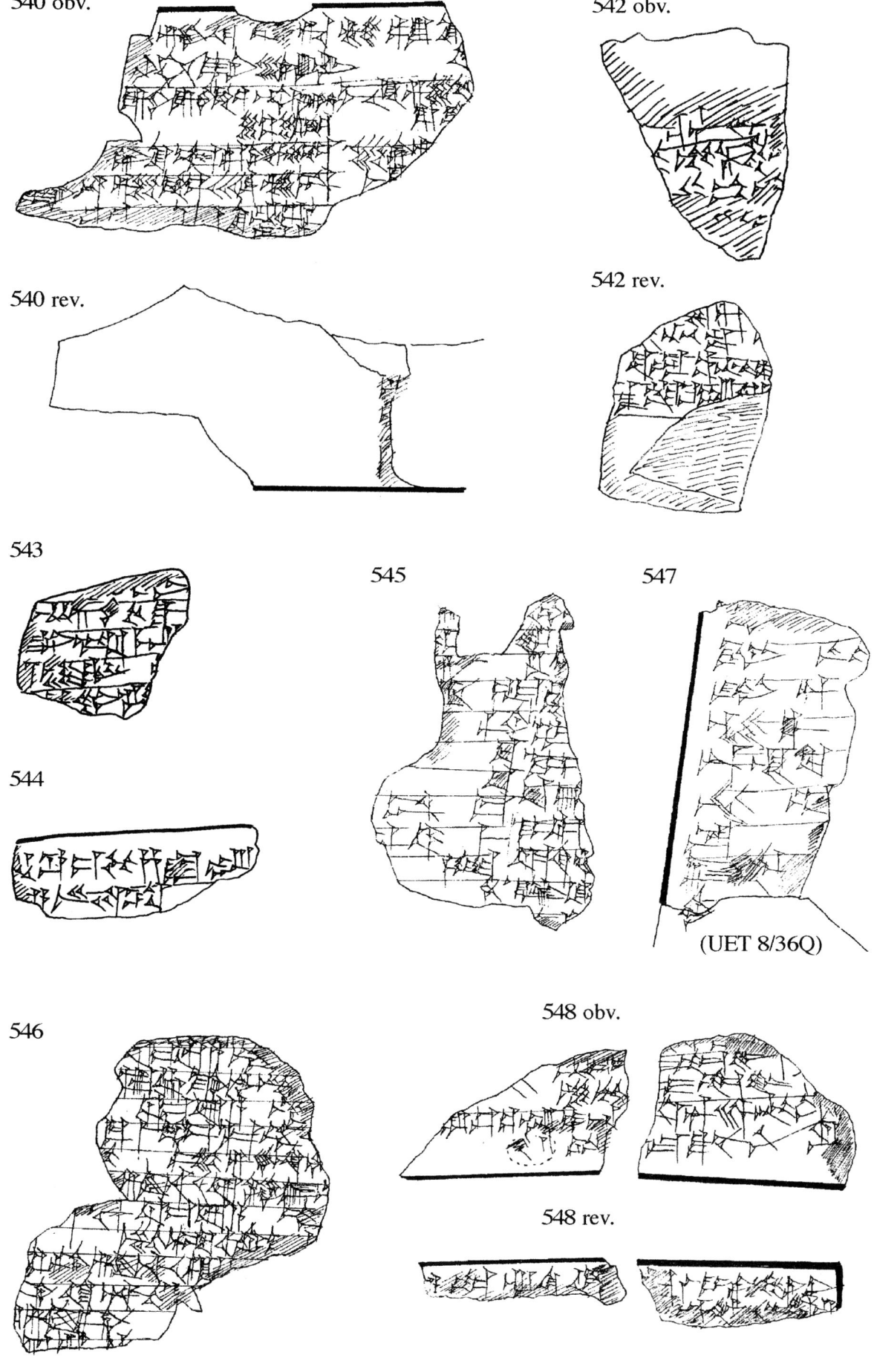

540 obv.

542 obv.

540 rev.

542 rev.

543

545

547

544

546

(UET 8/36Q)

548 obv.

548 rev.

Plate 26

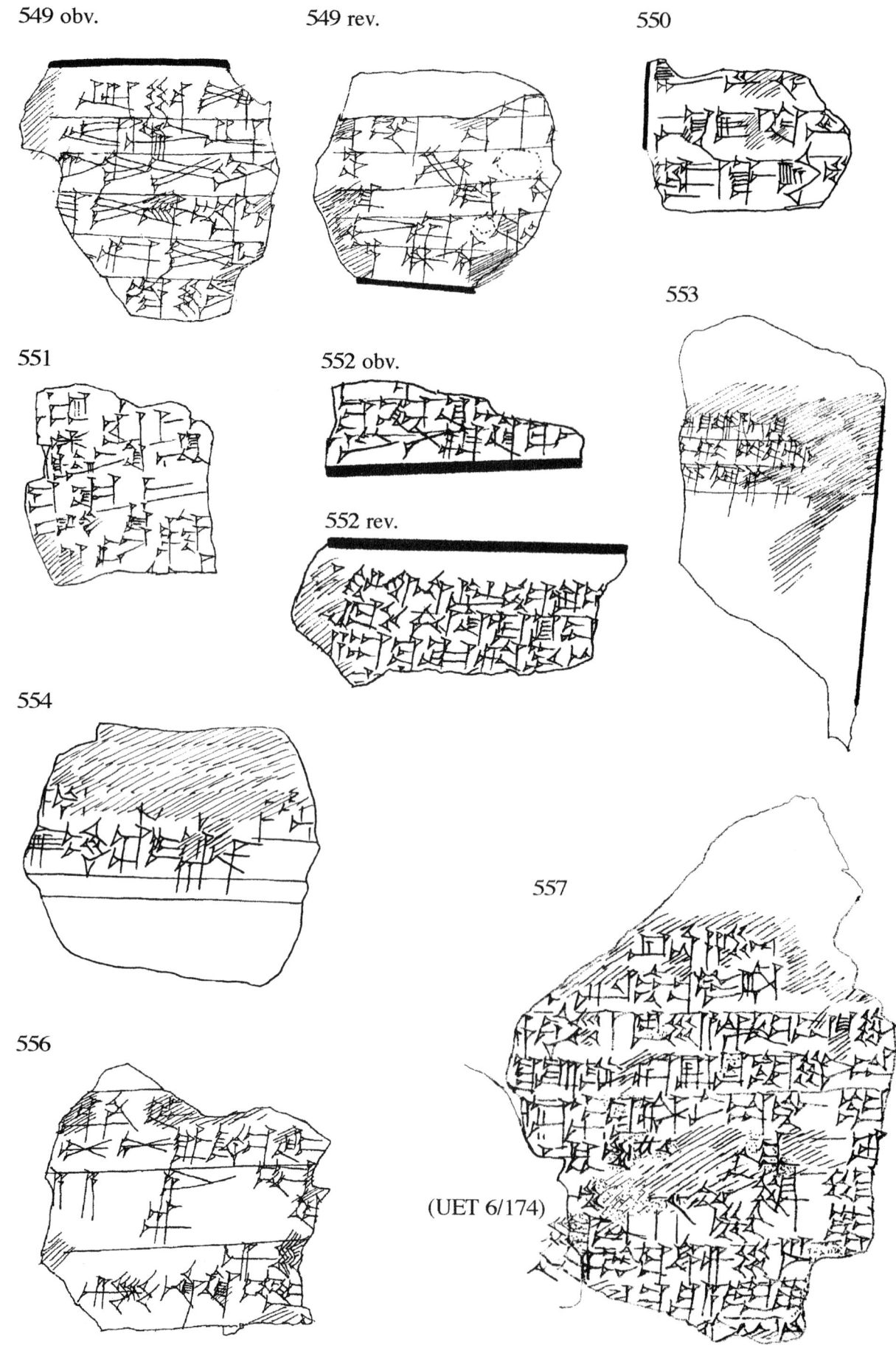

549 obv.

549 rev.

550

551

552 obv.

552 rev.

553

554

556

557

(UET 6/174)

Plate 27

555 obv.

555 rev.

558 obv.

558 rev.

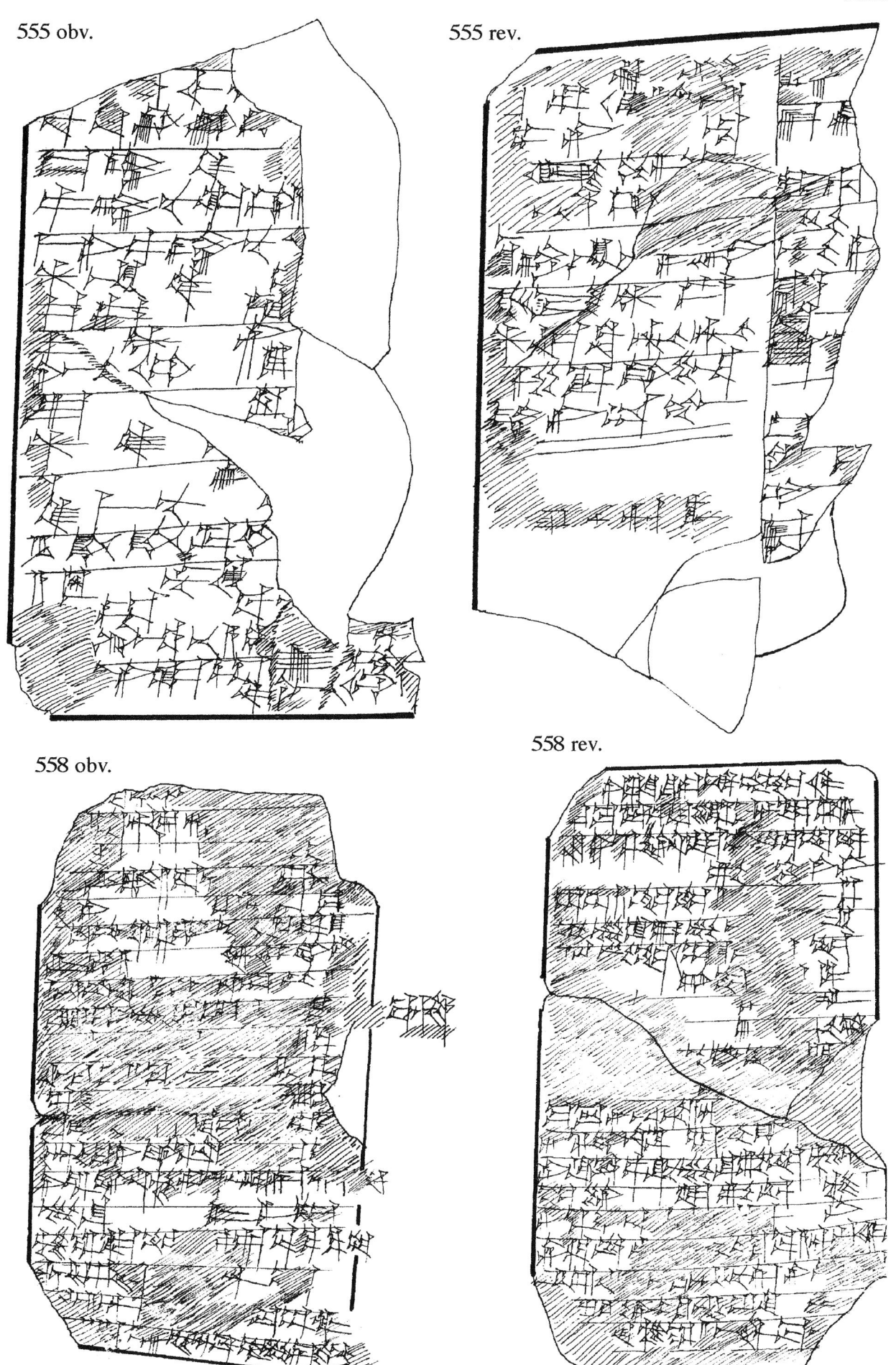

Plate 28

559   (UET 8/70 obv.)

560

561 rev.

561 obv.

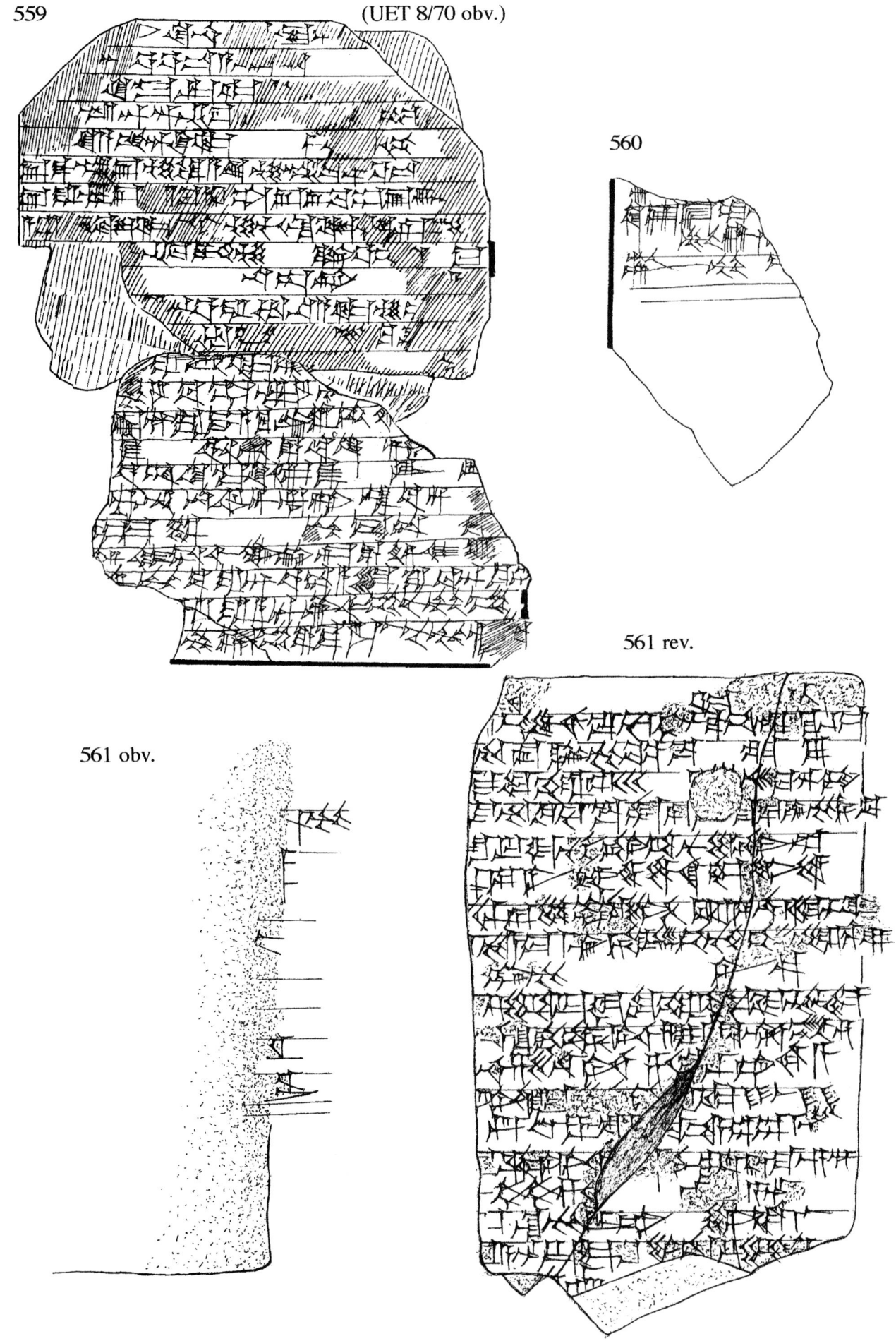

Plate 29

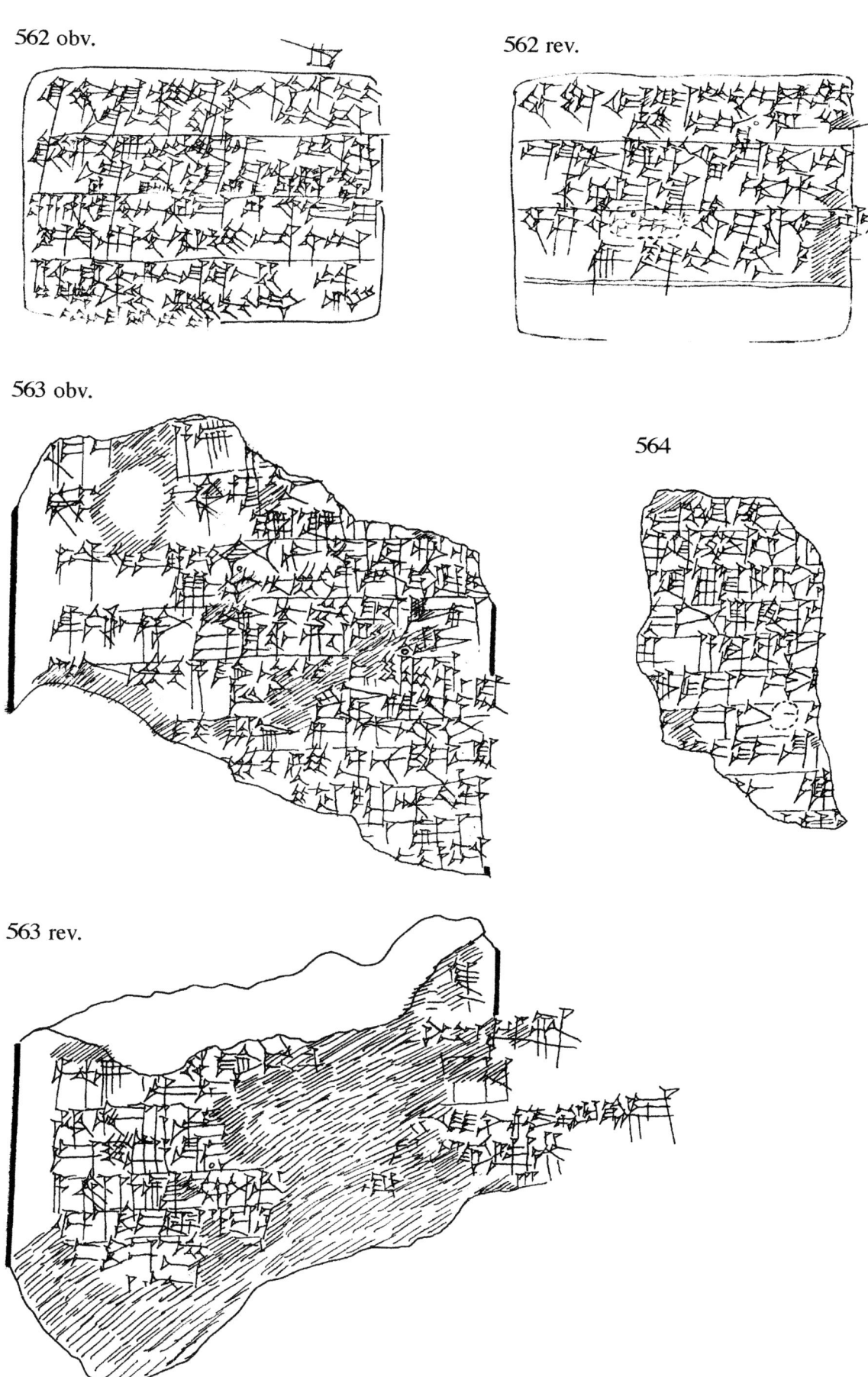

562 obv.

562 rev.

563 obv.

564

563 rev.

Plate 30

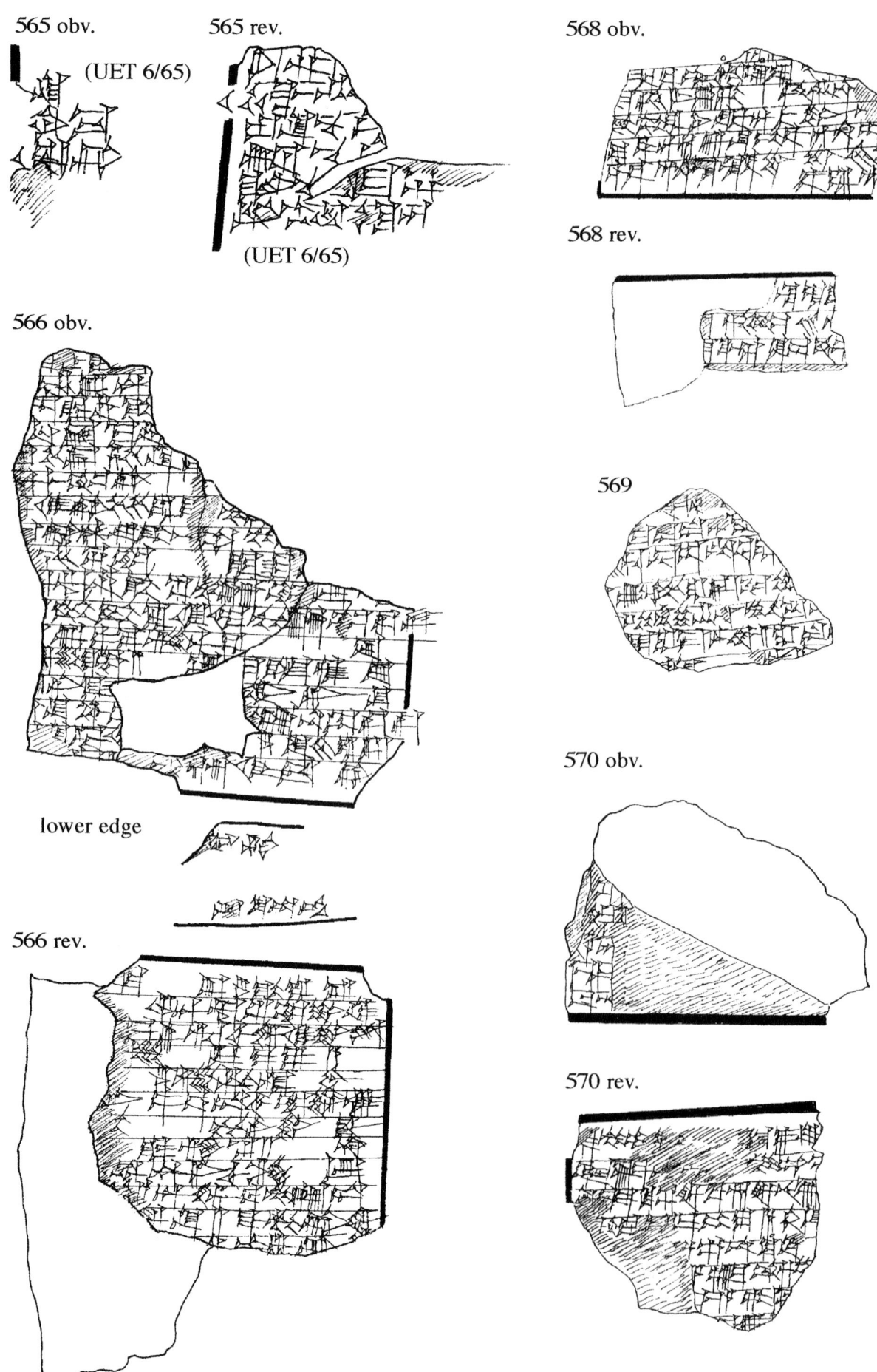

565 obv.

(UET 6/65)

565 rev.

(UET 6/65)

568 obv.

568 rev.

566 obv.

569

lower edge

570 obv.

566 rev.

570 rev.

Plate 31

567 U.8820 obv.

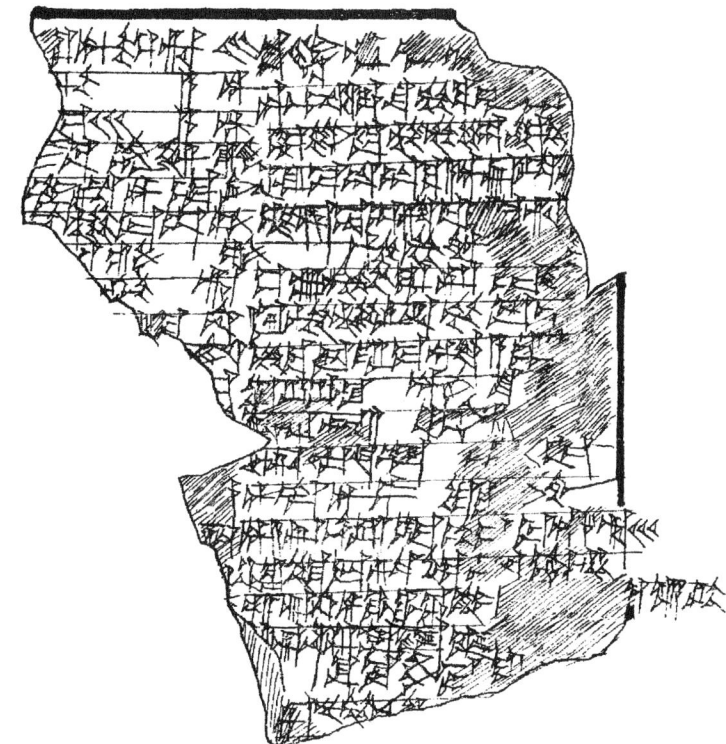

567 U.8820 rev.

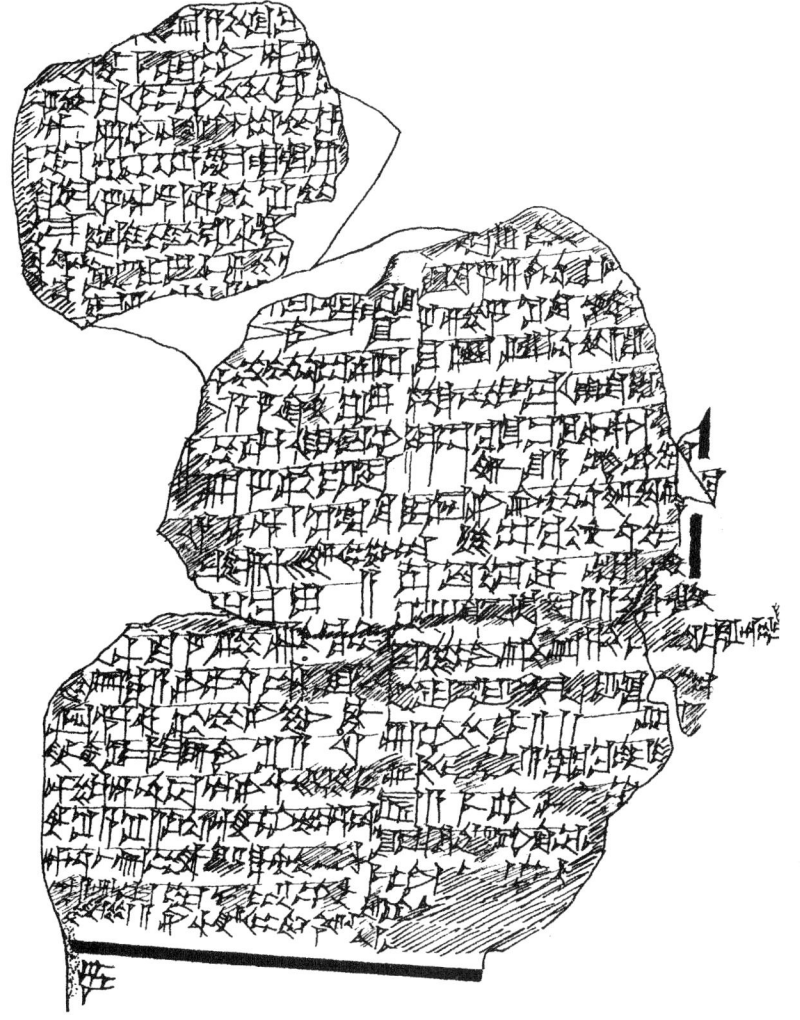

Plate 32

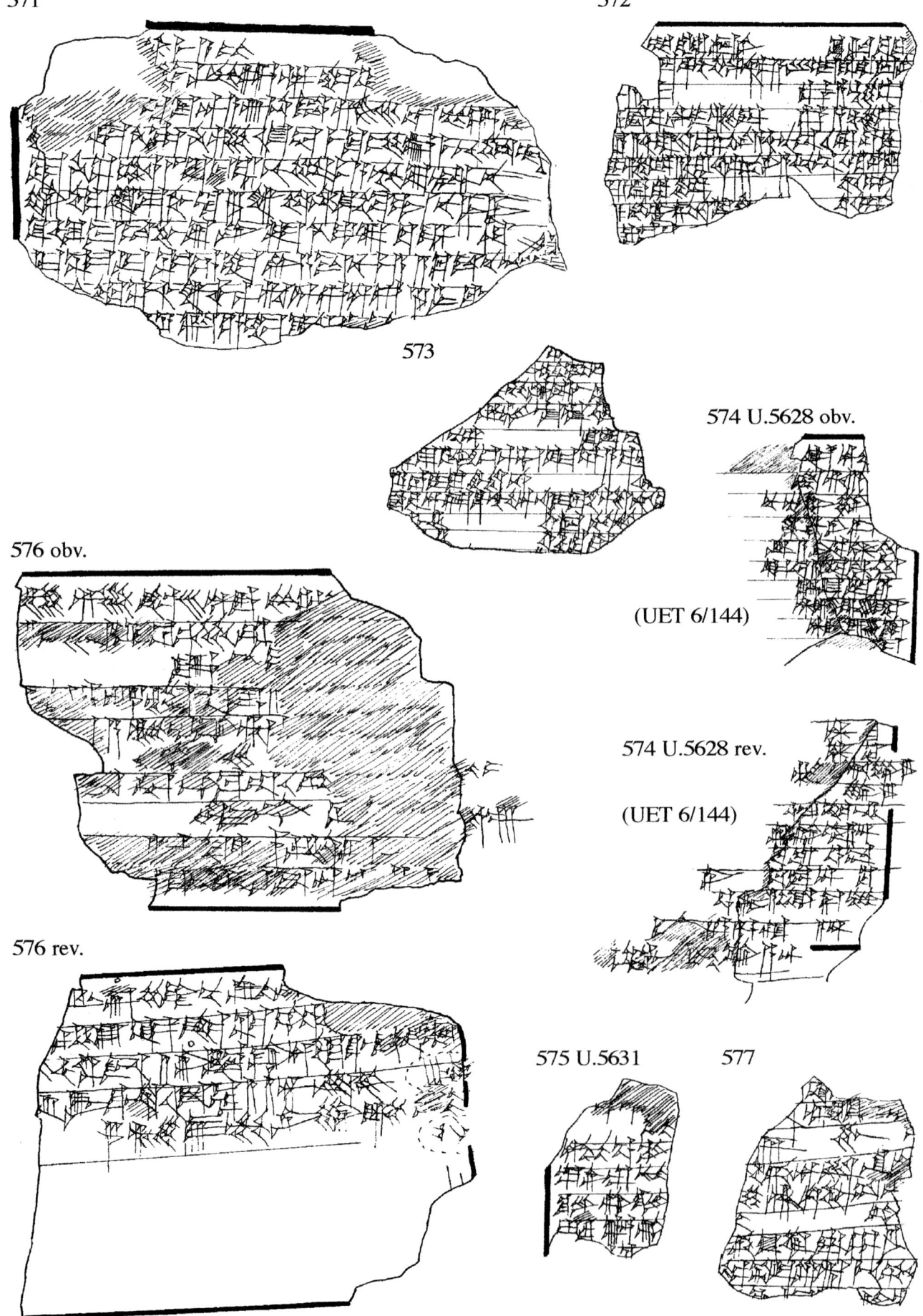

571

572

573

574 U.5628 obv.

(UET 6/144)

576 obv.

574 U.5628 rev.

(UET 6/144)

576 rev.

575 U.5631

577

Plate 33

578 obv.

578 rev.

579

(UET 6/388)

UET 8/92

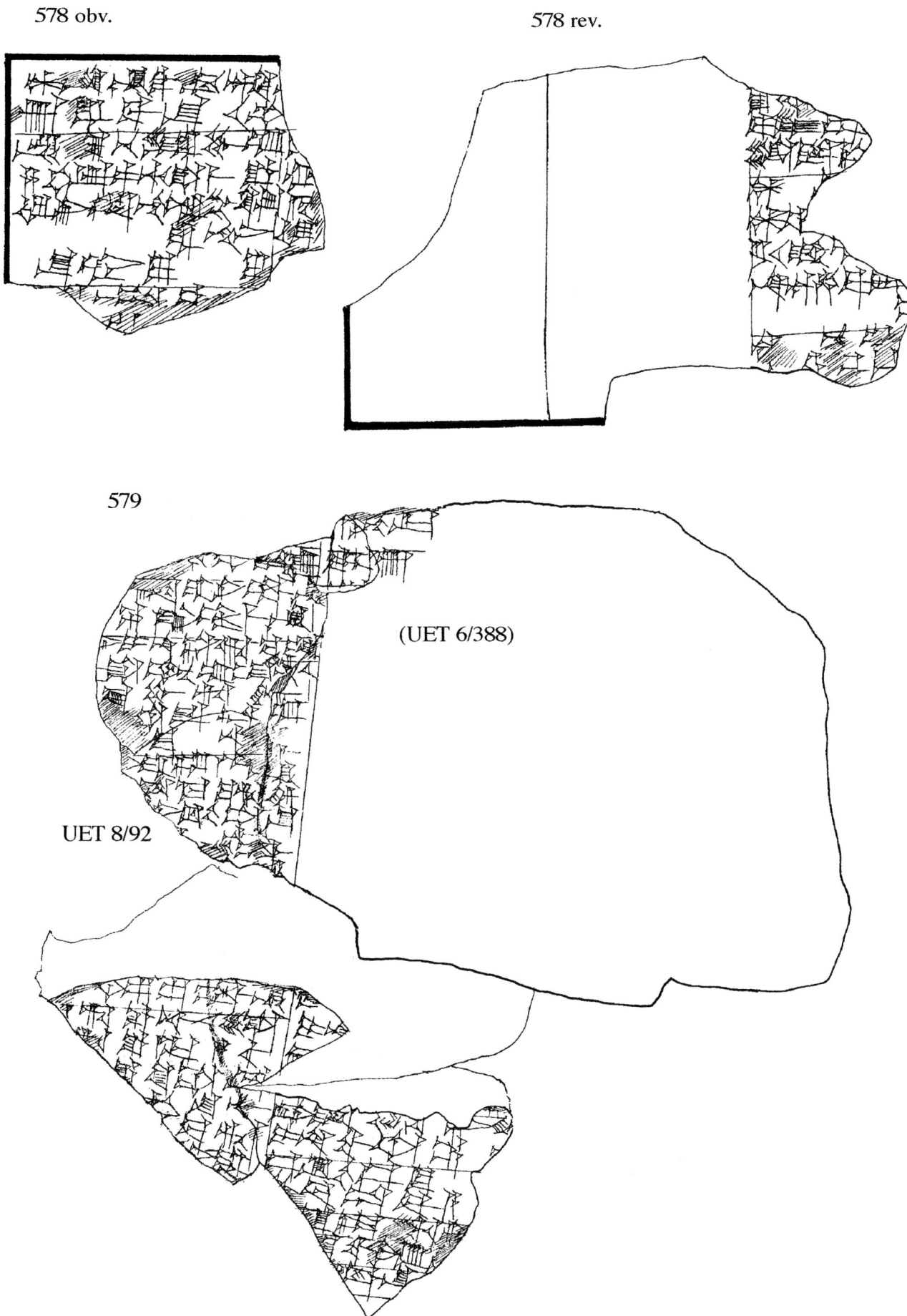

Plate 34

580 obv.

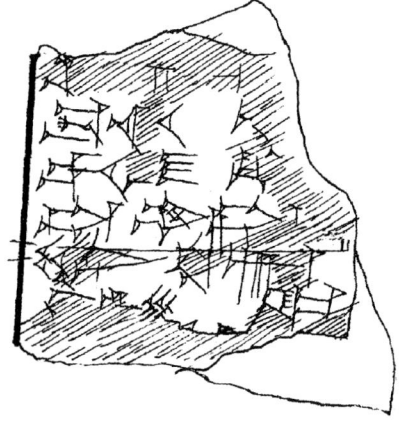

580 rev.

584 obv.   584 rev.

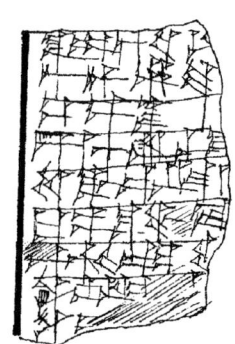

581

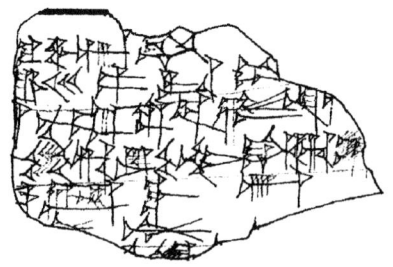

582 obv.

582 rev.

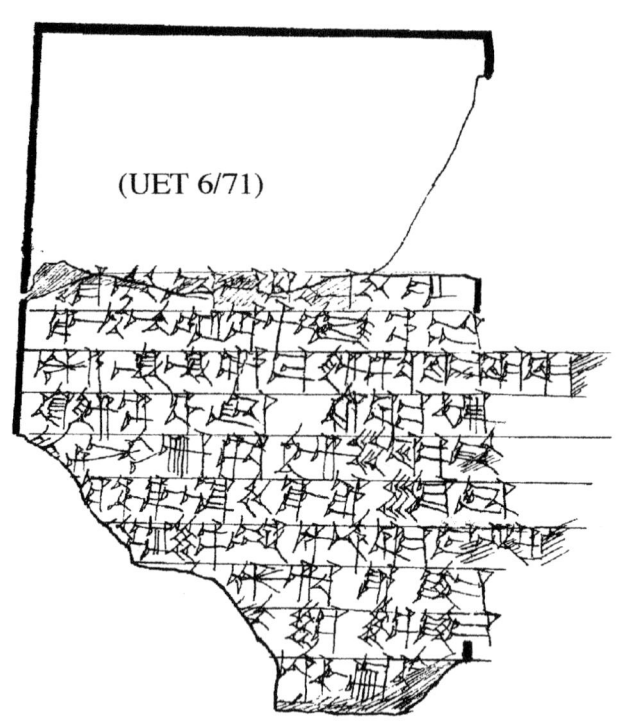

Plate 35

583 obv.

583 rev.

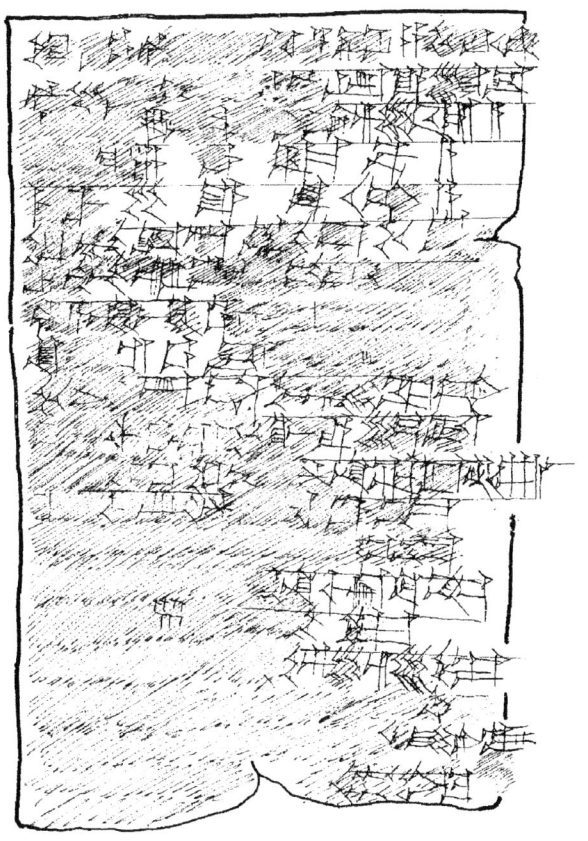

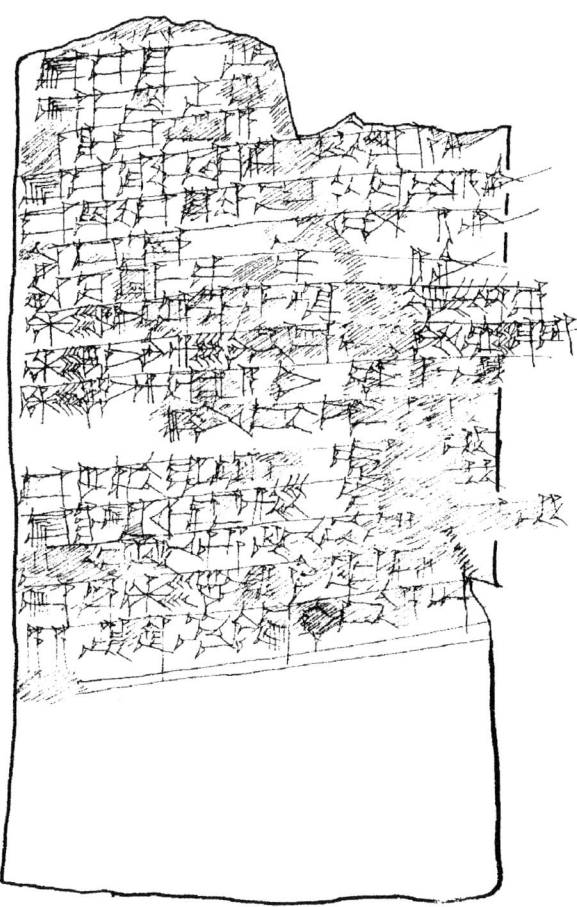

585

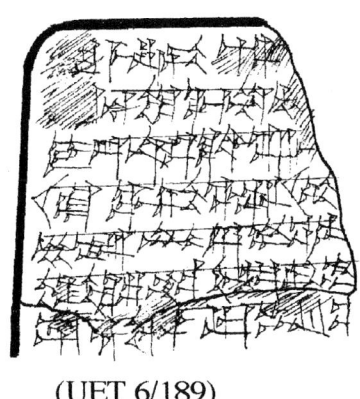

(UET 6/189)

586 obv.

586 rev.

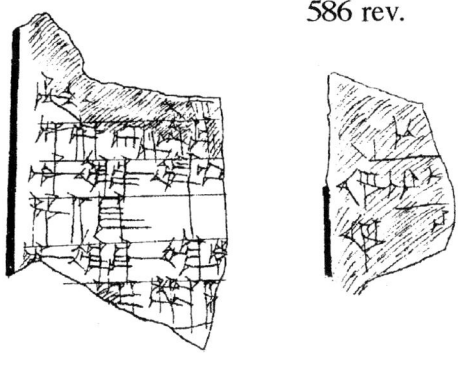

587 obv.

587 rev.

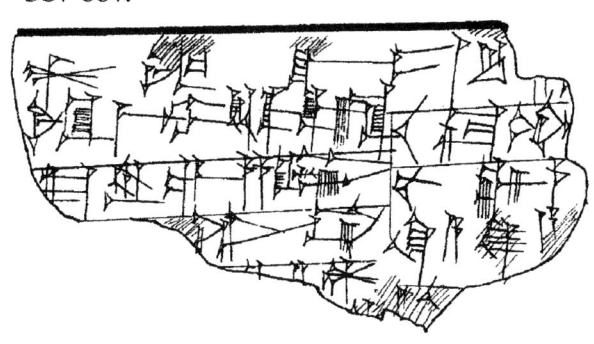

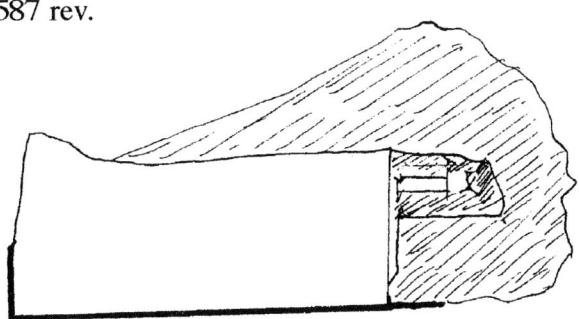

Plate 36

588 obv.

588 rev.

589 obv.

589 rev.

590

591

592 obv.

592 rev.

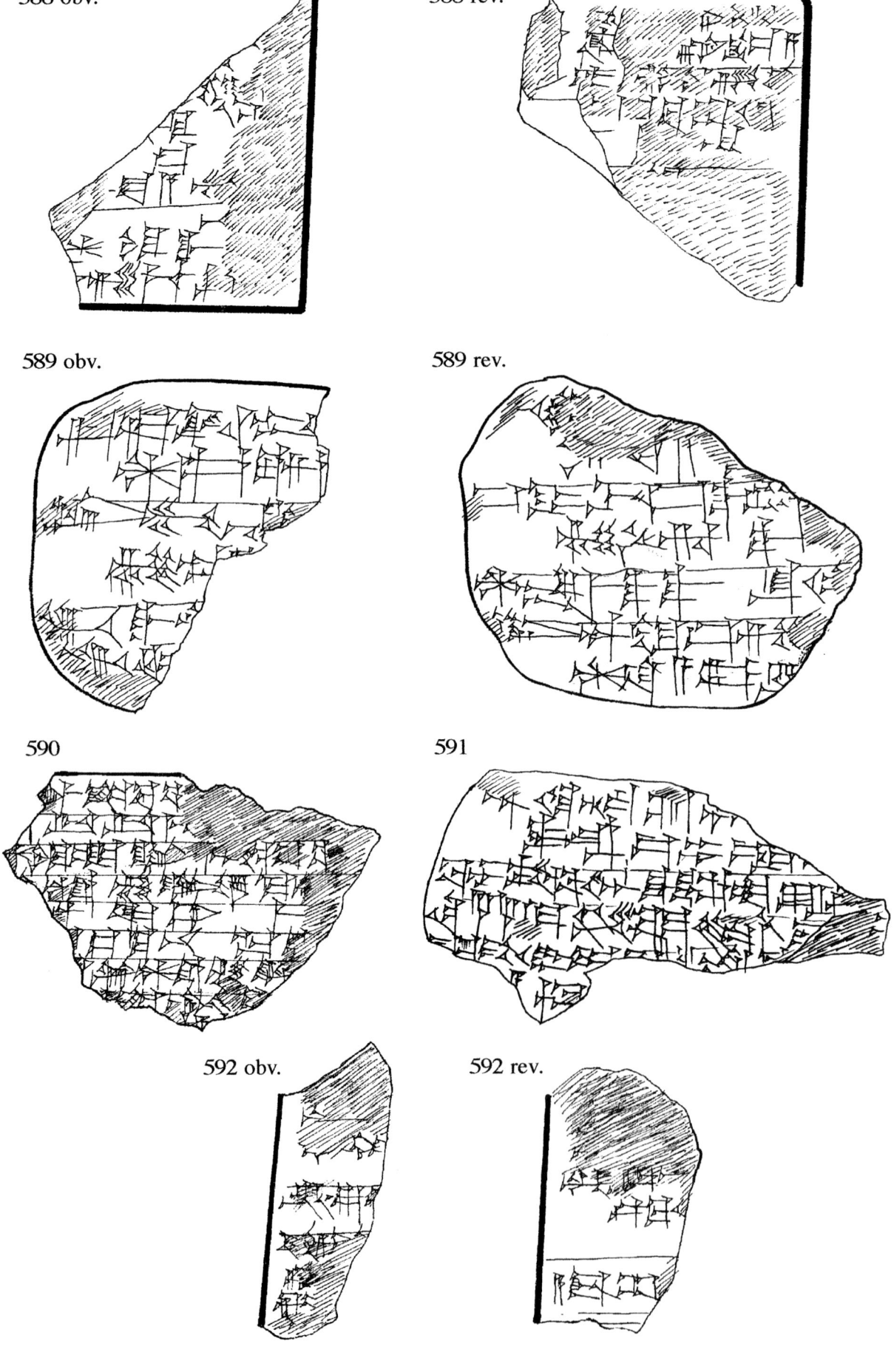

Plate 37

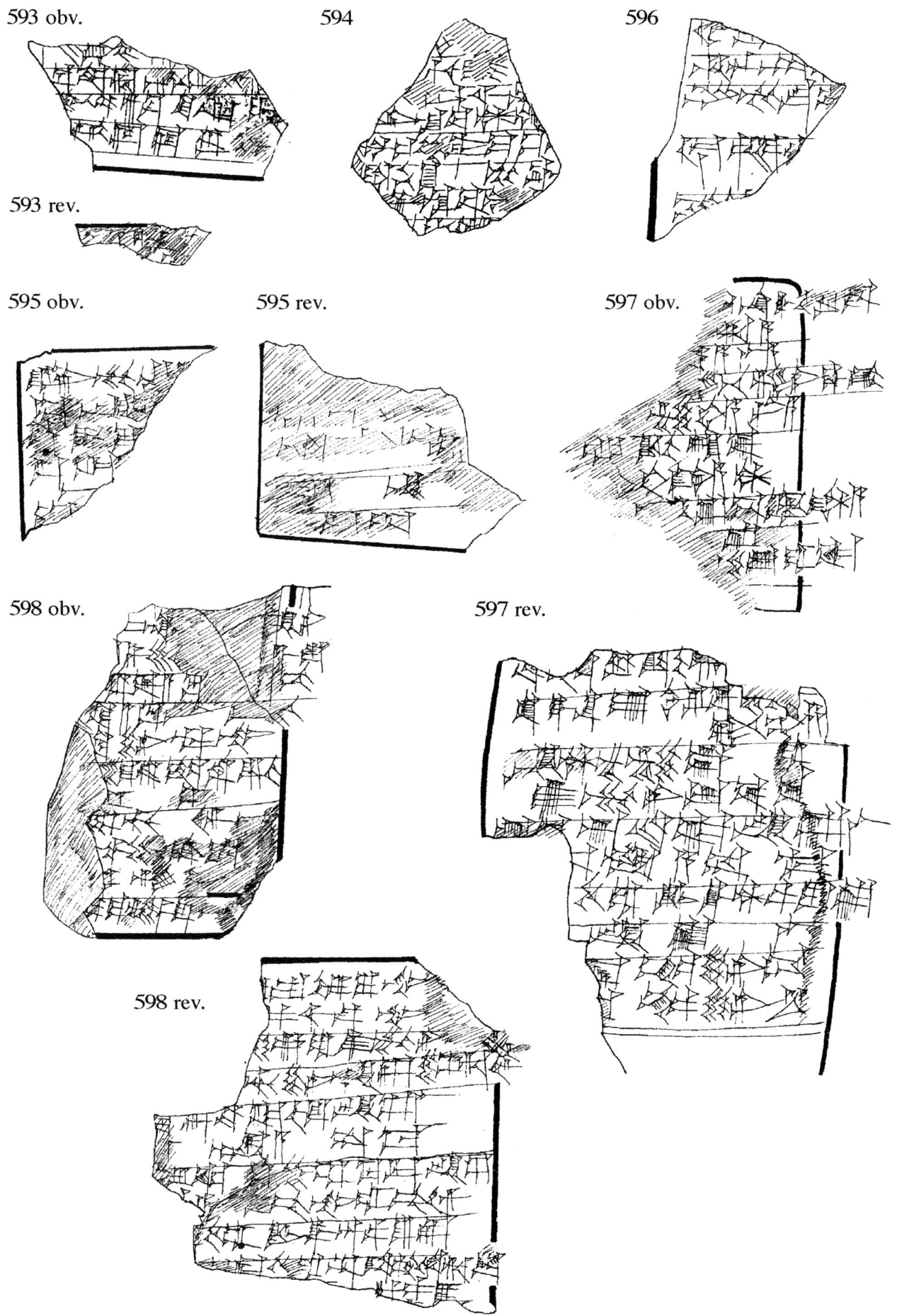

593 obv.

593 rev.

594

596

595 obv.

595 rev.

597 obv.

598 obv.

597 rev.

598 rev.

Plate 38

599 U.7782 obv.

599 U.7782 rev.

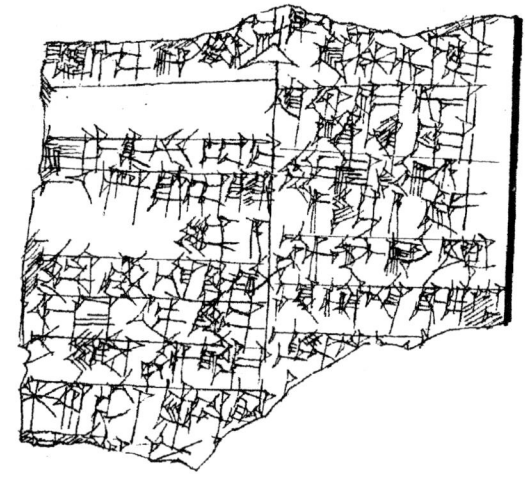

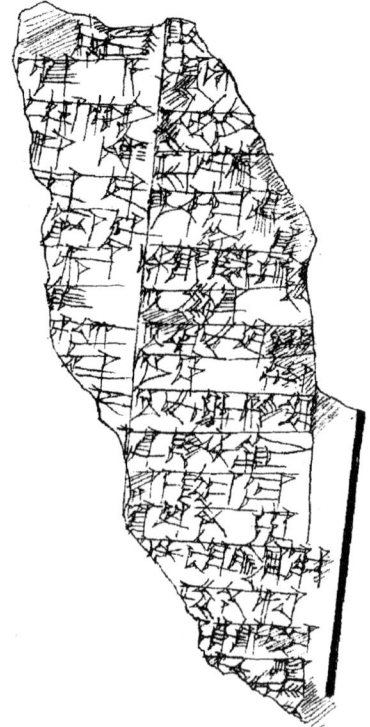

600 obv.

600 rev.

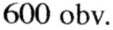

602 obv.

(UET 6/116)

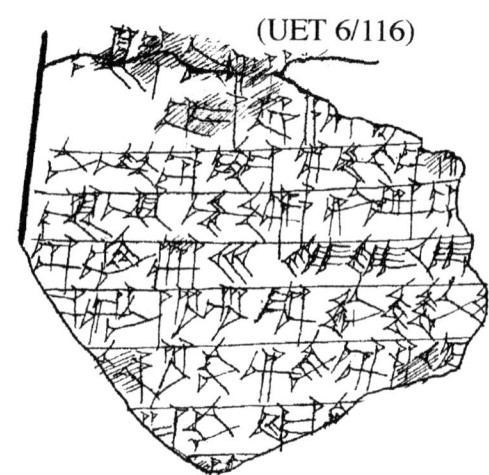

601

602 rev.

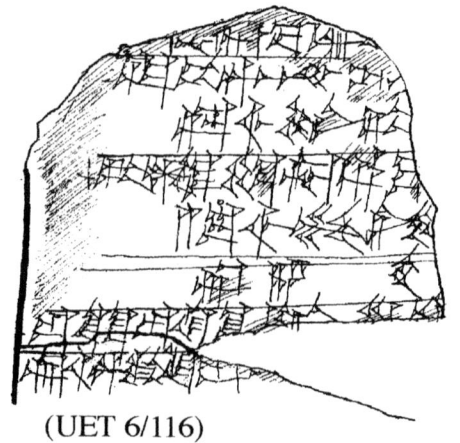

(UET 6/116)

Plate 39

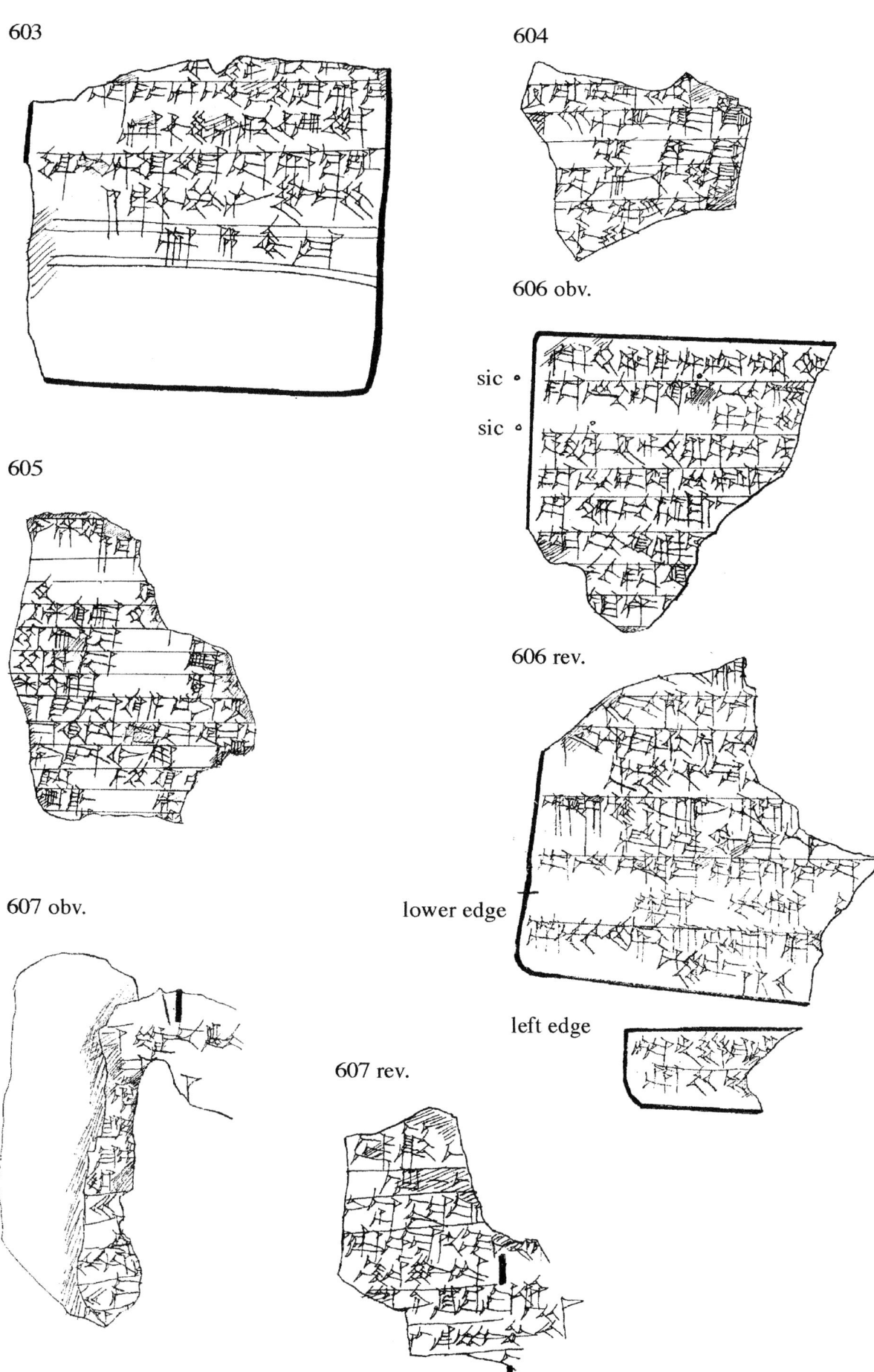

603

604

605

606 obv.

sic

sic

606 rev.

607 obv.

lower edge

left edge

607 rev.

Plate 40

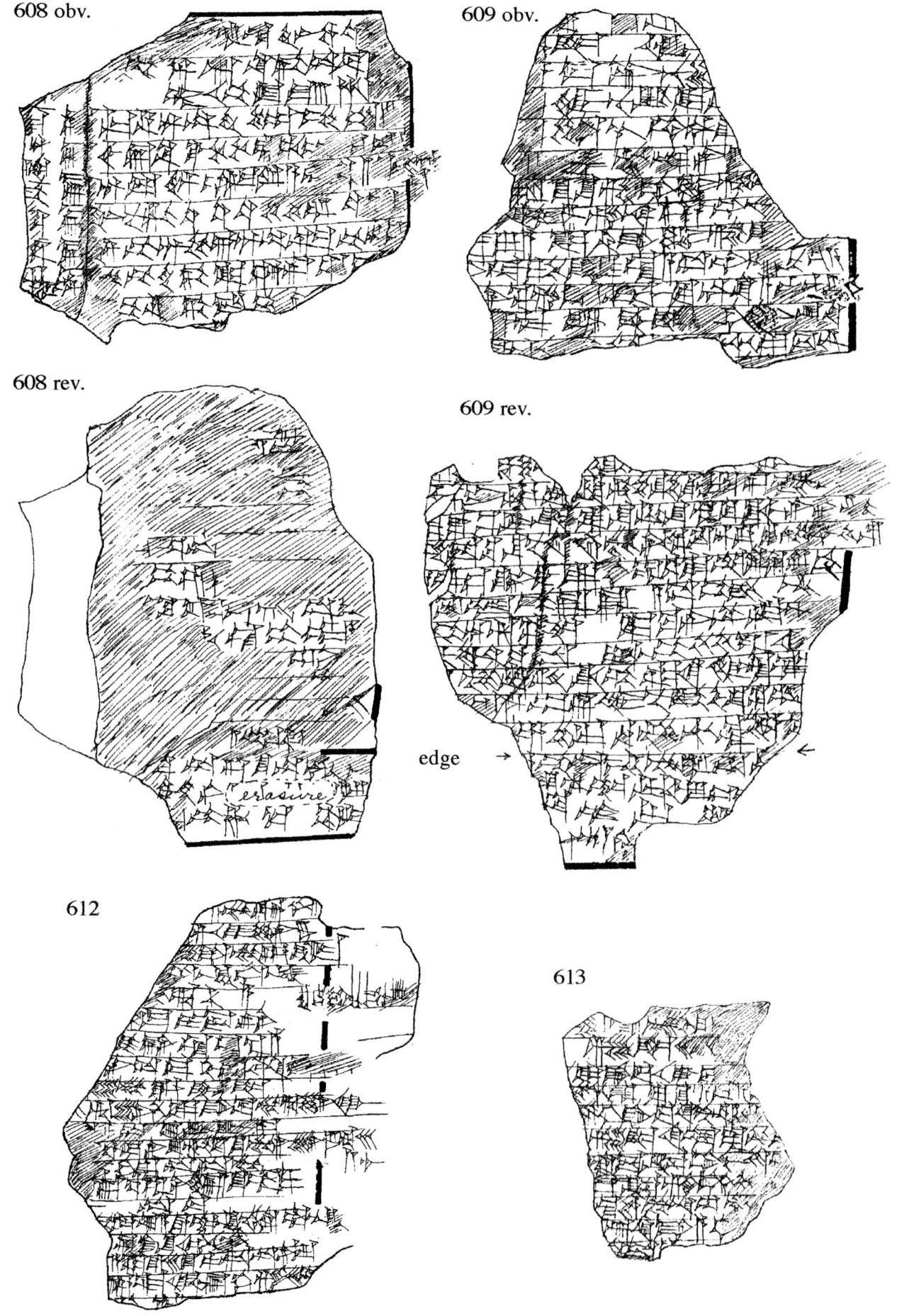

608 obv.

609 obv.

608 rev.

609 rev.

edge →

612

613

Plate 41

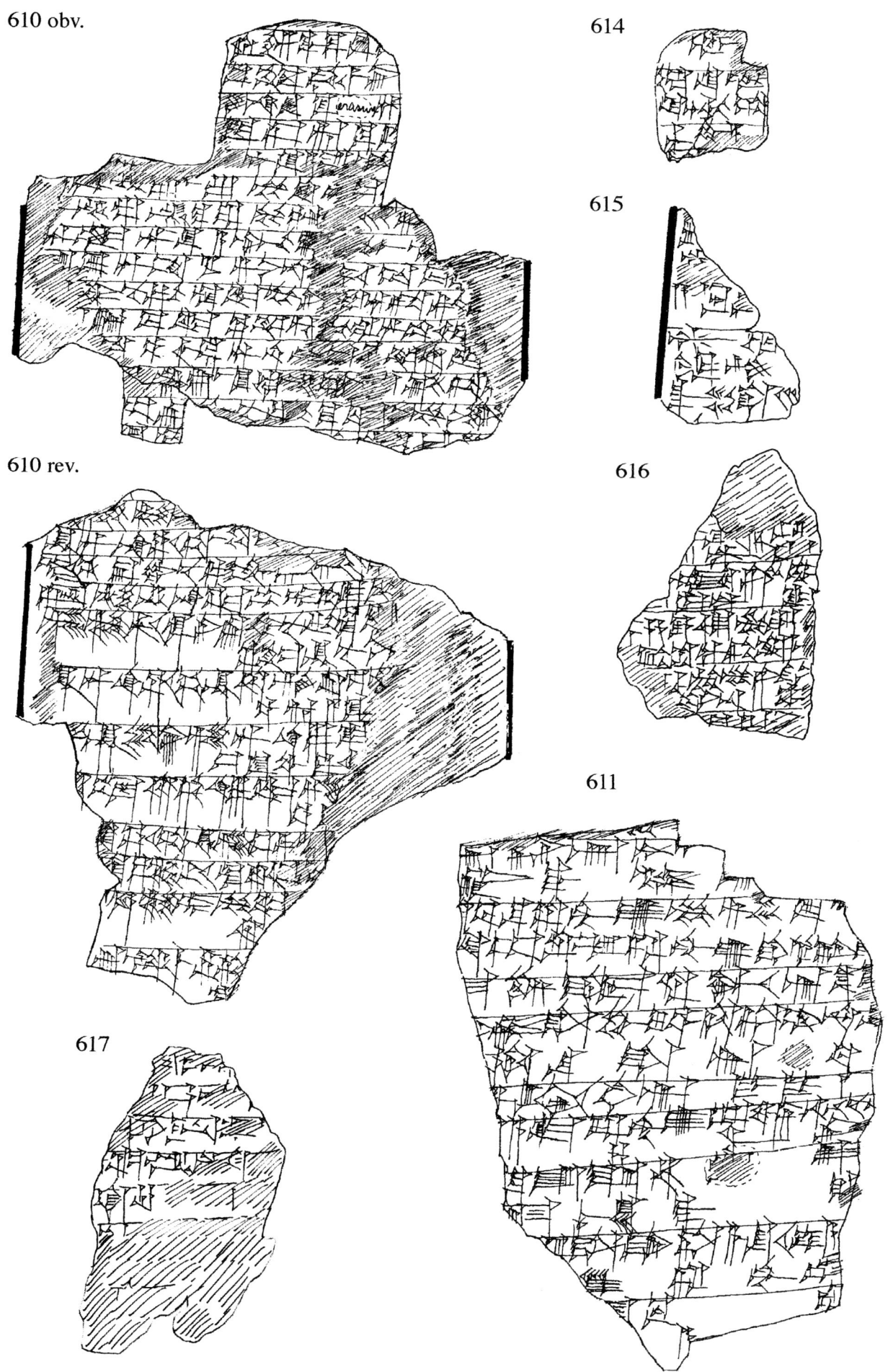

610 obv.

614

615

610 rev.

616

611

617

Plate 42

618 obv.

618 rev.

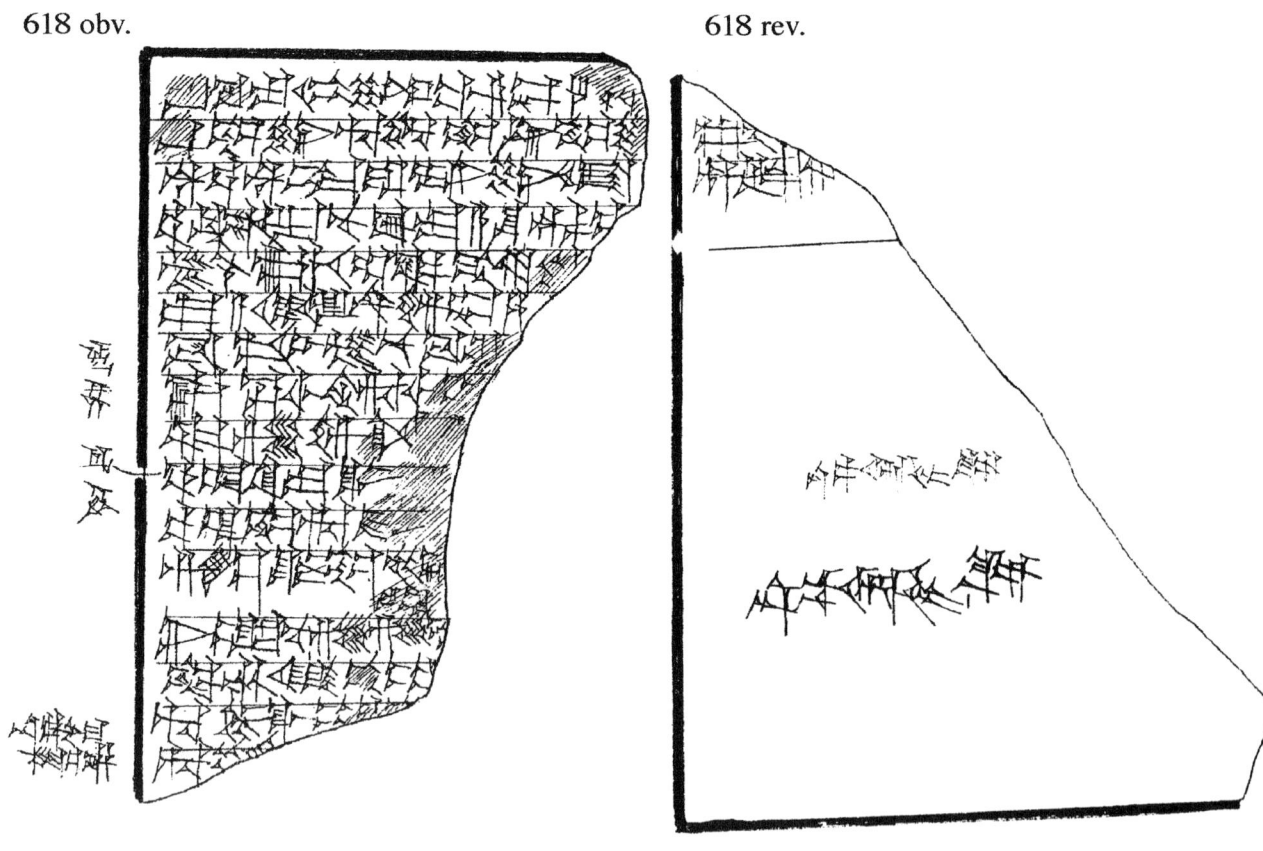

619 obv.

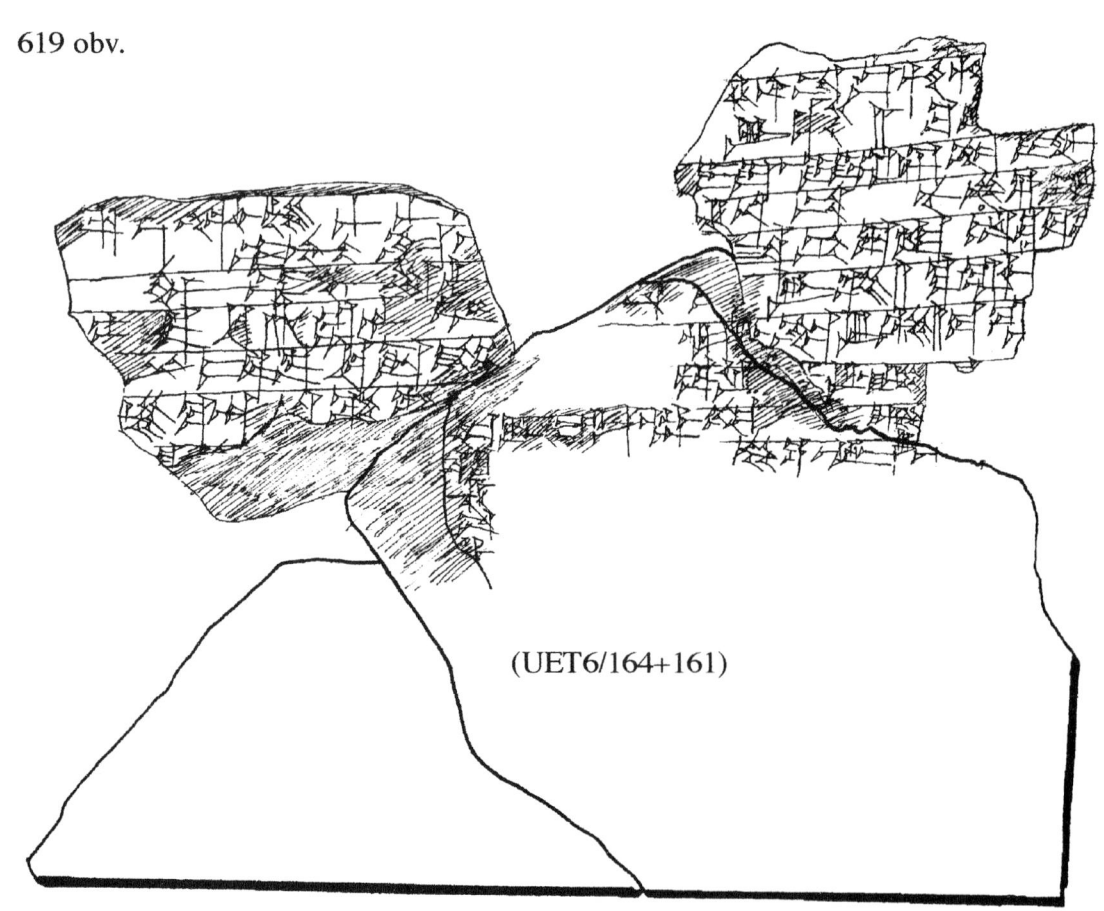

(UET6/164+161)

Plate 43

619 rev.

(UET 6/164+161)

620 obv.

620 rev.

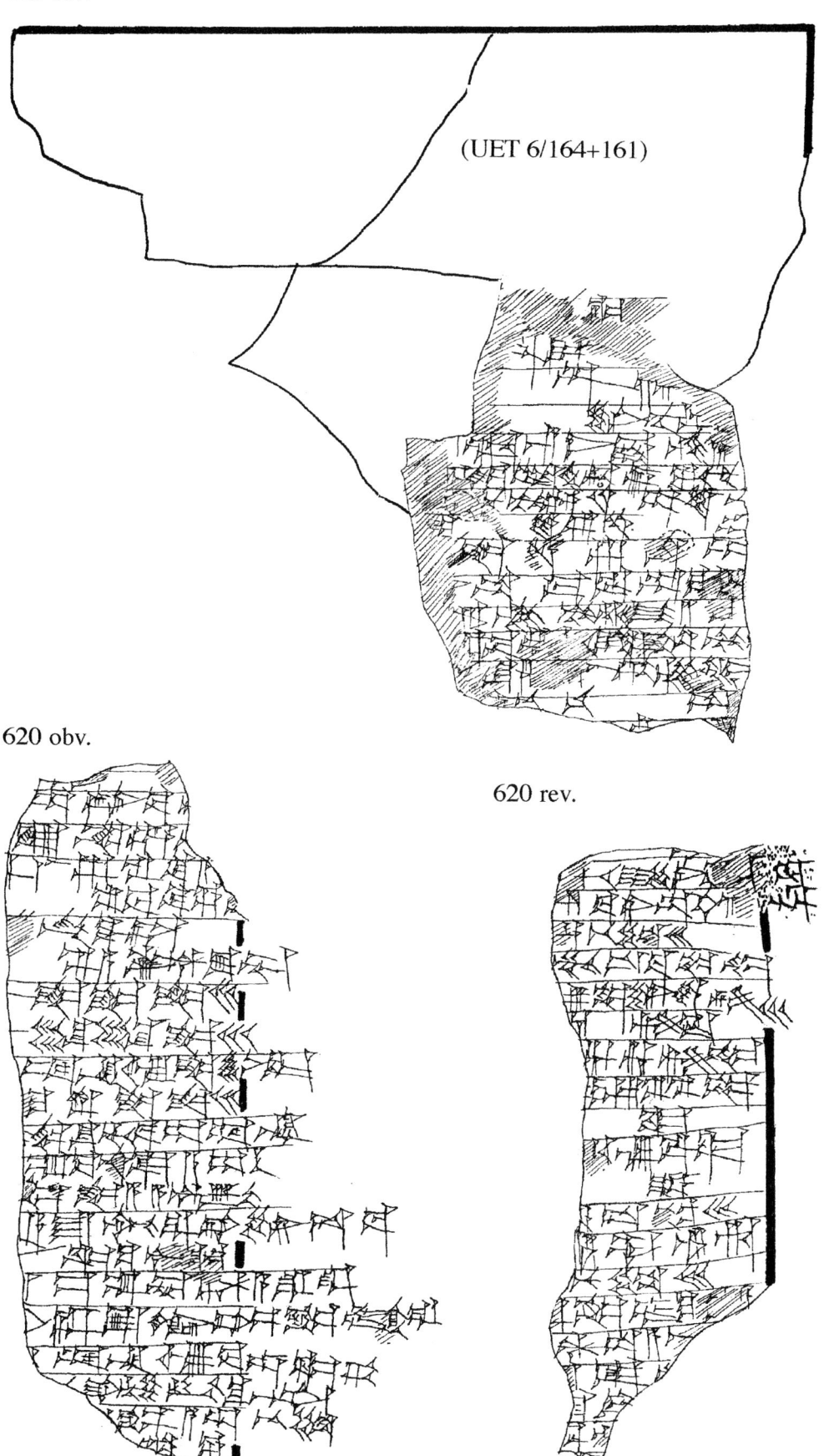

Plate 44

621 obv.

623 obv.

621 rev.

623 rev.

622

624 obv.

624 rev.

Plate 45

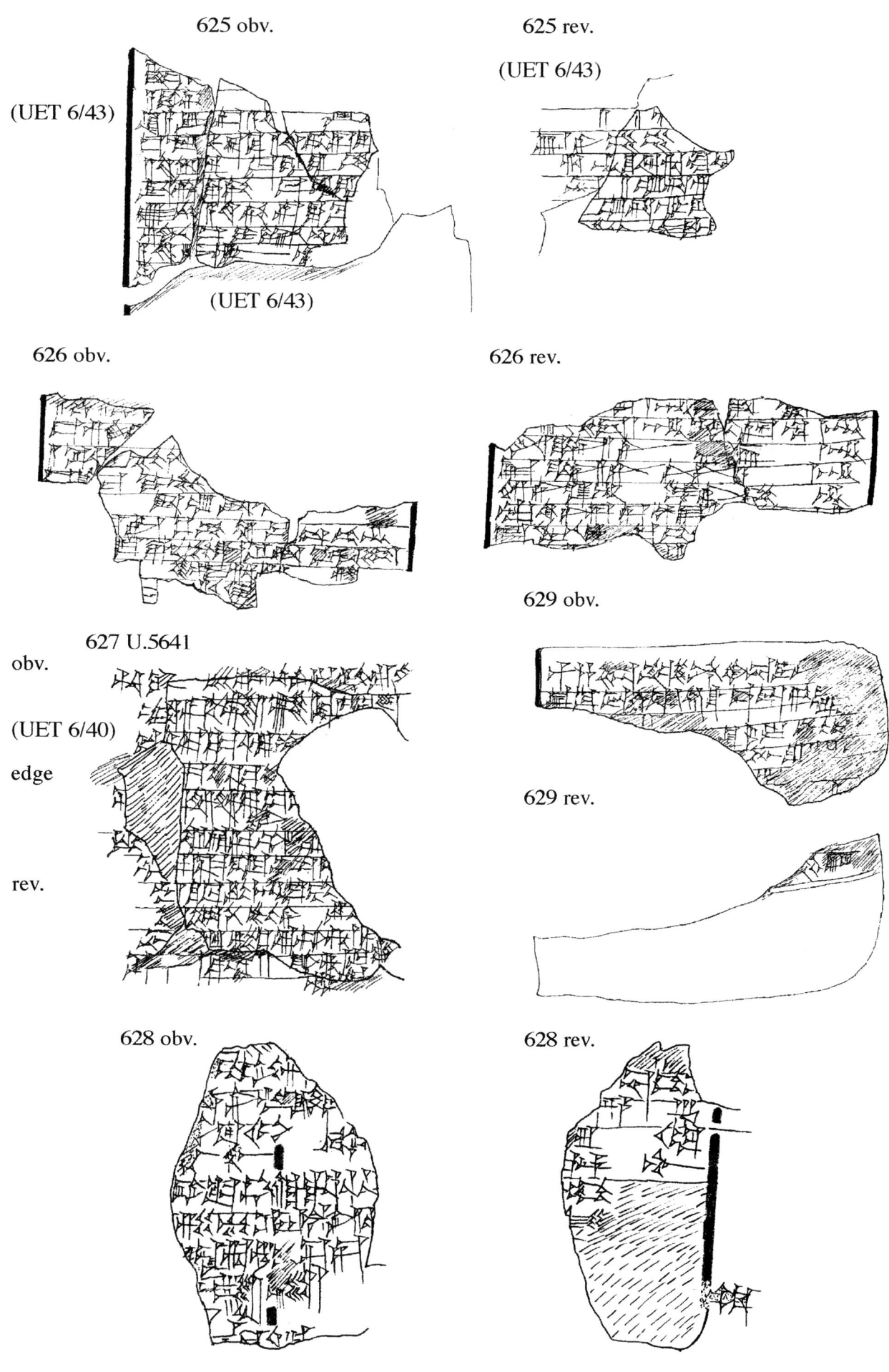

625 obv.

625 rev.

(UET 6/43)

(UET 6/43)

(UET 6/43)

626 obv.

626 rev.

629 obv.

627 U.5641

obv.

(UET 6/40)

edge

rev.

629 rev.

628 obv.

628 rev.

Plate 46

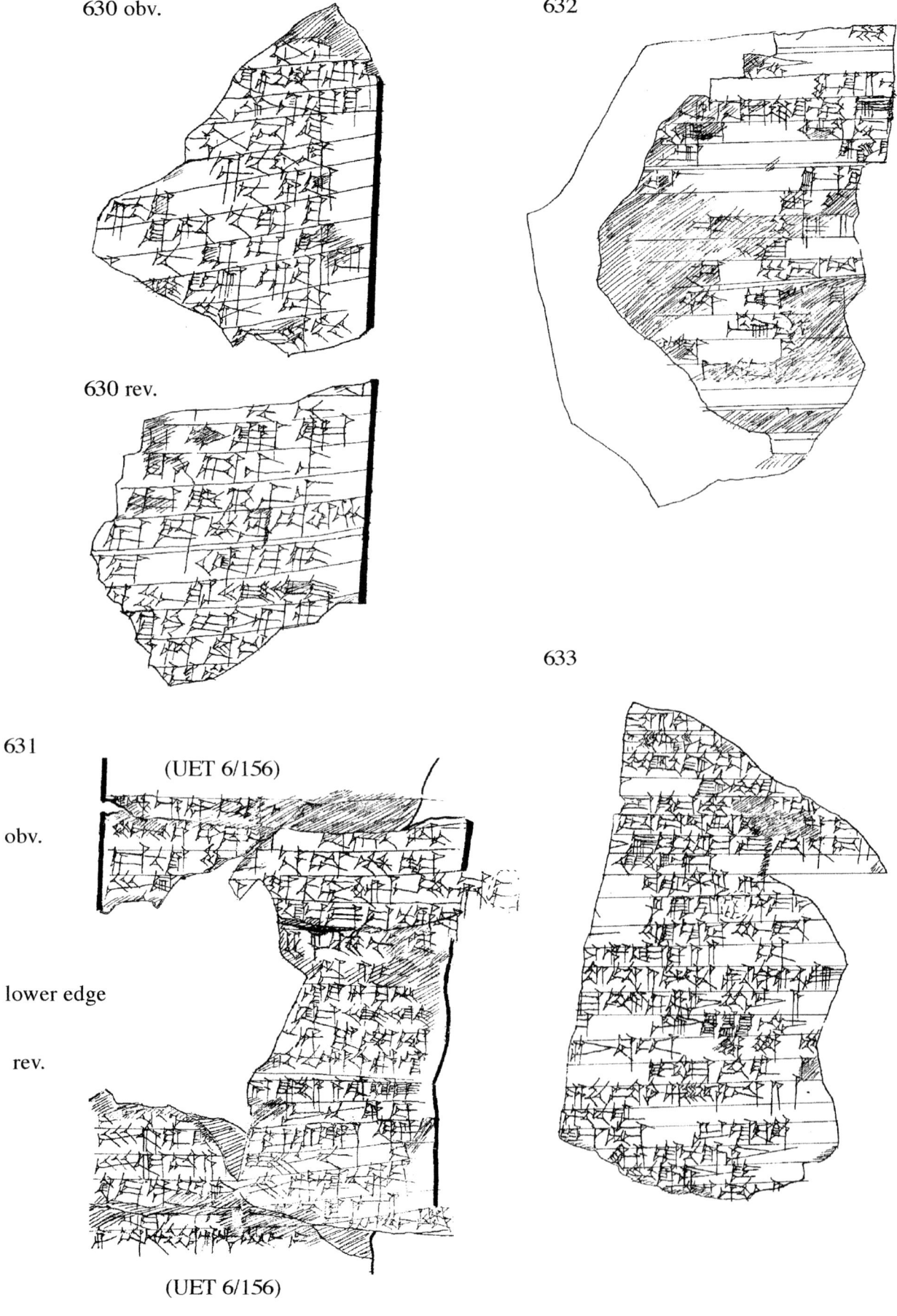

630 obv.

630 rev.

631

(UET 6/156)

obv.

lower edge

rev.

(UET 6/156)

632

633

Plate 47

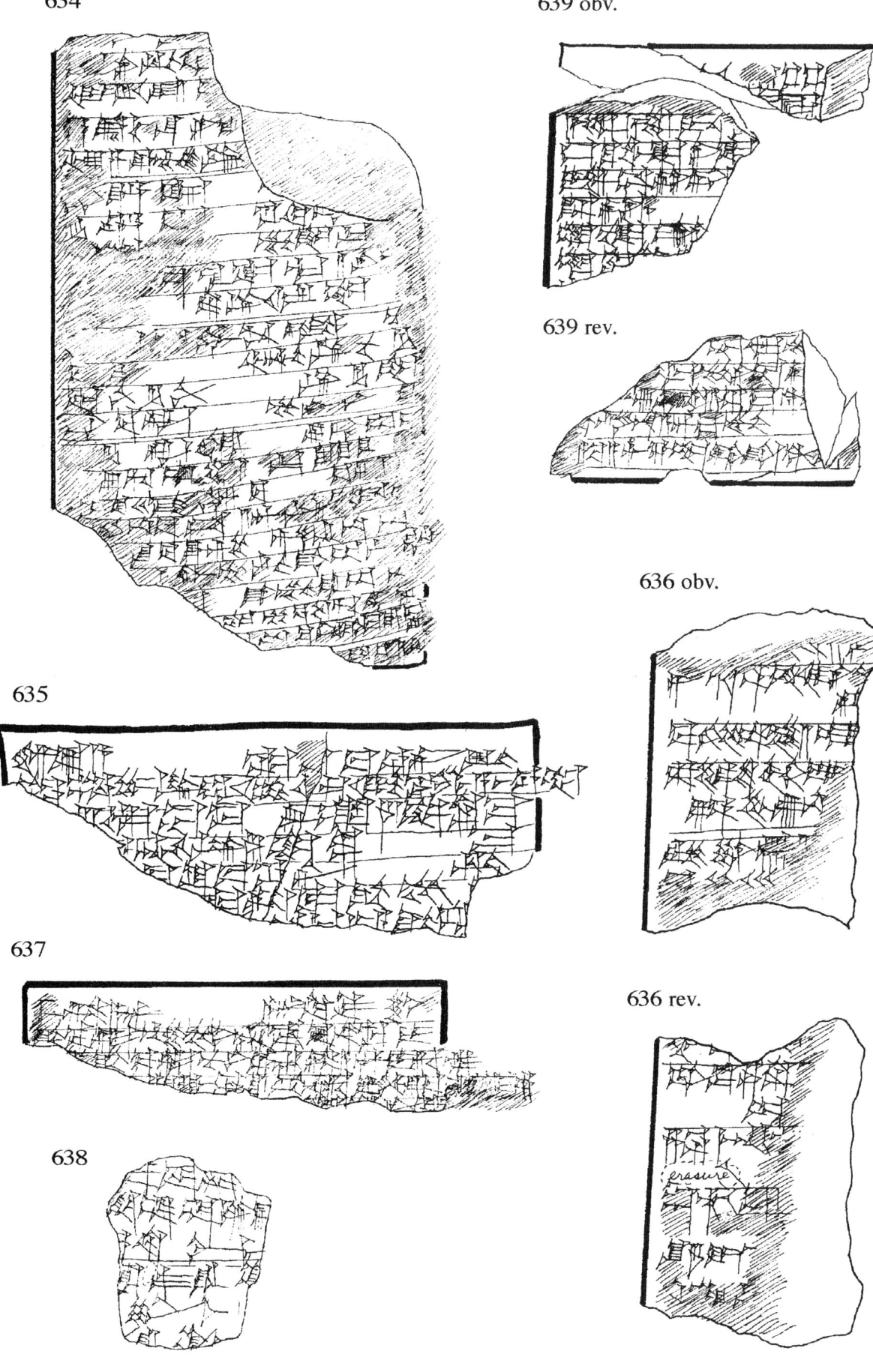

634

639 obv.

639 rev.

636 obv.

635

637

636 rev.

638

Plate 48

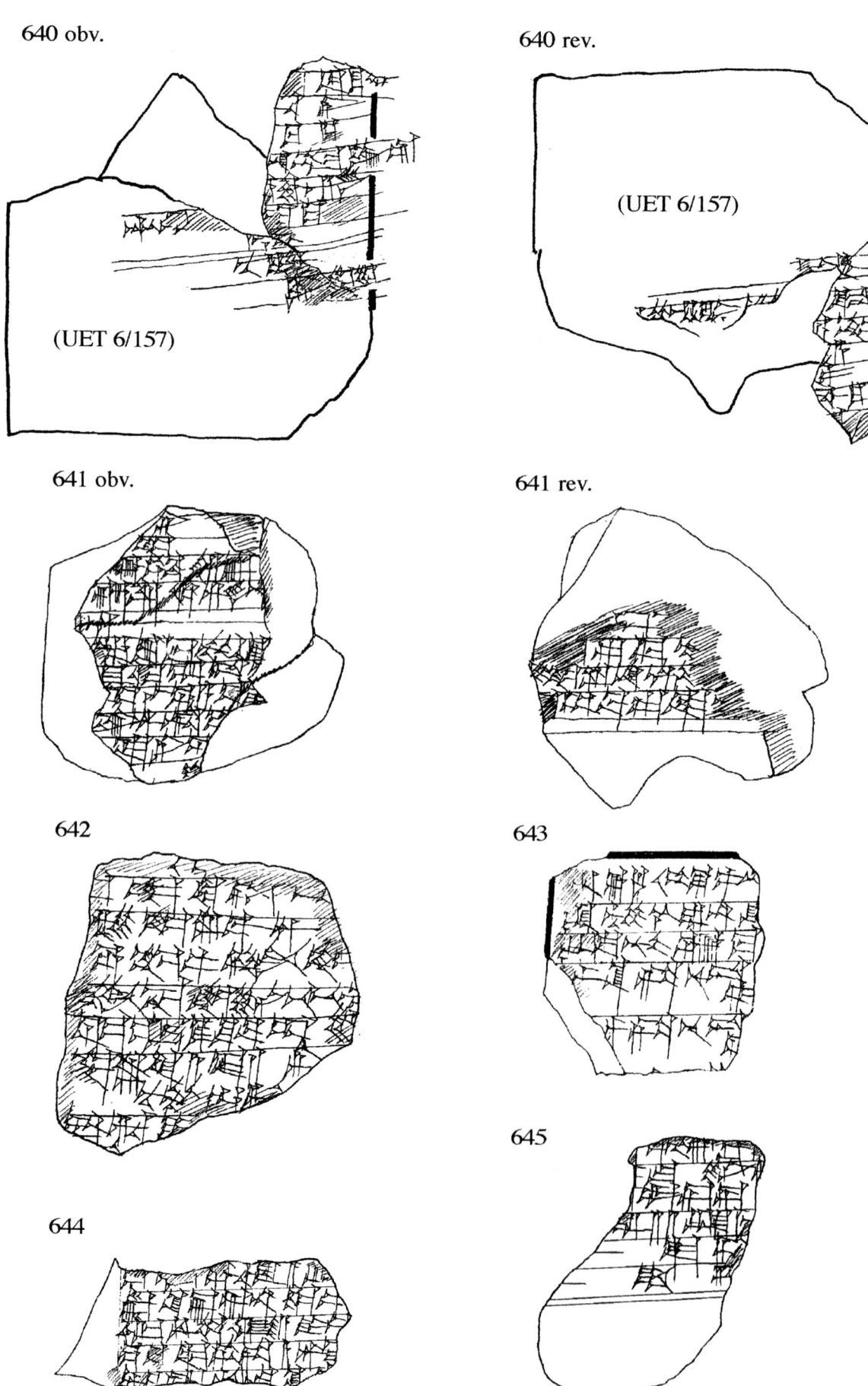

640 obv.

640 rev.

(UET 6/157)

(UET 6/157)

641 obv.

641 rev.

642

643

644

645

Plate 49

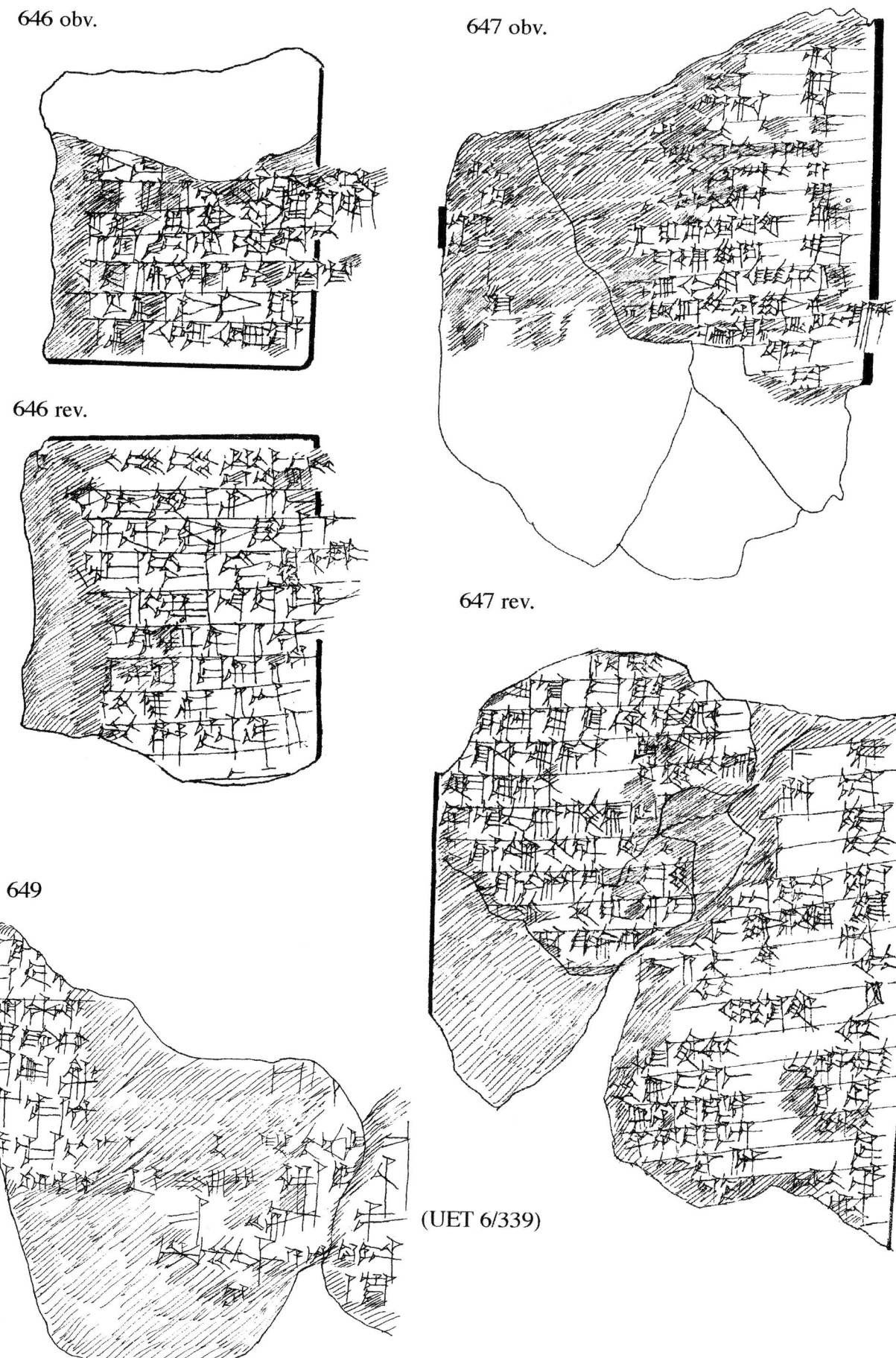

646 obv.

647 obv.

646 rev.

647 rev.

649

(UET 6/339)

Plate 50

648 U.7827y obv.

650

651

652 obv.

652 rev.

648 U.7827y rev.

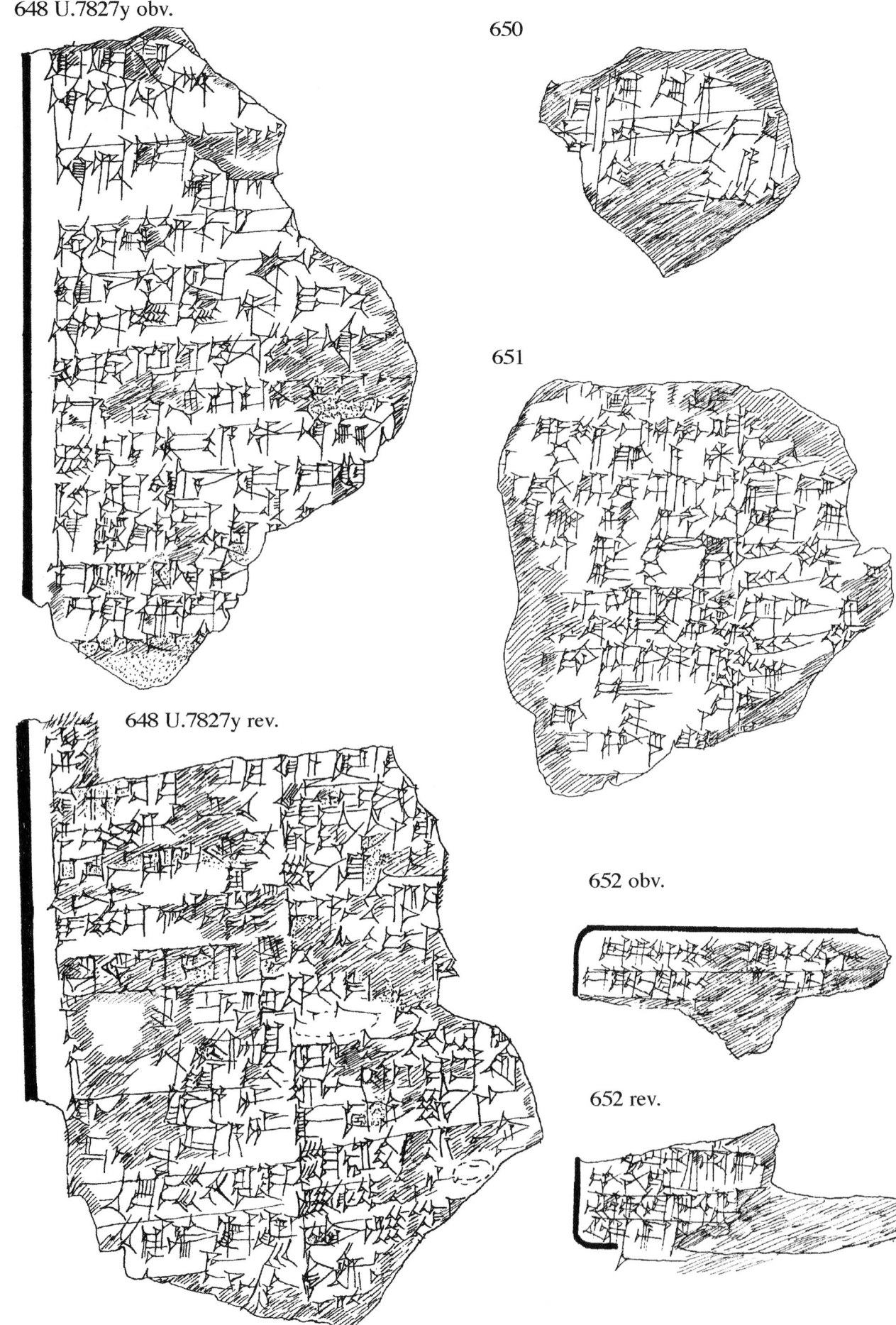

Plate 51

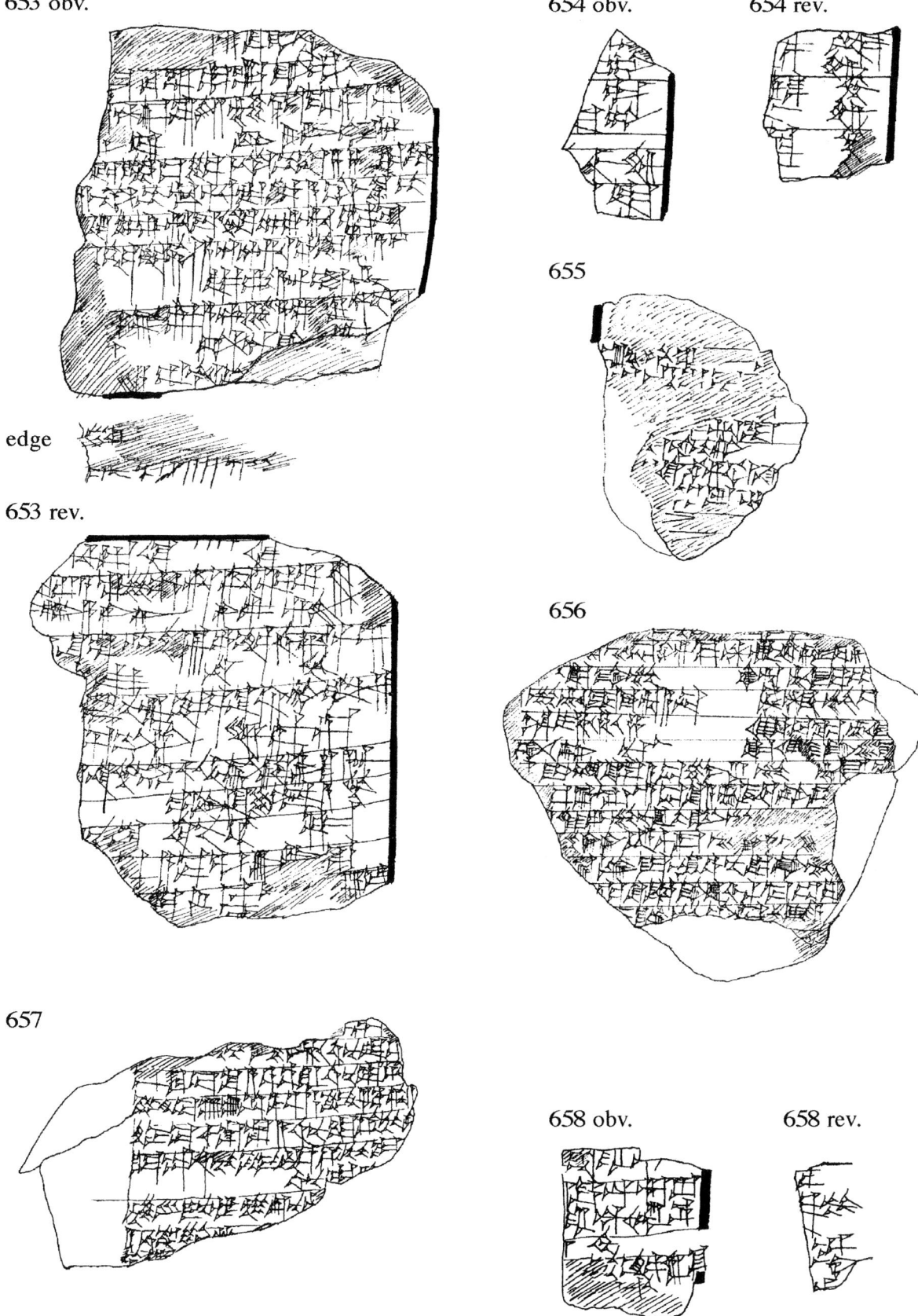

653 obv.

edge

653 rev.

654 obv.   654 rev.

655

656

657

658 obv.   658 rev.

Plate 52

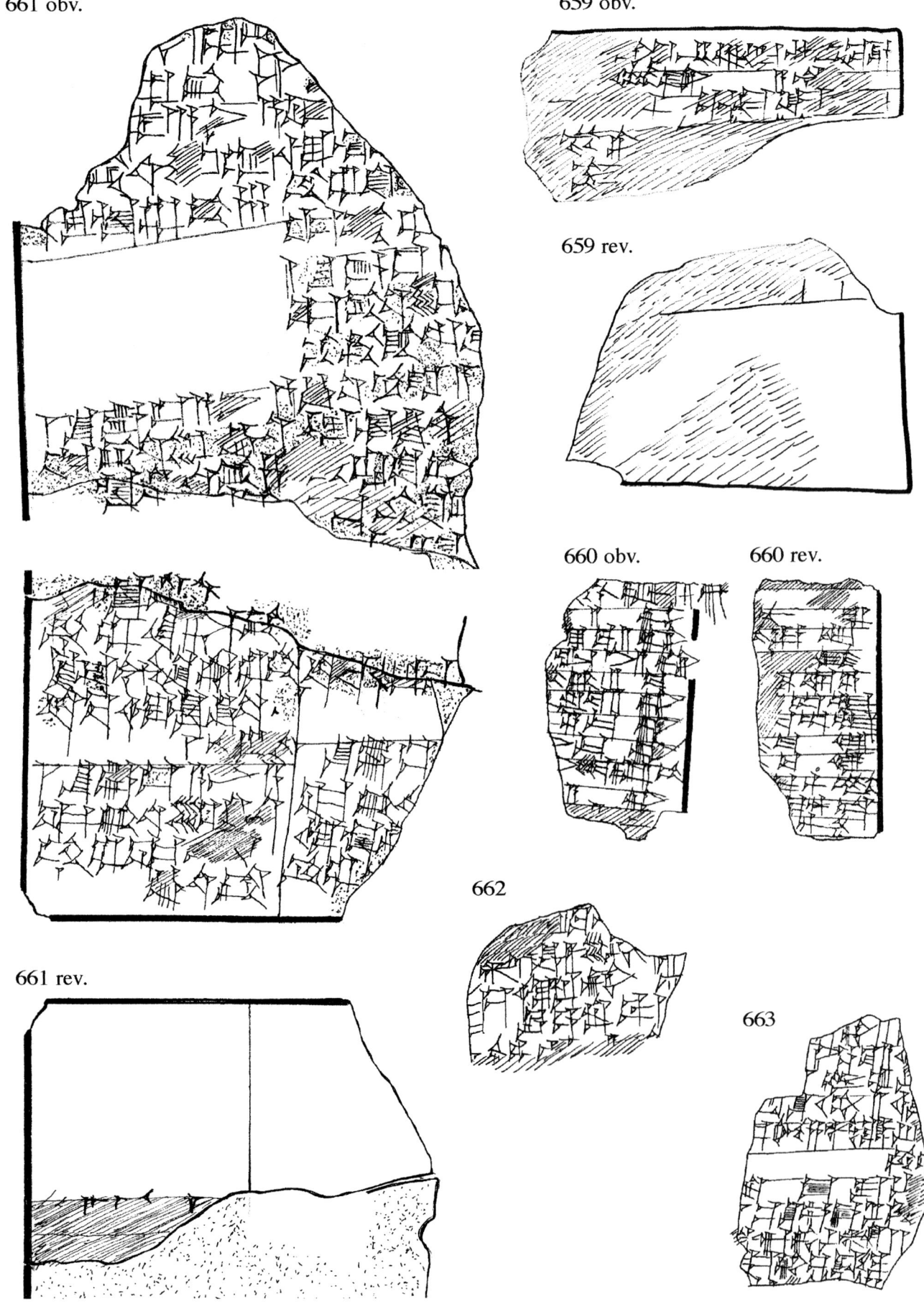

661 obv.

659 obv.

659 rev.

660 obv.

660 rev.

662

661 rev.

663

Plate 53

664 obv.

664 rev.

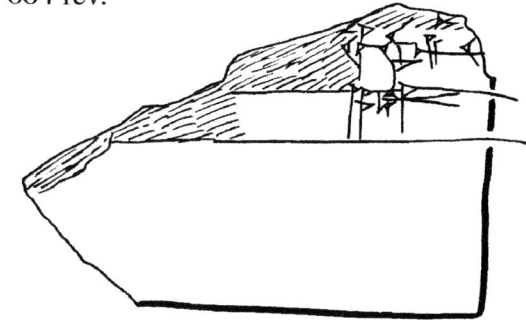

665 obv.

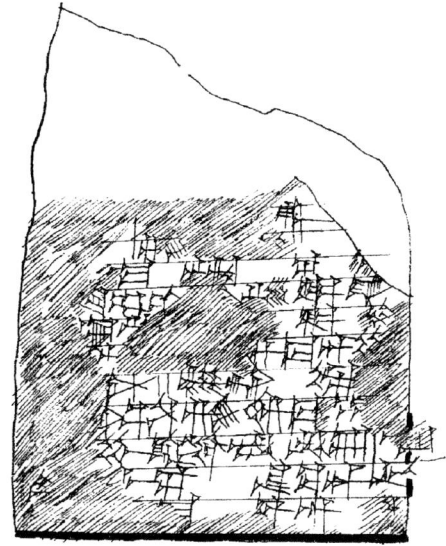

666

665 rev.

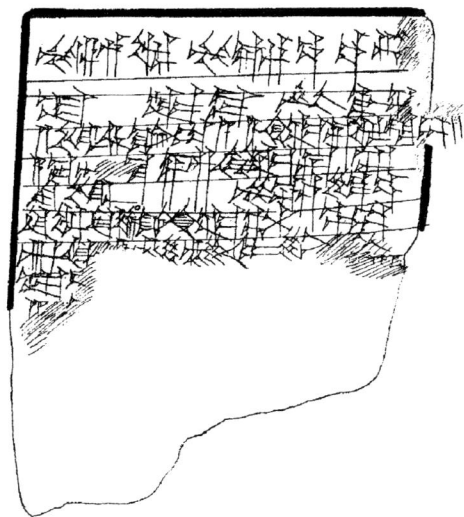

667 obv.

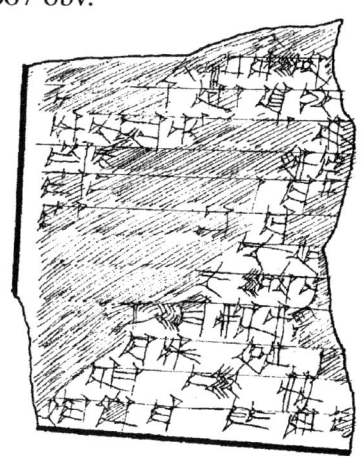

667 rev.

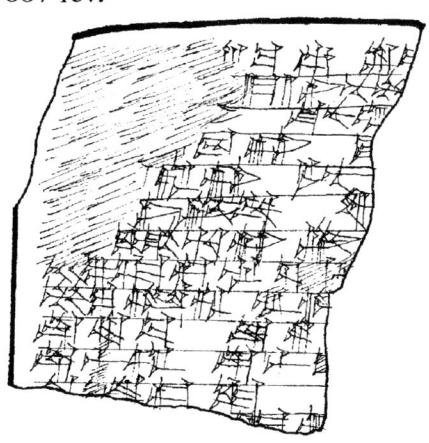

Plate 54

668 obv.

668 rev.

670 obv.

669

670 rev.

671

Plate 55

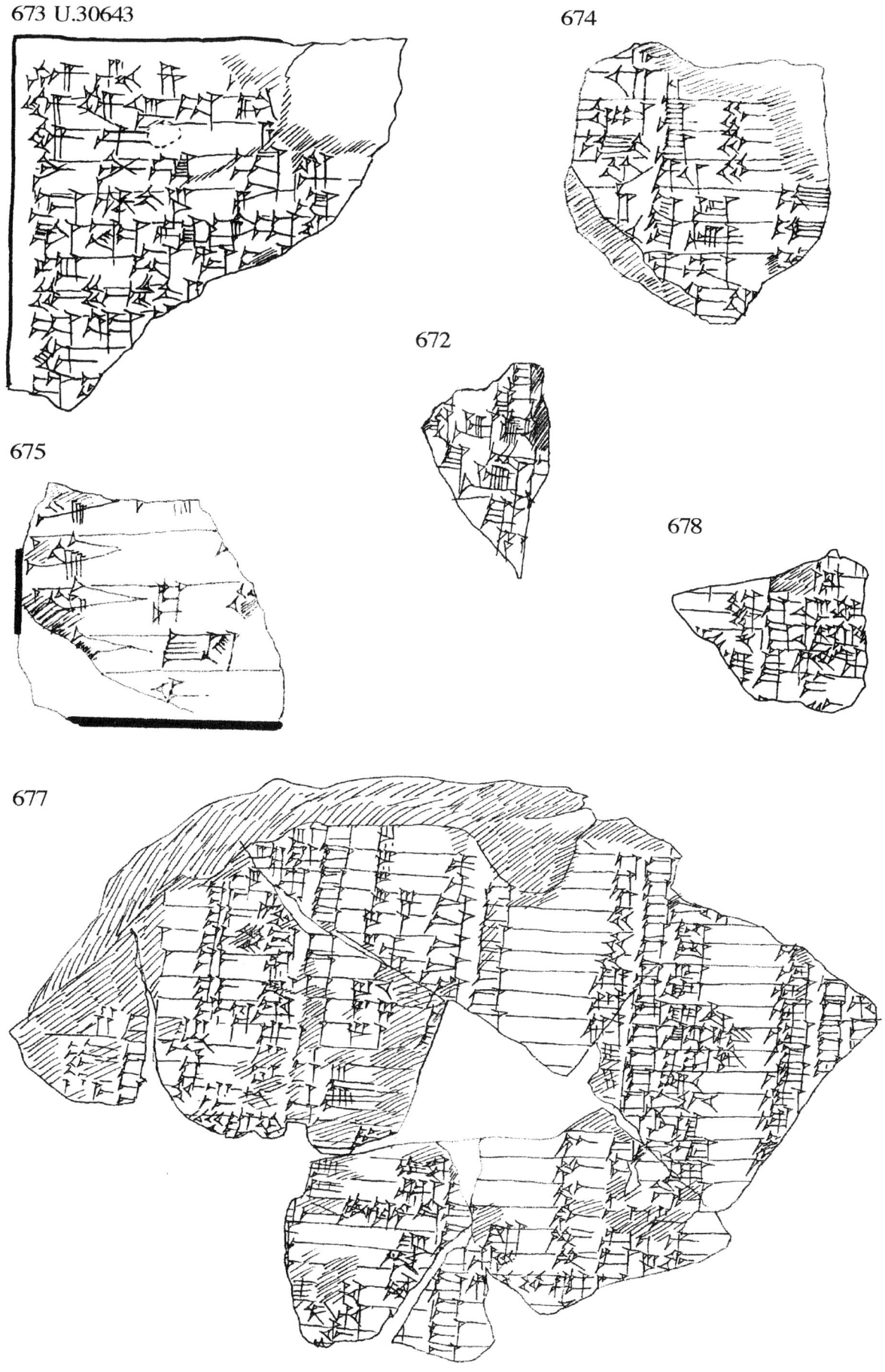

673 U.30643

674

672

675

678

677

Plate 56

676 obv.   679   682 U.30497

676 rev.   681

680 obv.

680 rev.

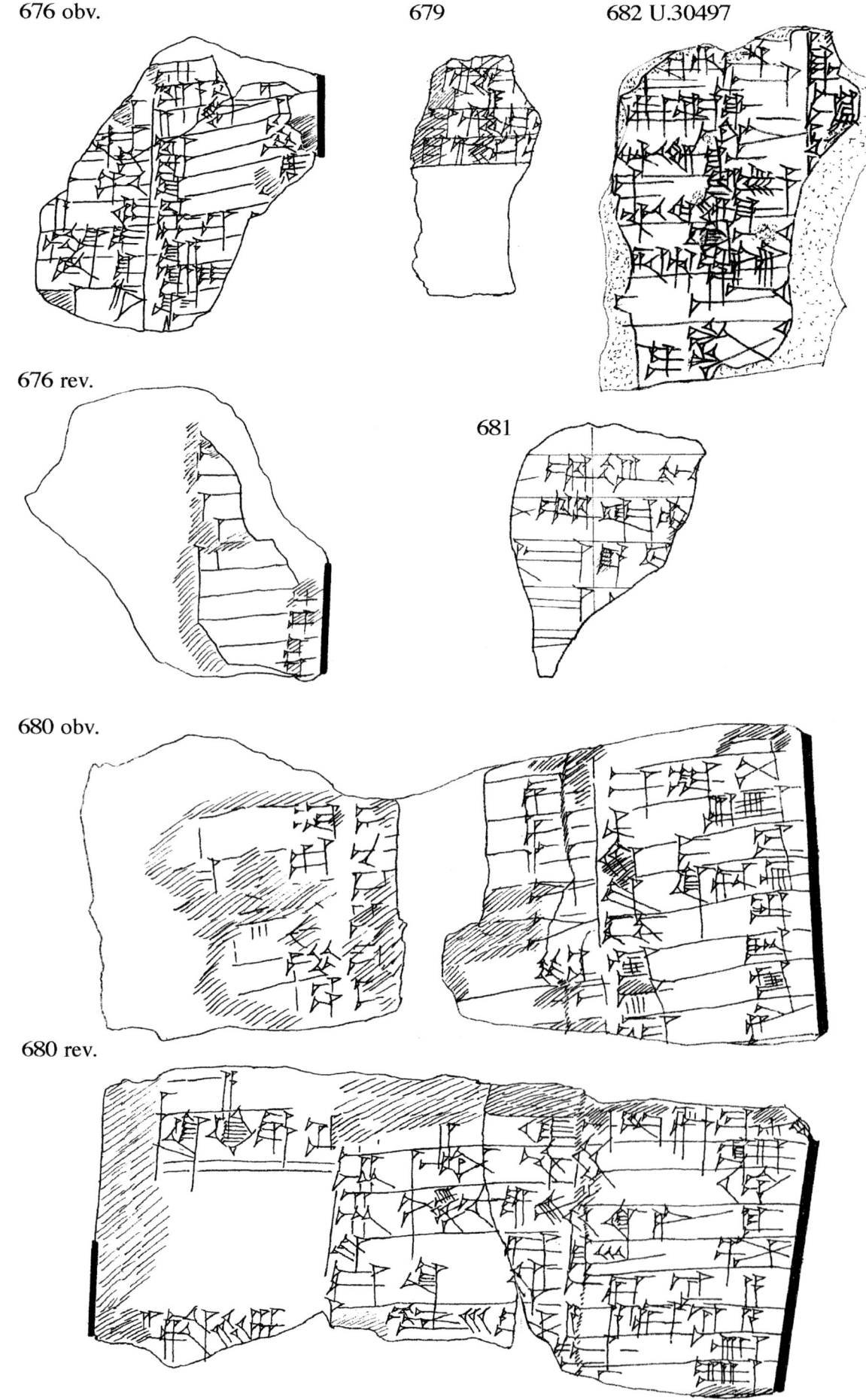

Plate 57

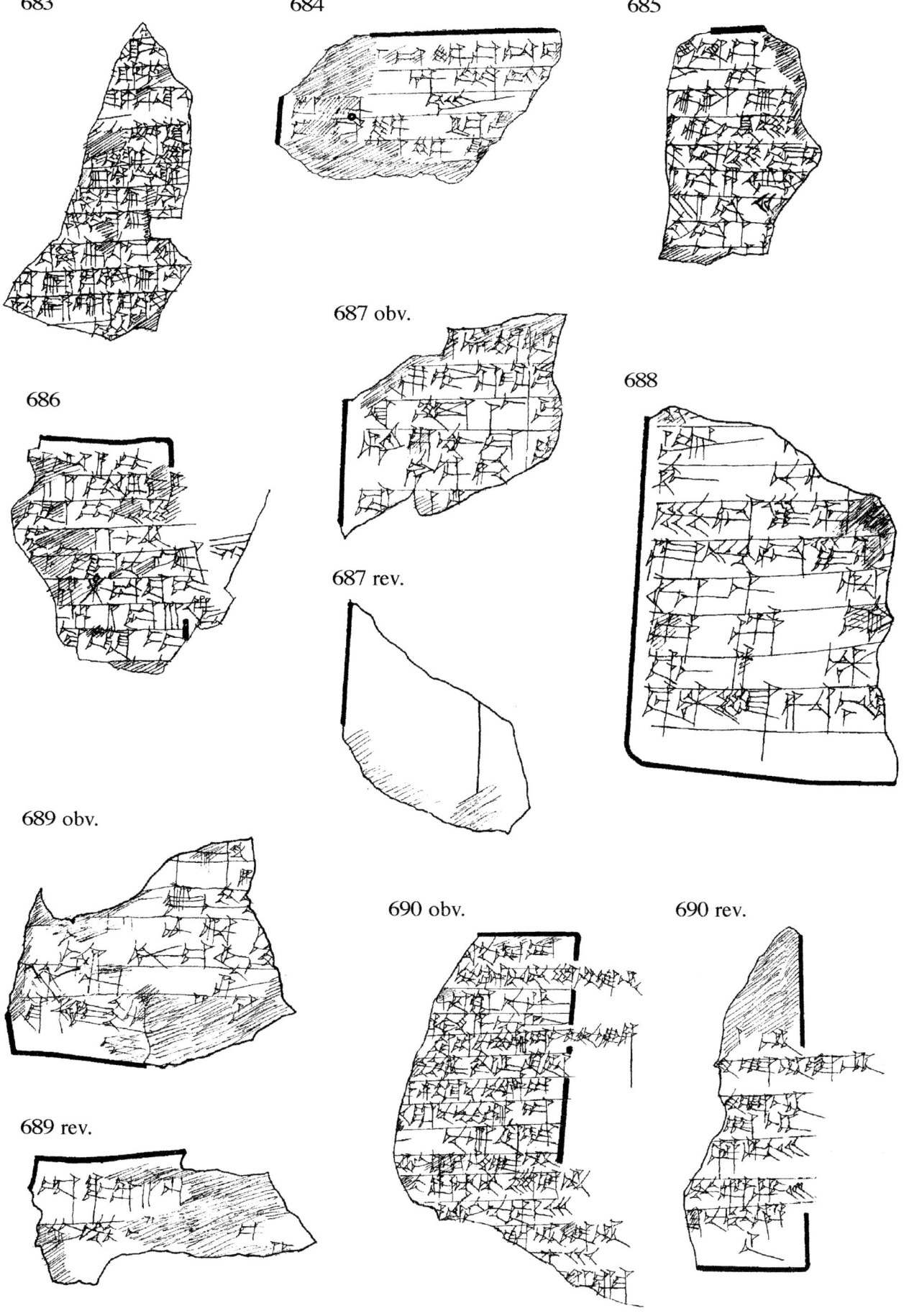

683

684

685

687 obv.

686

688

687 rev.

689 obv.

690 obv.

690 rev.

689 rev.

Plate 58

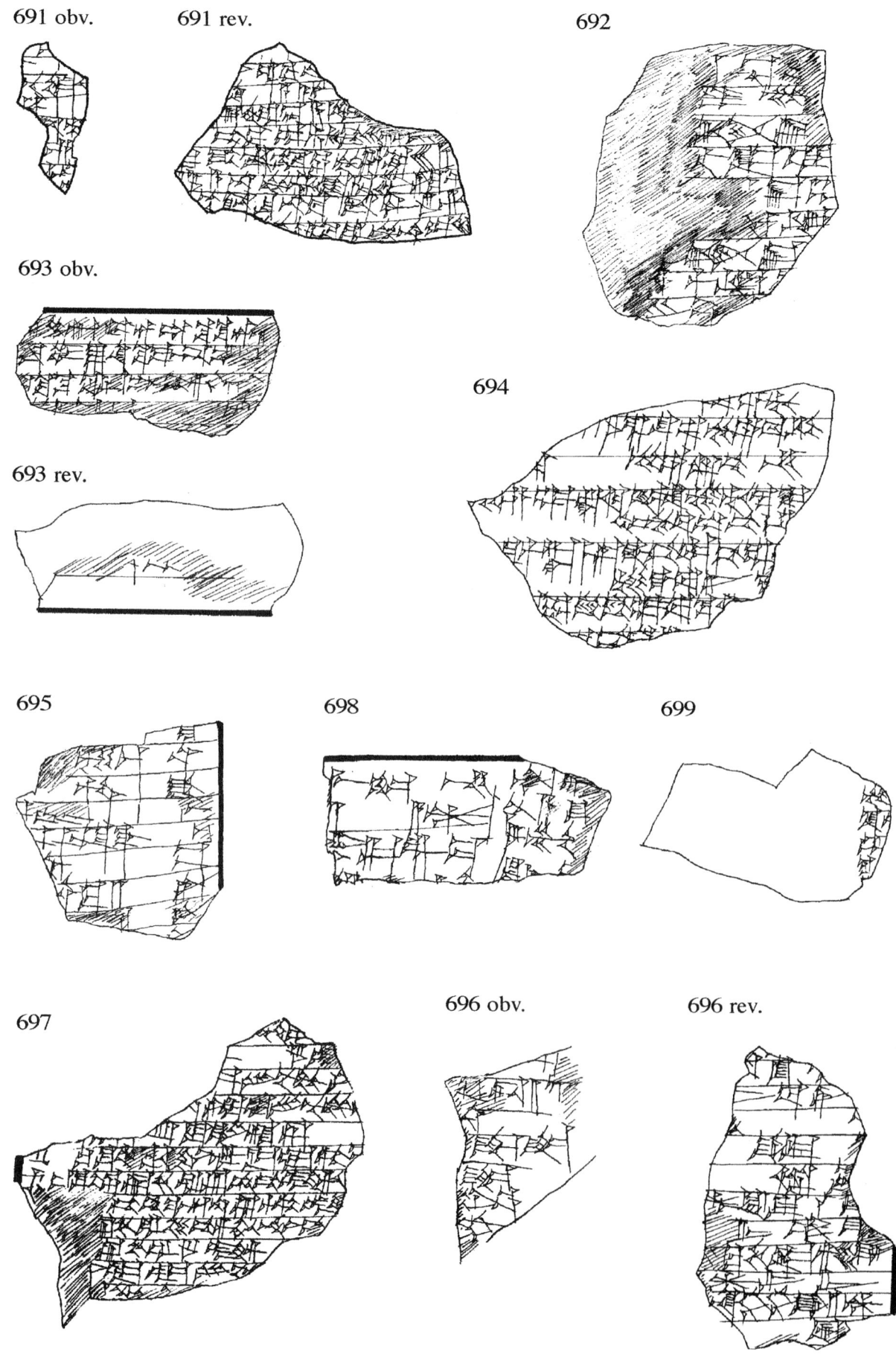

691 obv. 691 rev. 692

693 obv.

693 rev. 694

695 698 699

697 696 obv. 696 rev.

Plate 59

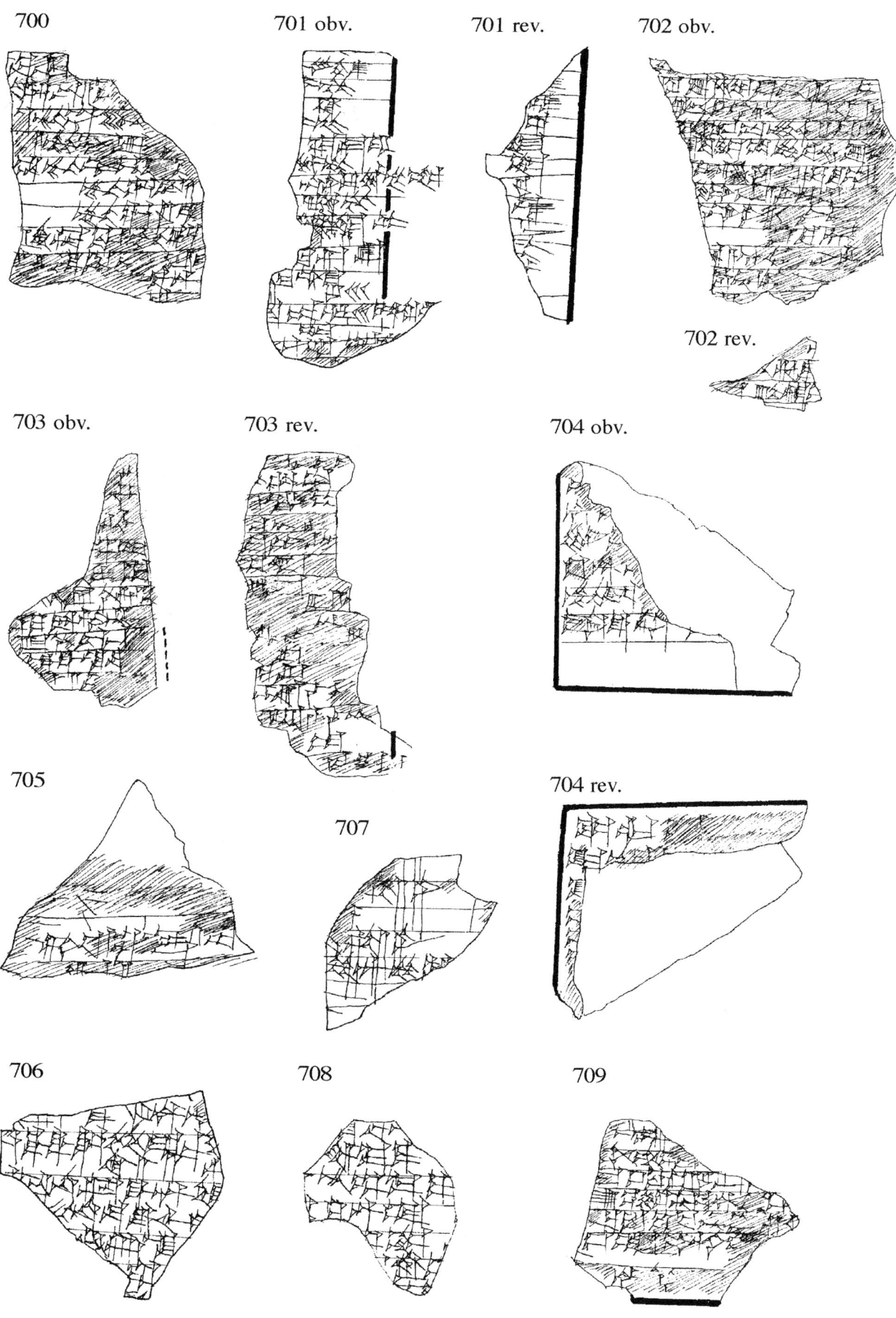

700

701 obv.

701 rev.

702 obv.

702 rev.

703 obv.

703 rev.

704 obv.

705

707

704 rev.

706

708

709

Plate 60

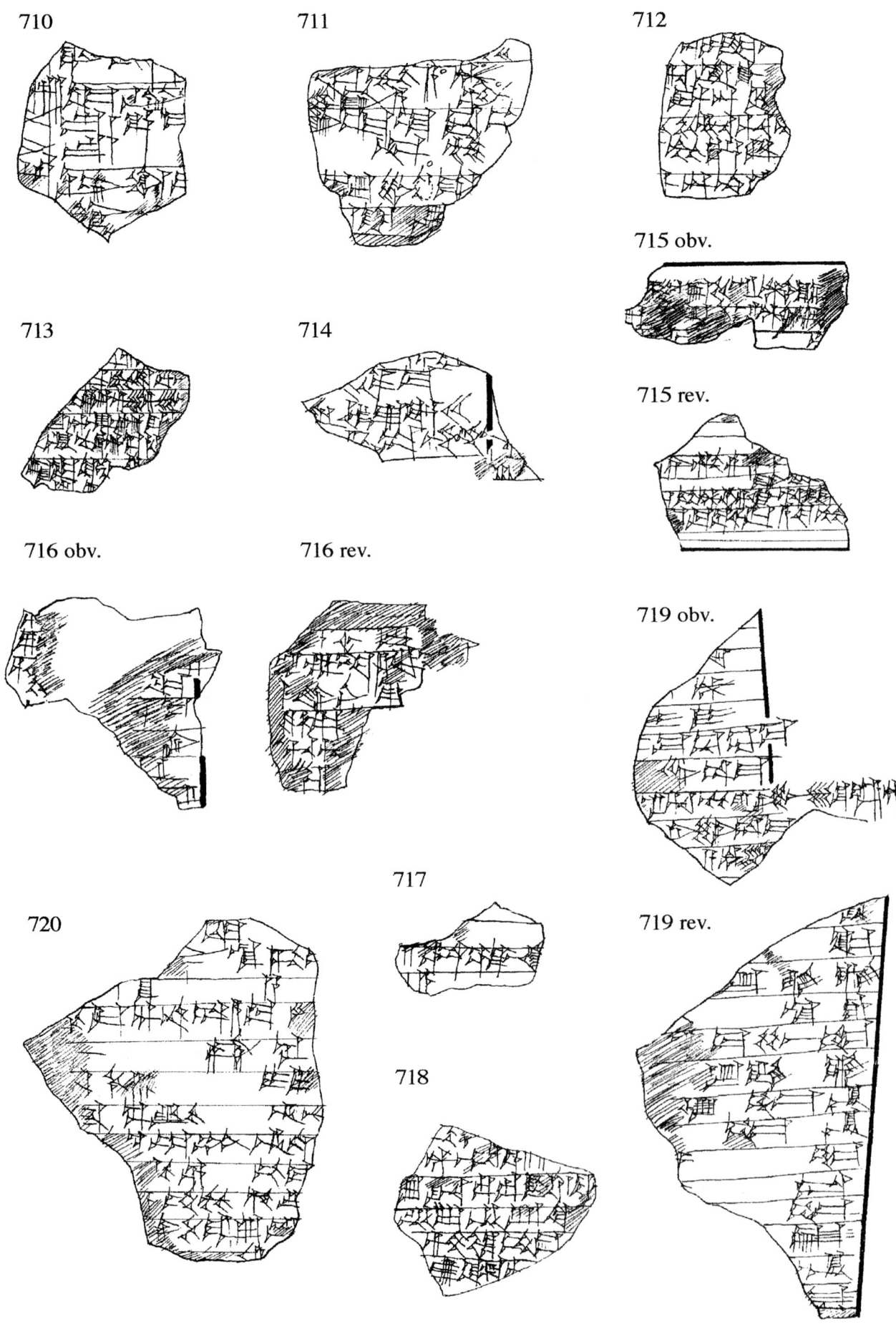

710

711

712

715 obv.

713

714

715 rev.

716 obv.

716 rev.

719 obv.

717

720

719 rev.

718

Plate 61

721 obv.

721 rev.

722 obv.

723 obv.

722 rev.

726 obv.   726 rev.

723 rev.

725

727   728

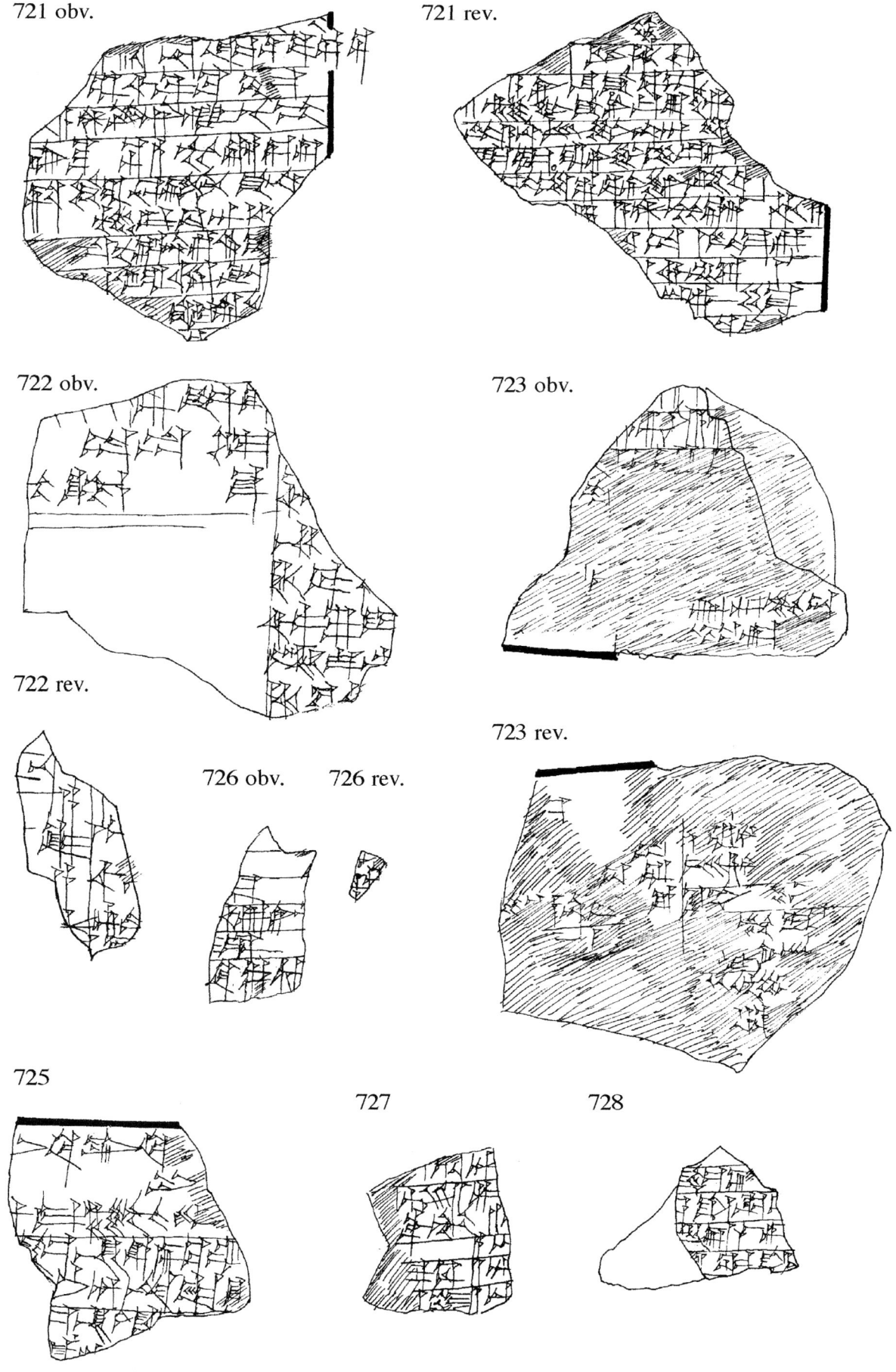

Plate 62

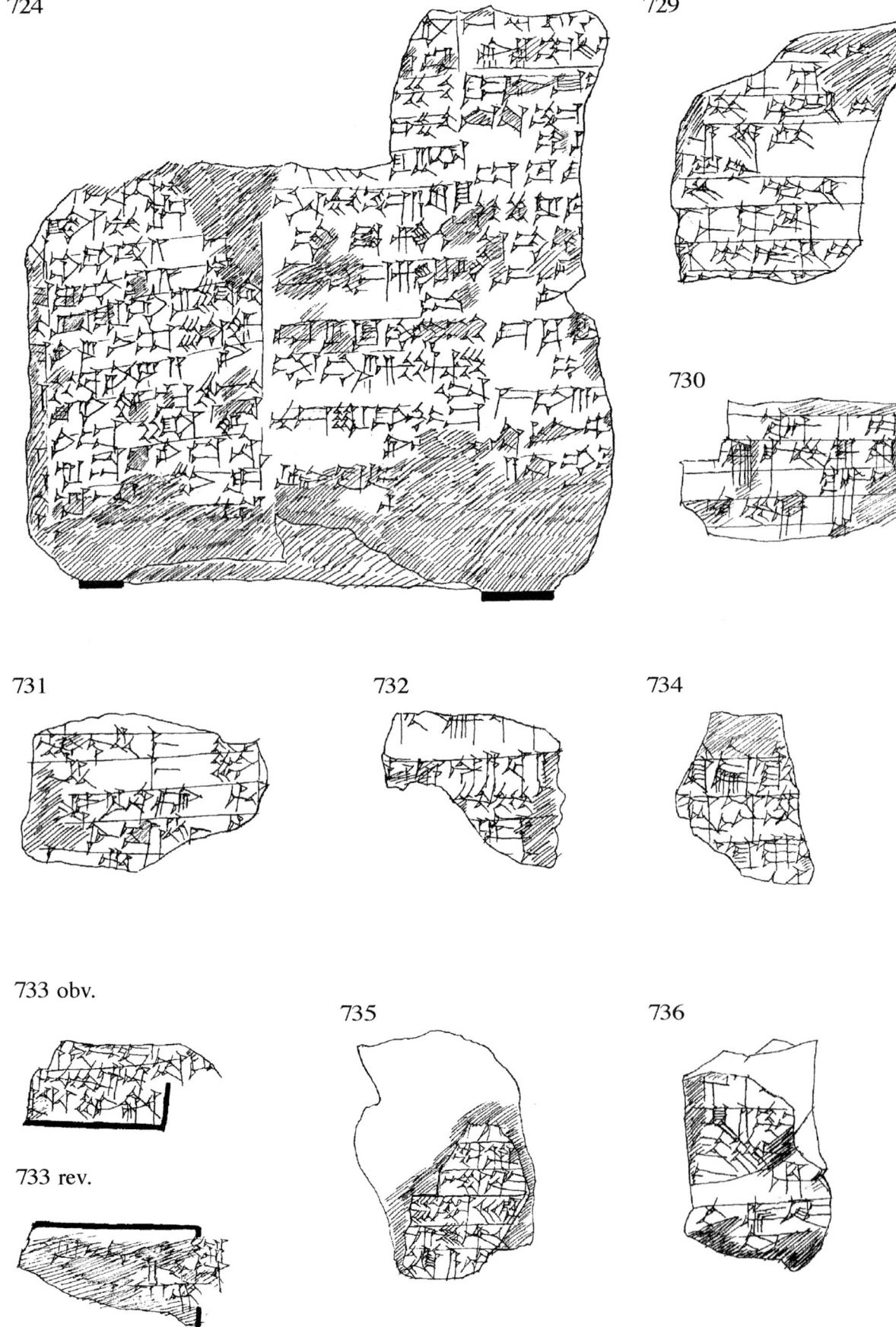

724

729

730

731

732

734

733 obv.

733 rev.

735

736

Plate 63

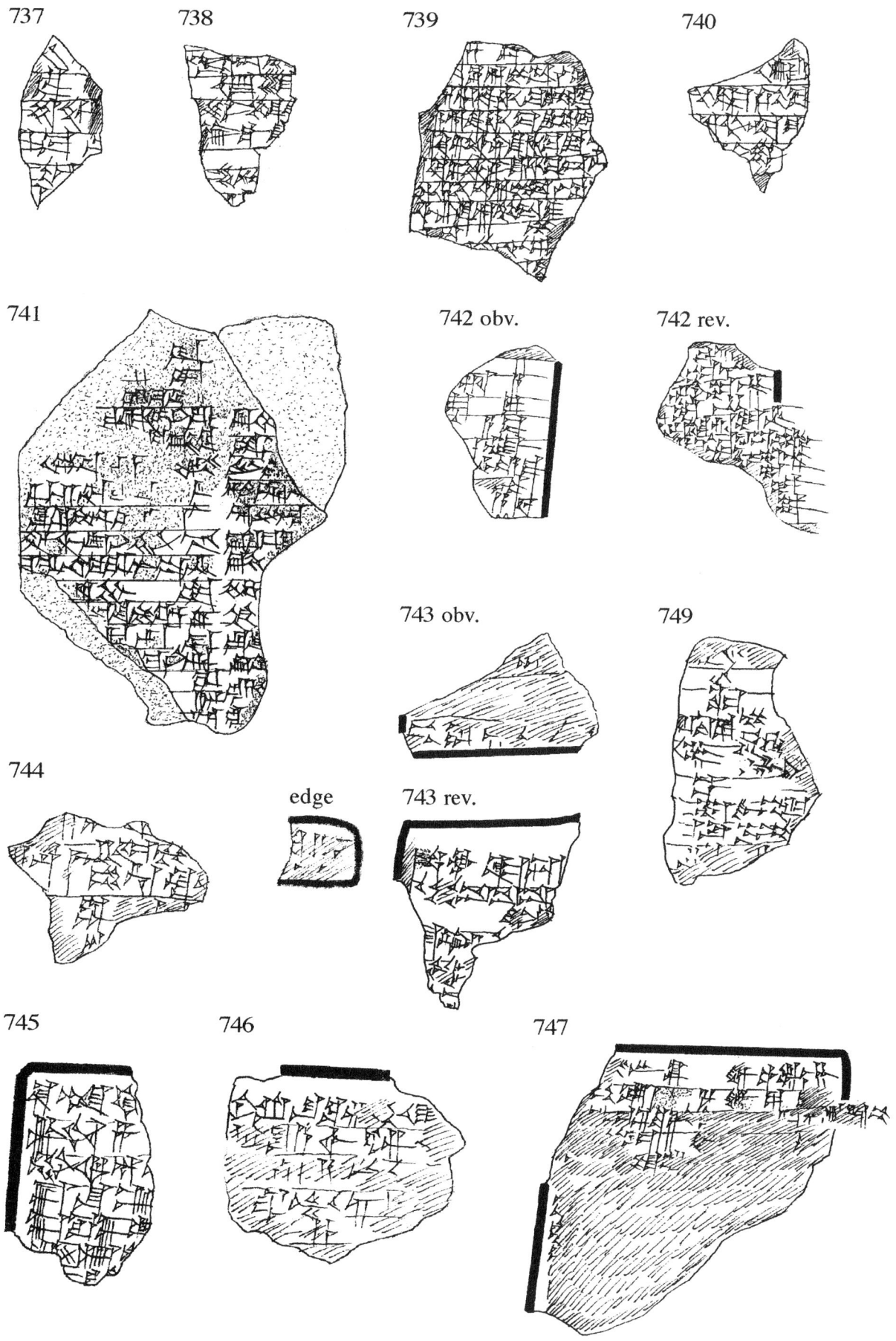

737

738

739

740

741

742 obv.

742 rev.

743 obv.

749

744

edge

743 rev.

745

746

747

Plate 64

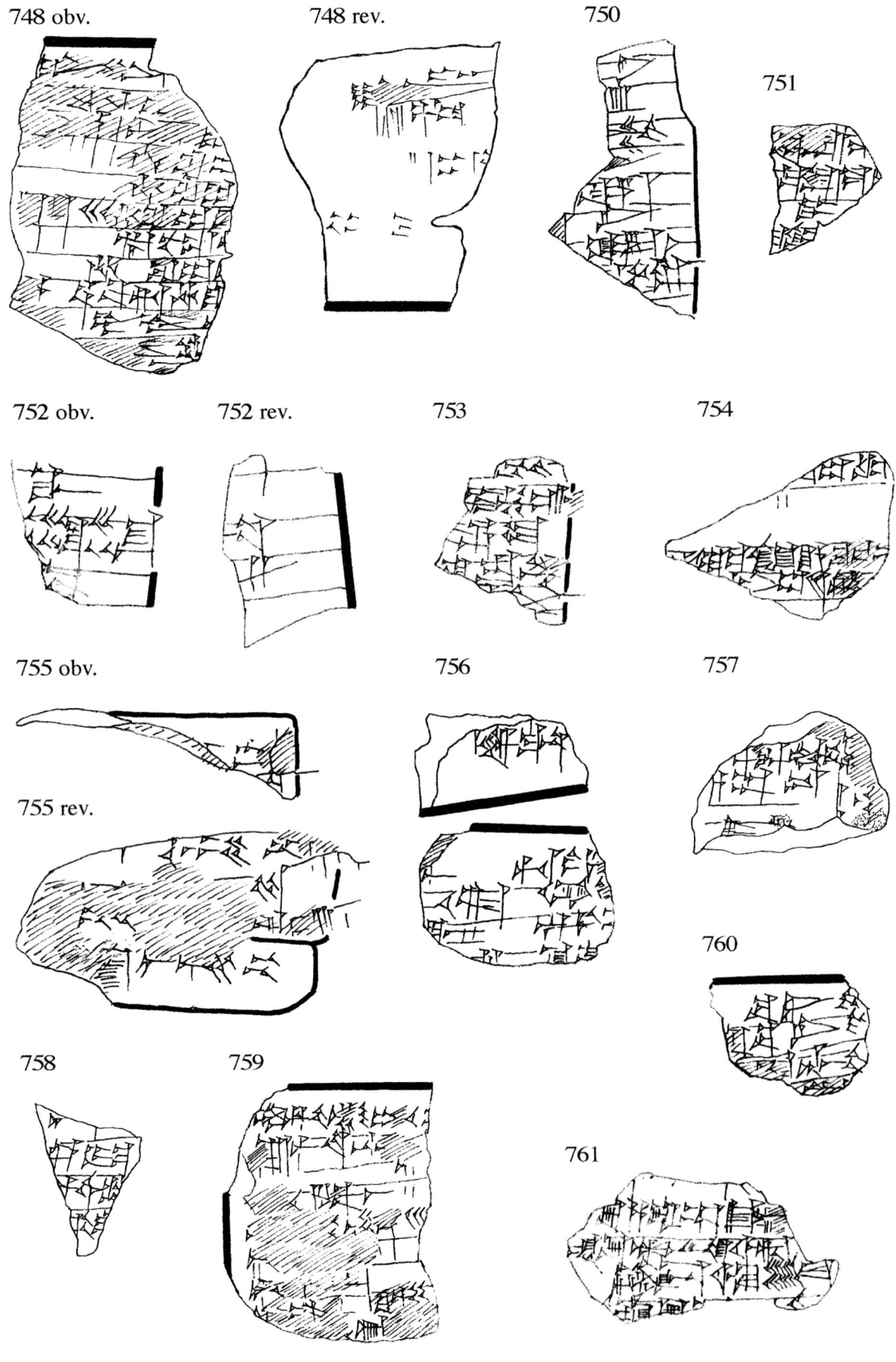

748 obv.

748 rev.

750

751

752 obv.

752 rev.

753

754

755 obv.

756

757

755 rev.

760

758

759

761

Plate 65

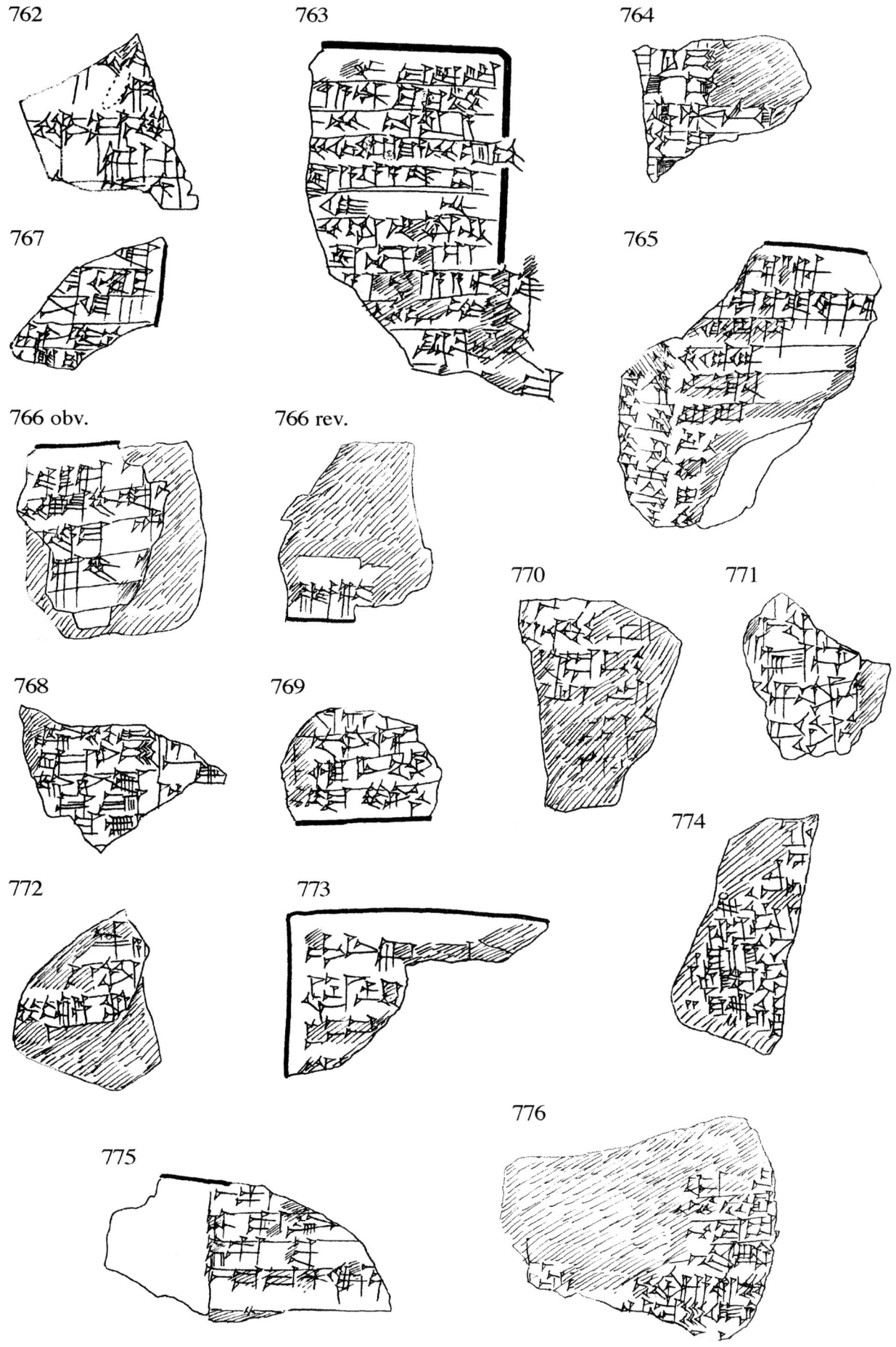

762

763

764

767

765

766 obv.

766 rev.

770

771

768

769

772

773

774

775

776

Plate 66

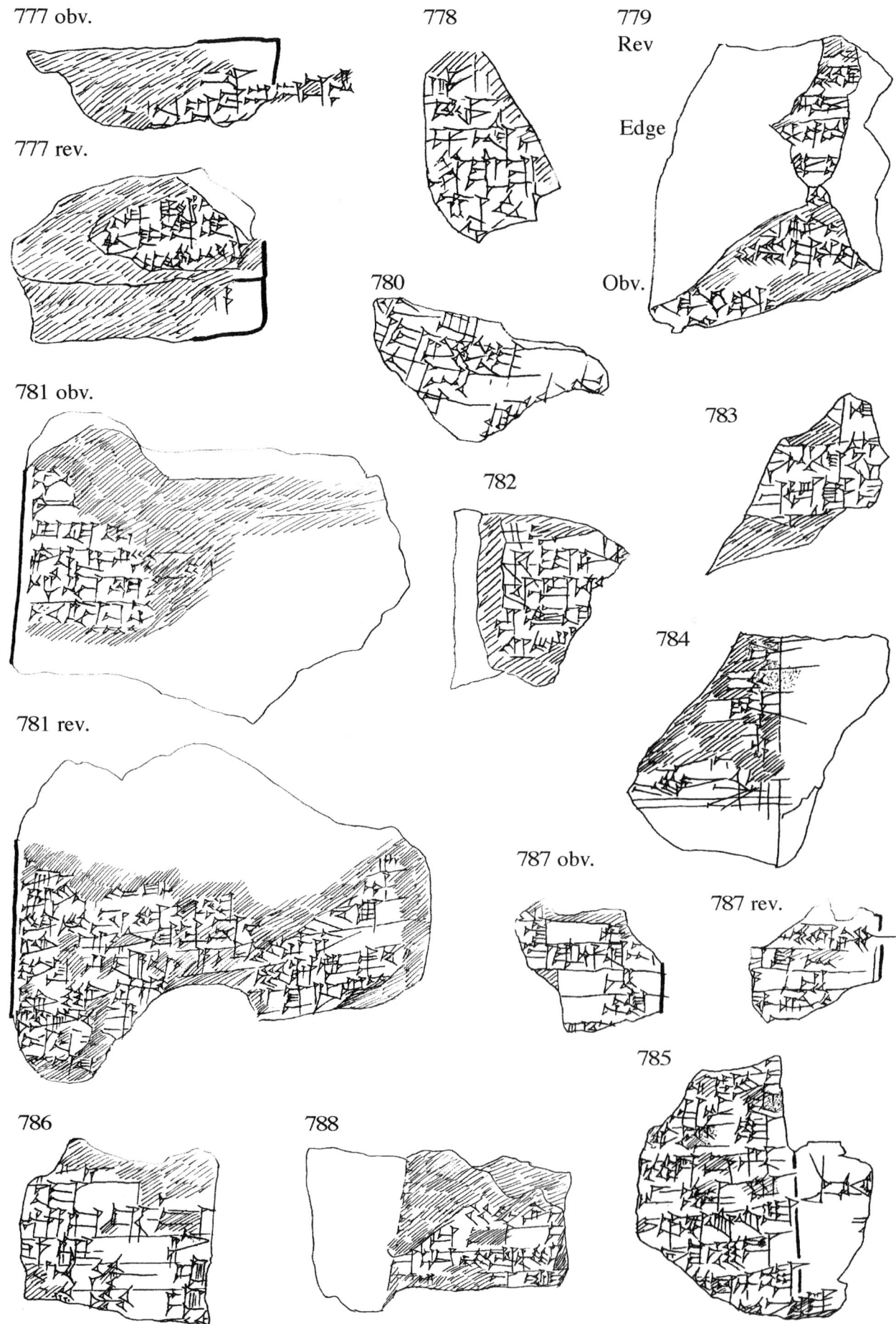

777 obv.

777 rev.

778

779
Rev

Edge

Obv.

780

781 obv.

782

783

784

781 rev.

787 obv.

787 rev.

785

786

788

Plate 67

789 obv.

789 rev.

790

791

792 obv.

792 rev.

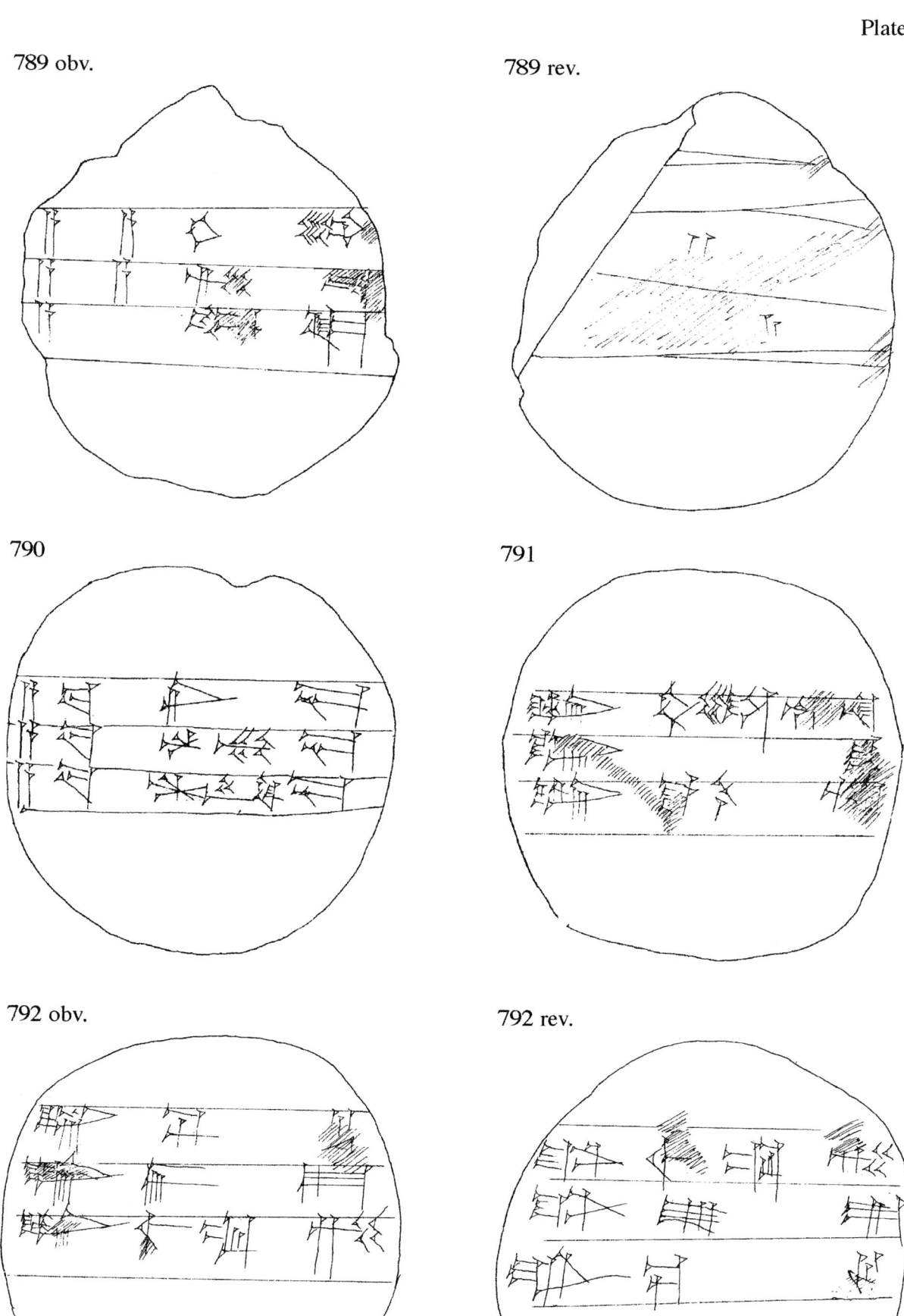

Plate 68

793

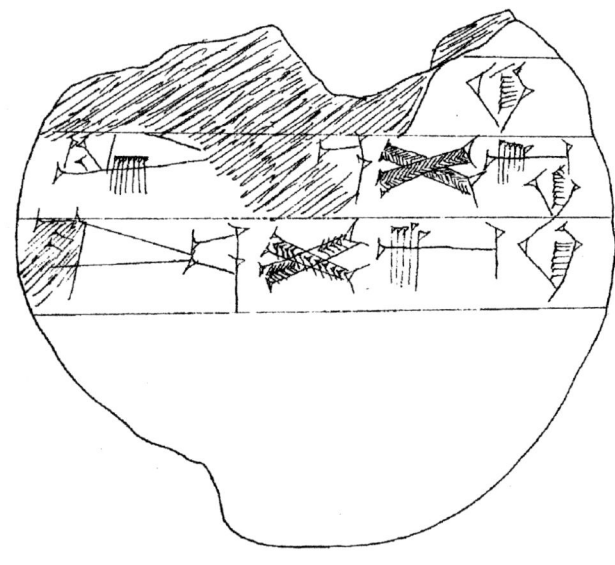

794

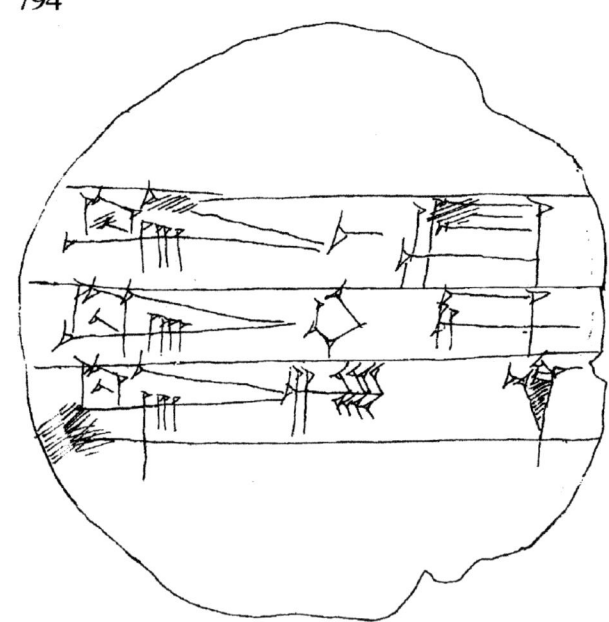

795

796

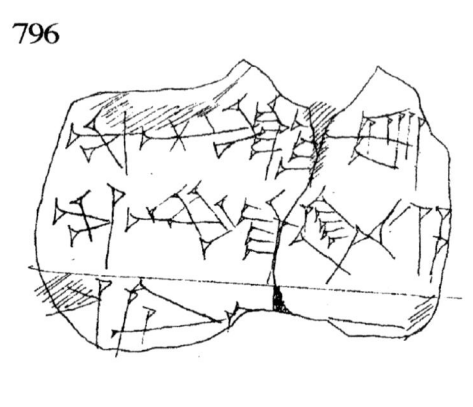

797 obv.

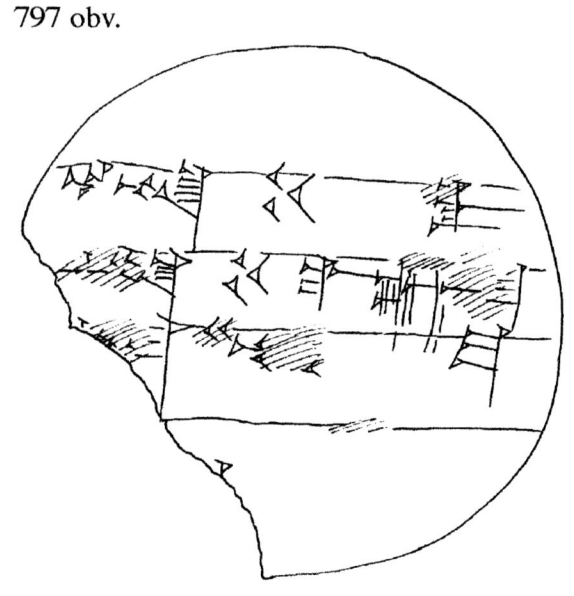

797 rev.

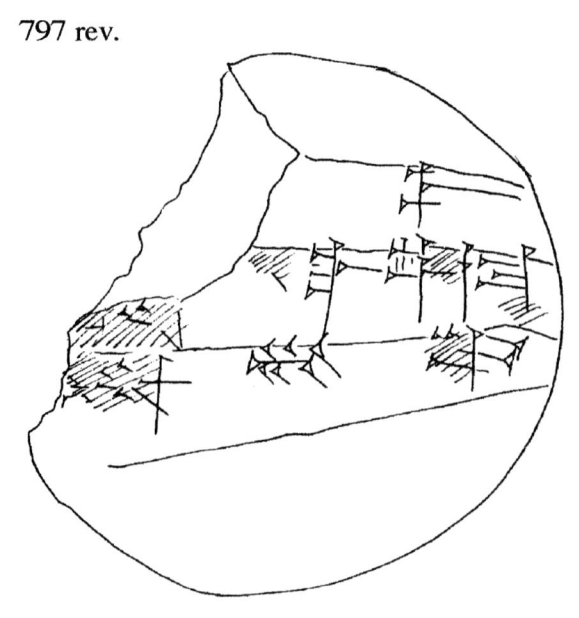

Plate 69

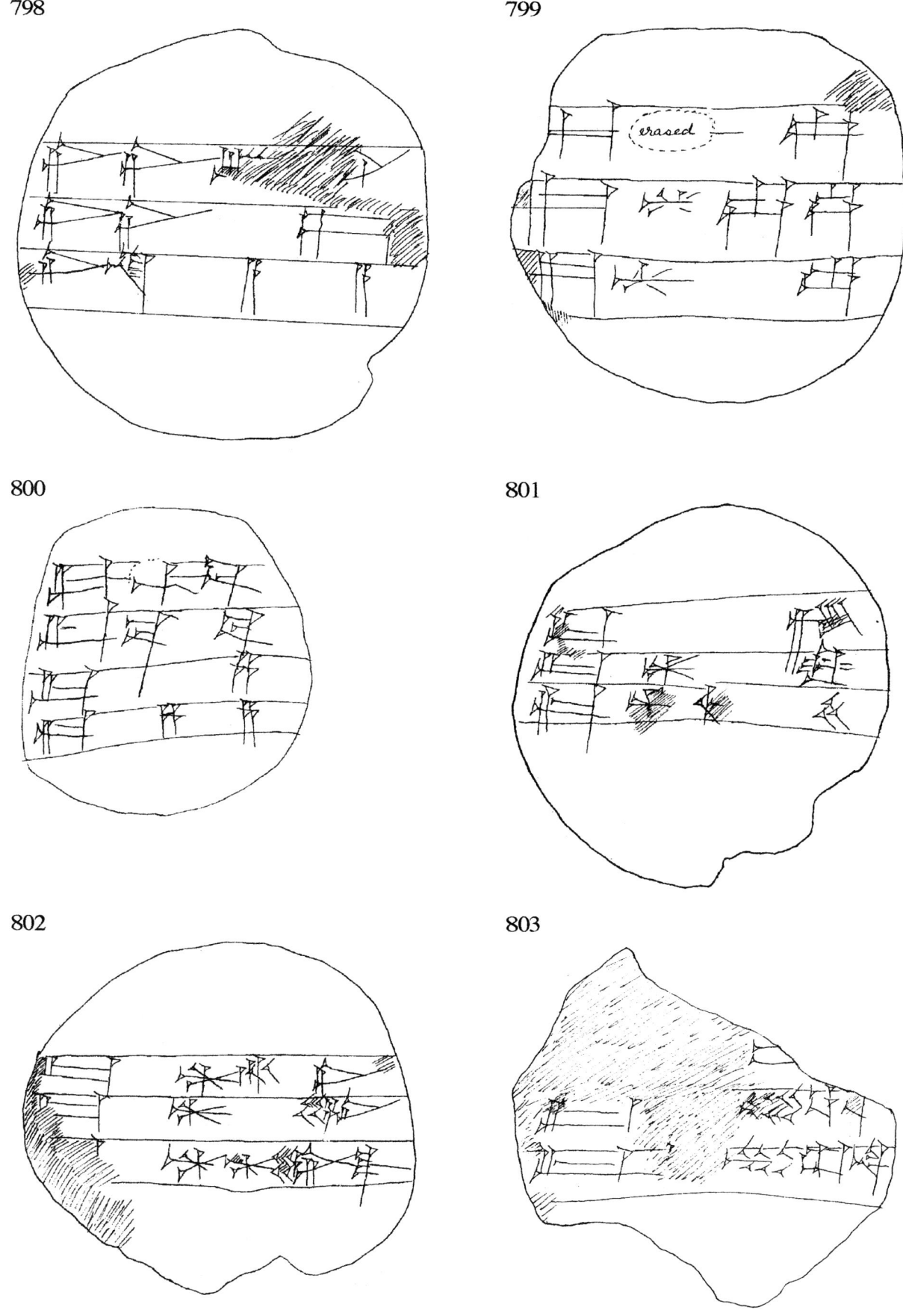

798

799

800

801

802

803

Plate 70

804 obv.

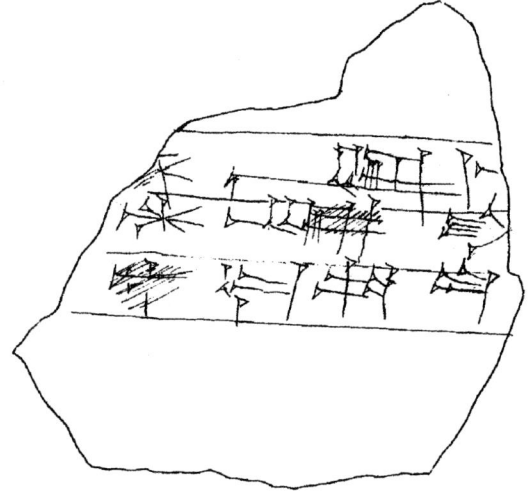

804 rev.

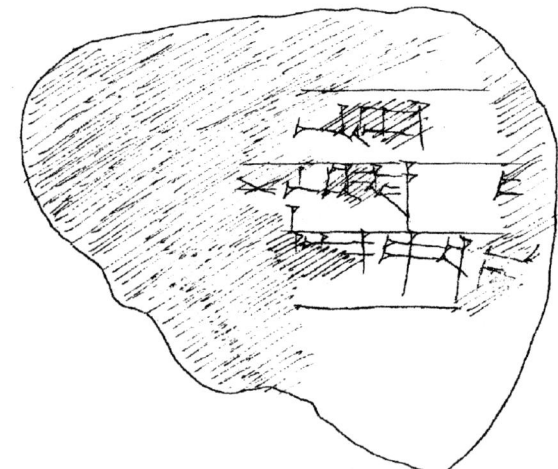

805 obv.

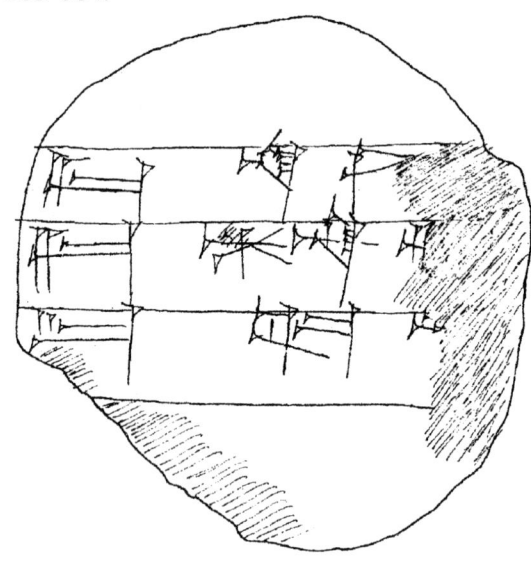

805 rev.

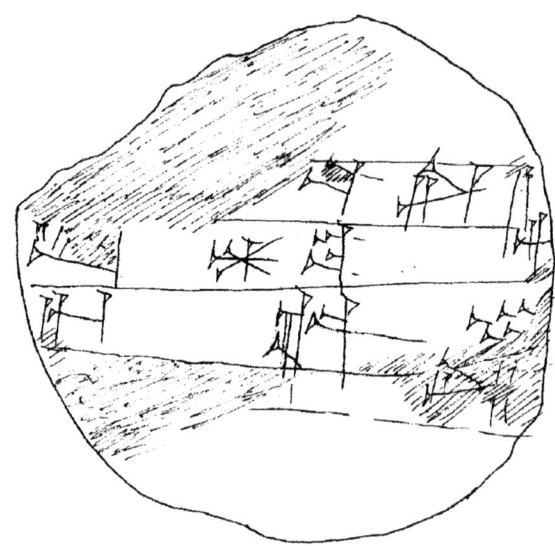

806

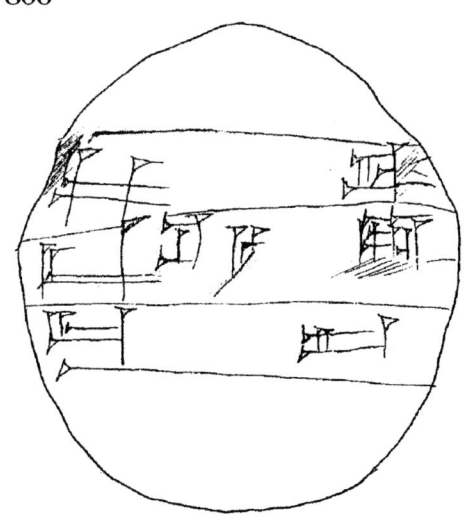

807

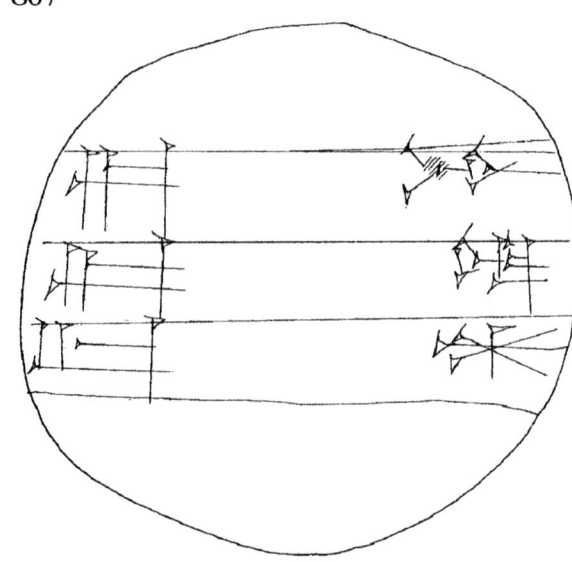

Plate 71

808 obv.

808 rev.

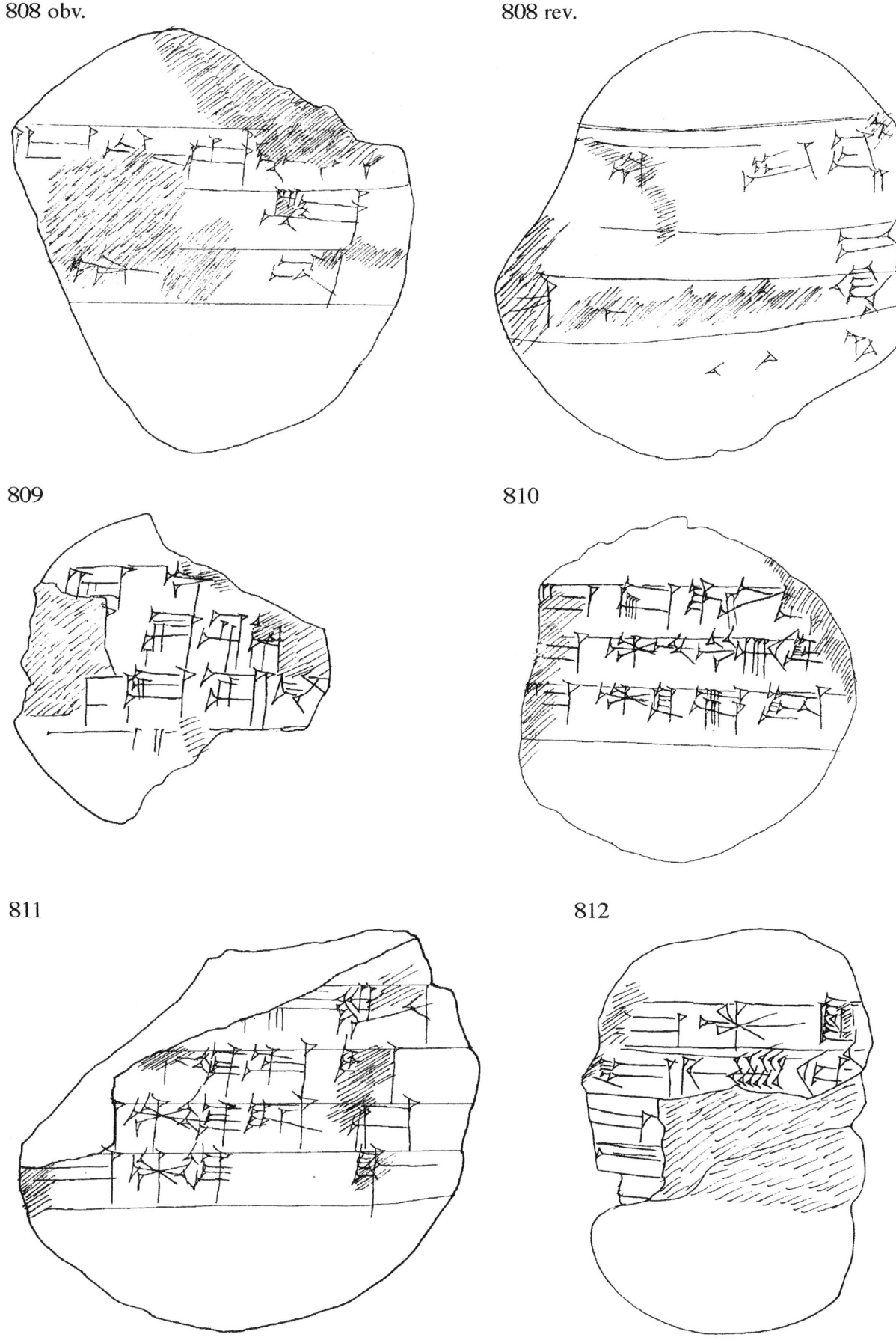

809

810

811

812

Plate 72

813 obv.

813 rev.

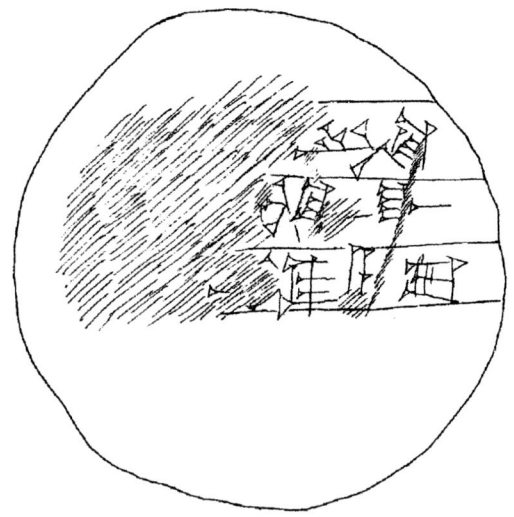

814

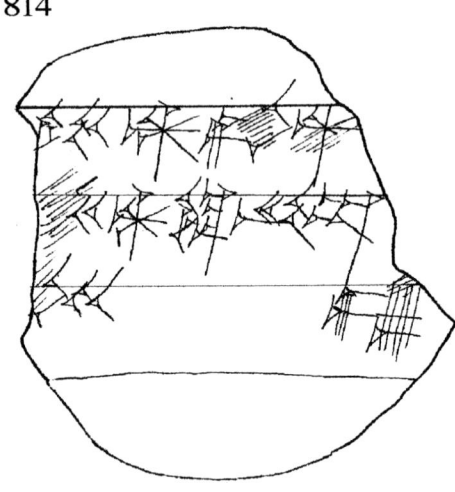

815

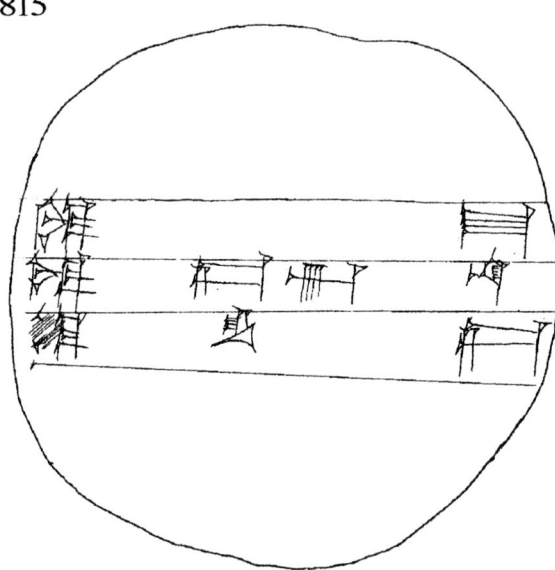

816 obv.

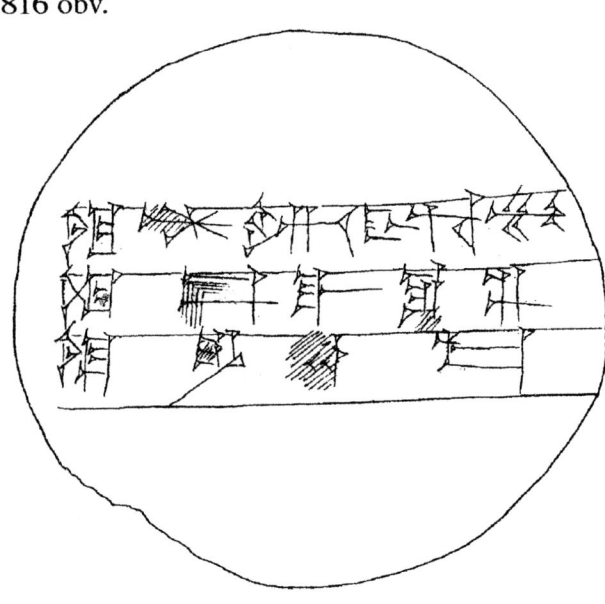

816 rev.

Plate 73

817 obv.

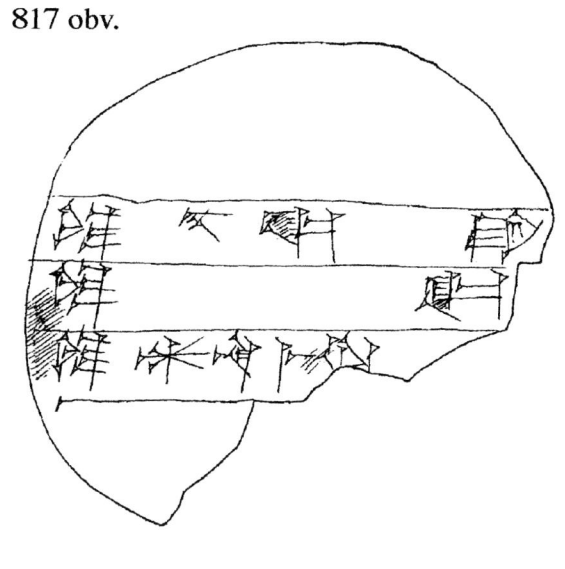

817 rev.

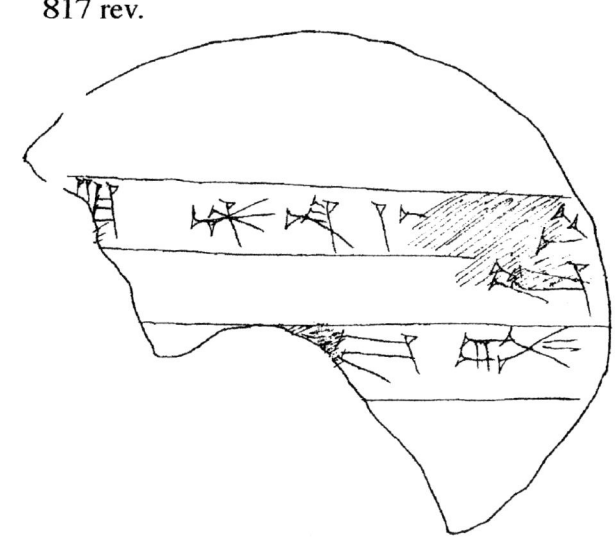

818 obv.

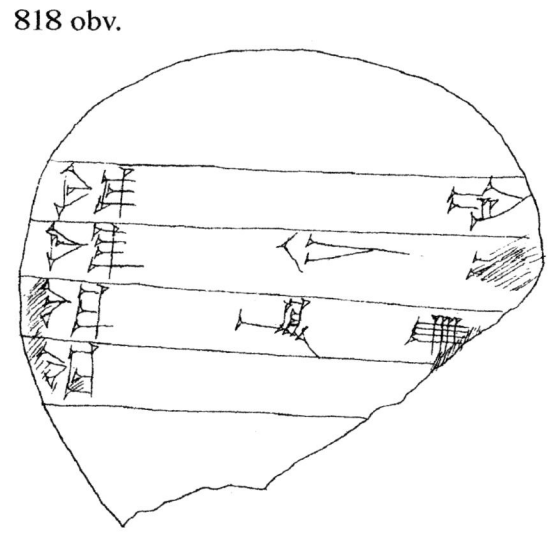

818 rev.

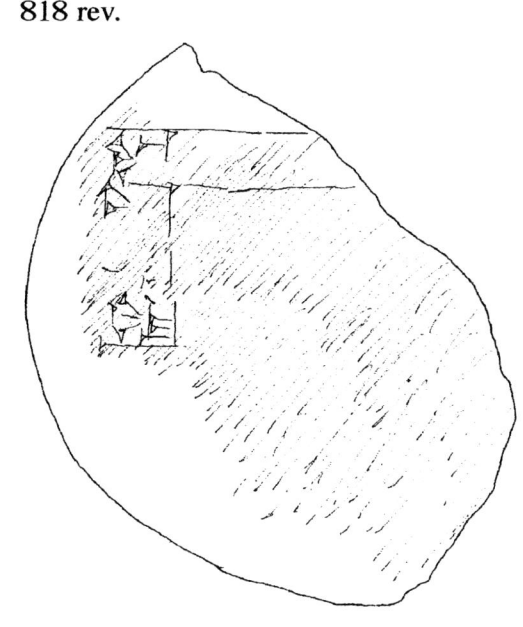

819 obv.

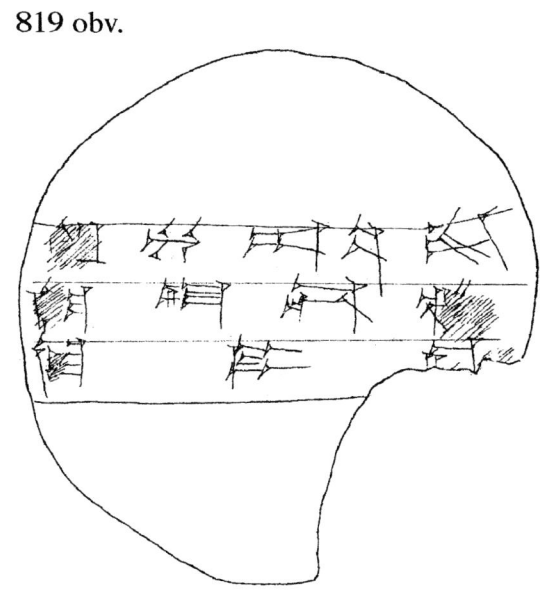

819 rev.

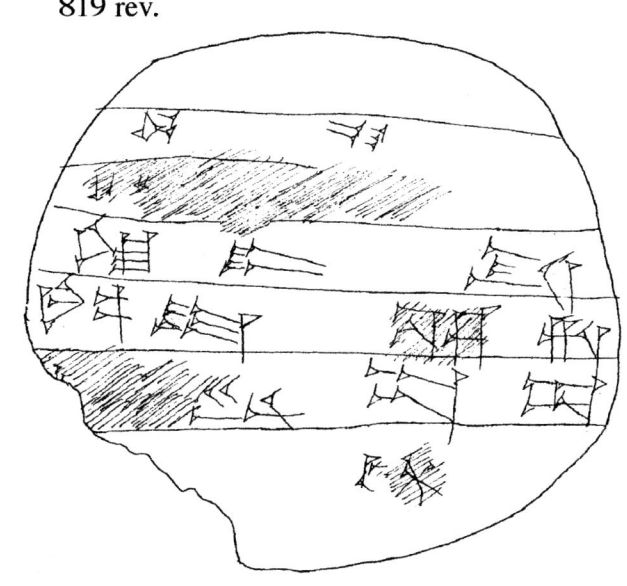

Plate 74

820 obv.

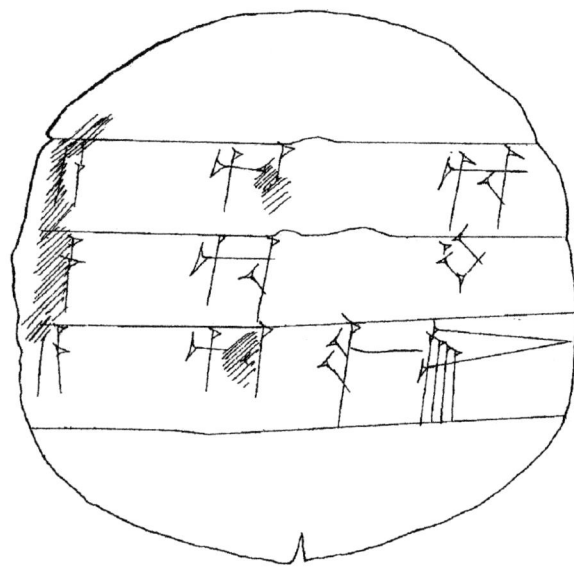

820 rev.

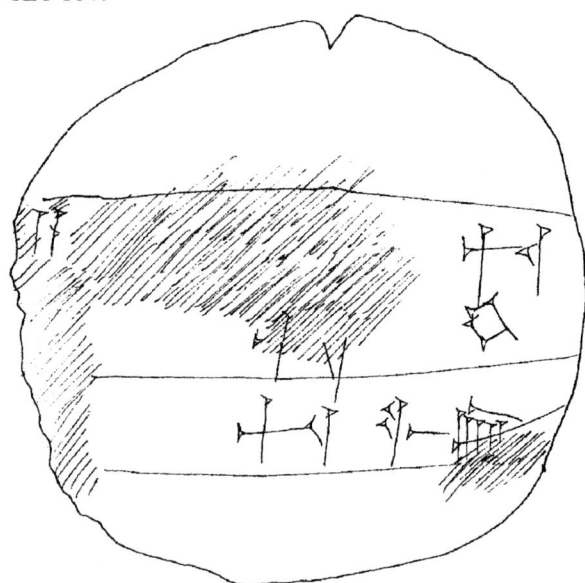

822

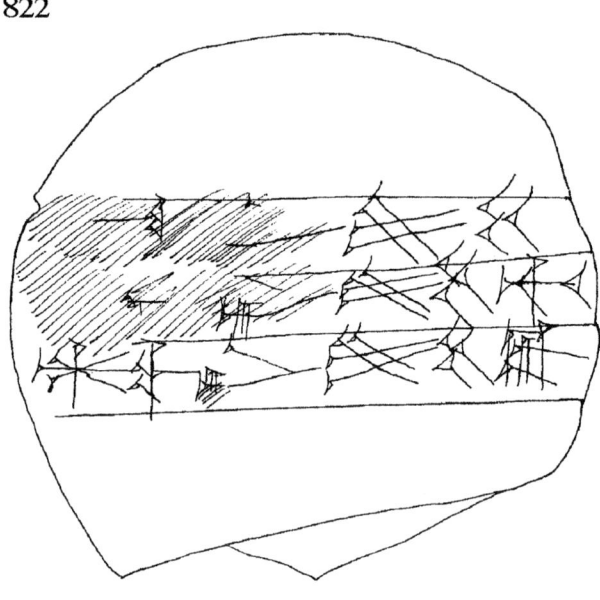

821 obv.

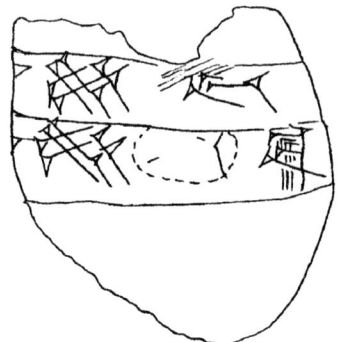

821 rev.

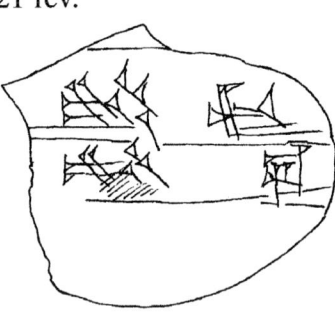

823 obv.

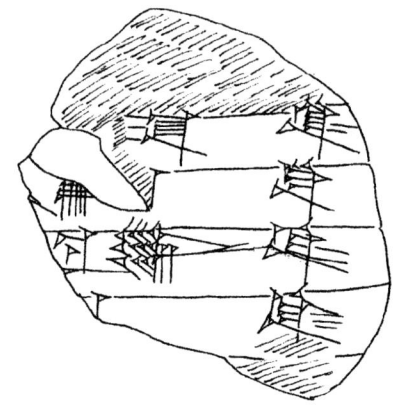

823 rev.

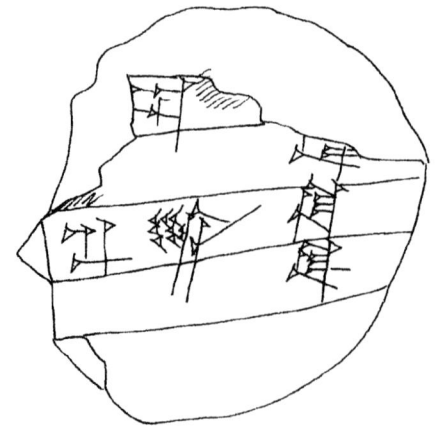

Plate 75

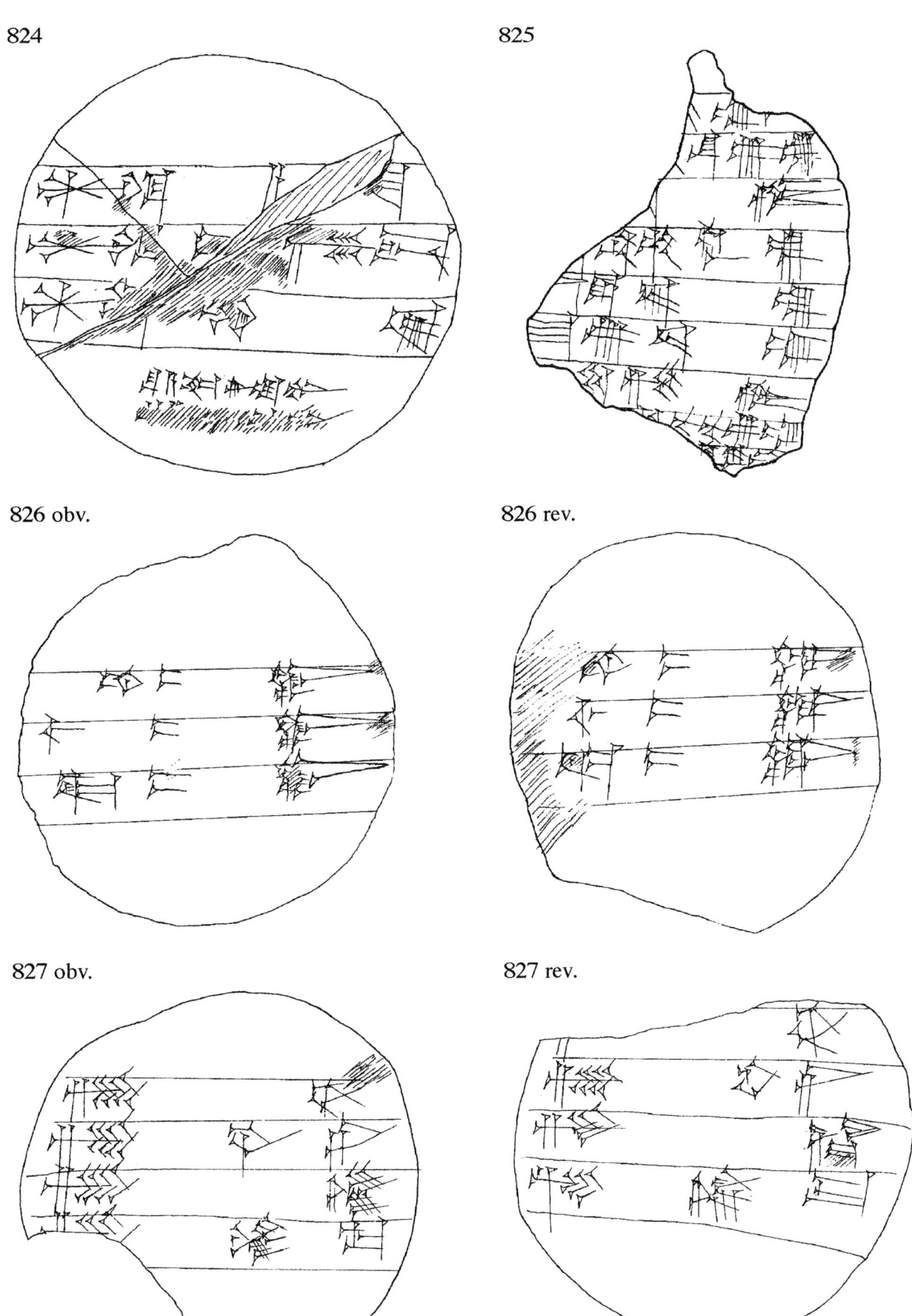

824

825

826 obv.

826 rev.

827 obv.

827 rev.

Plate 76

828 obv.

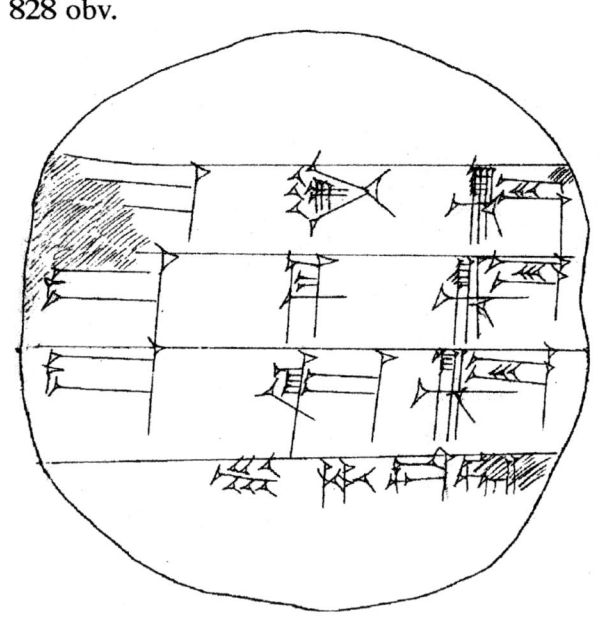

828 rev.

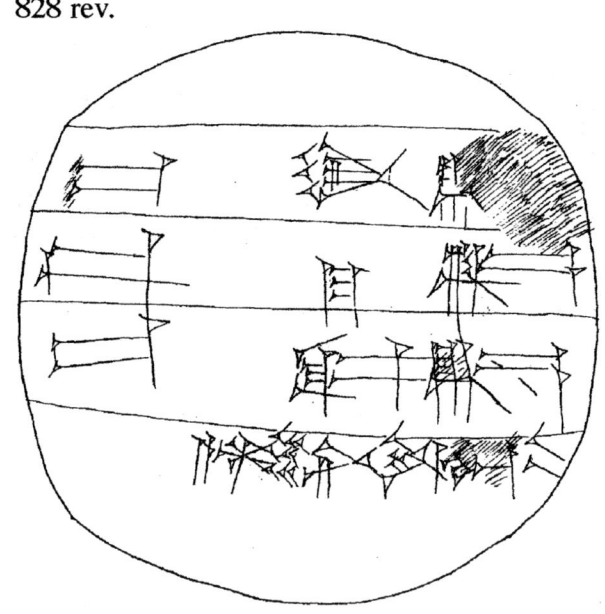

829

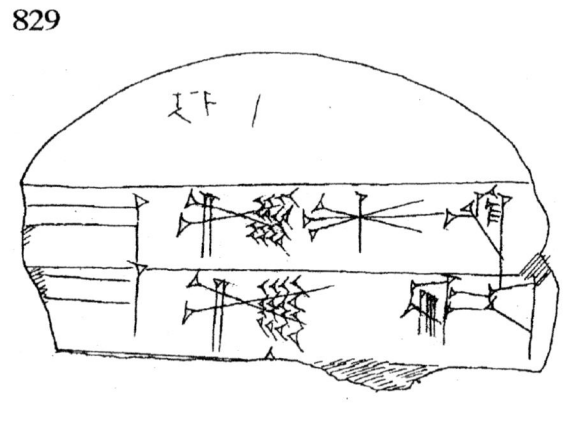

830

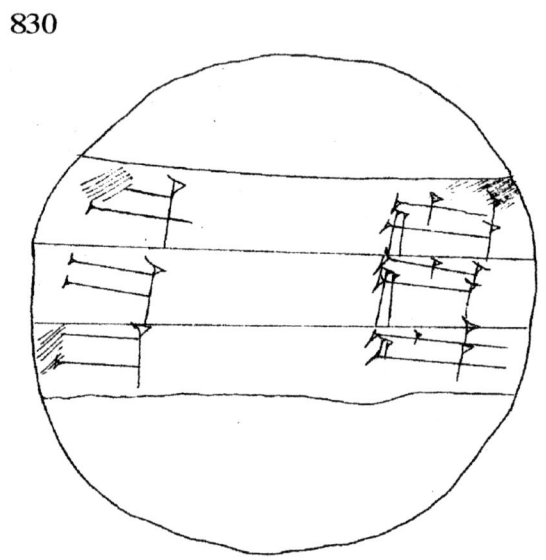

831 obv.

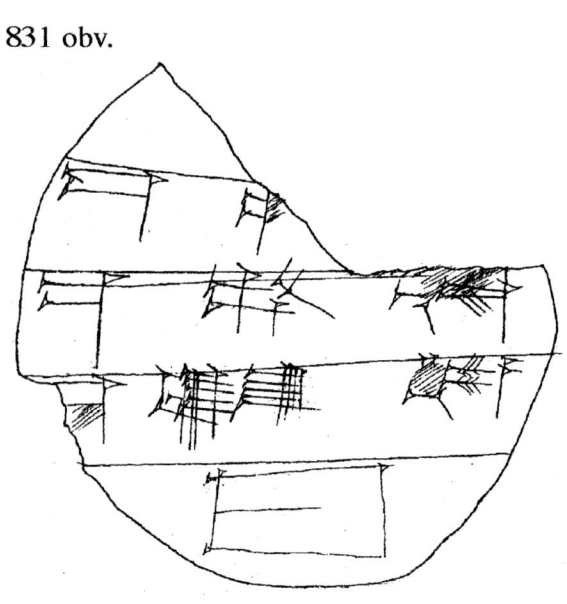

831 rev.

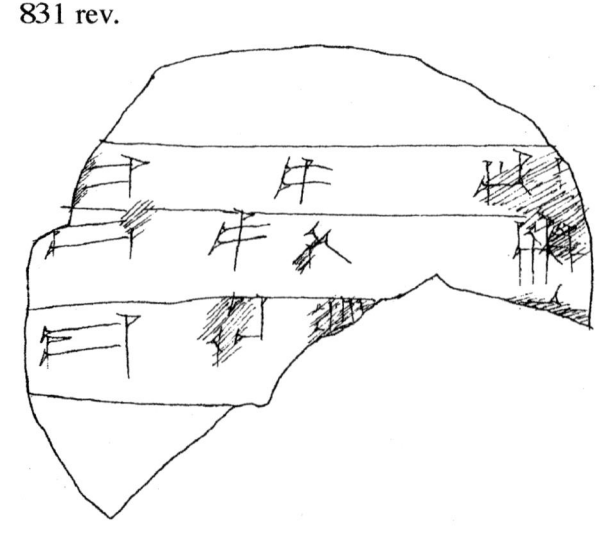

Plate 77

832

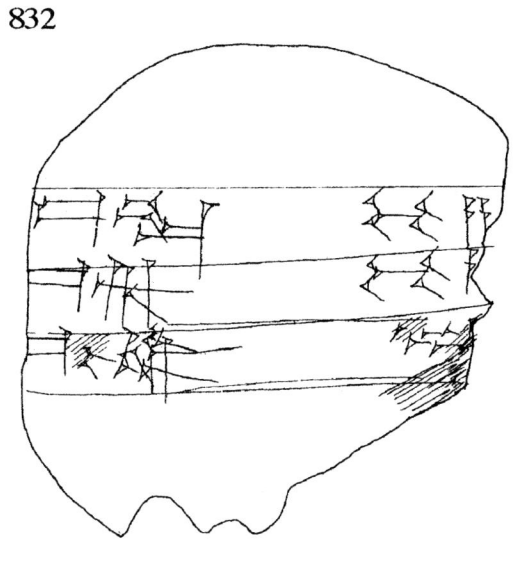

833

834 obv.

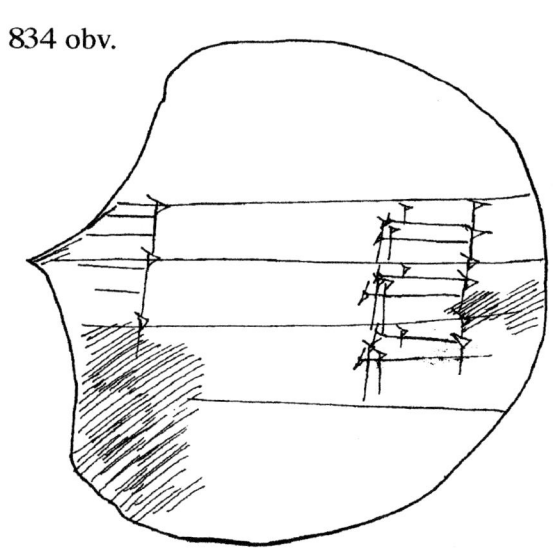

834 rev.

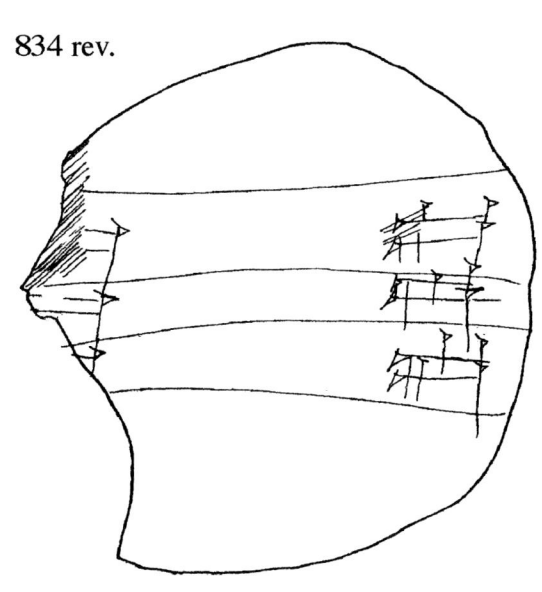

835 obv.

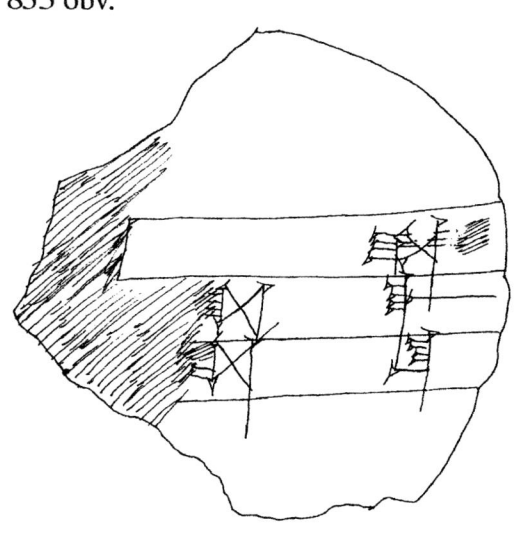

835 rev.

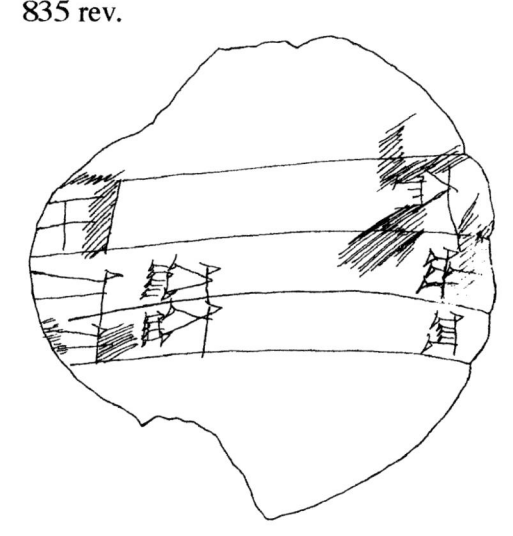

Plate 78

836 obv.

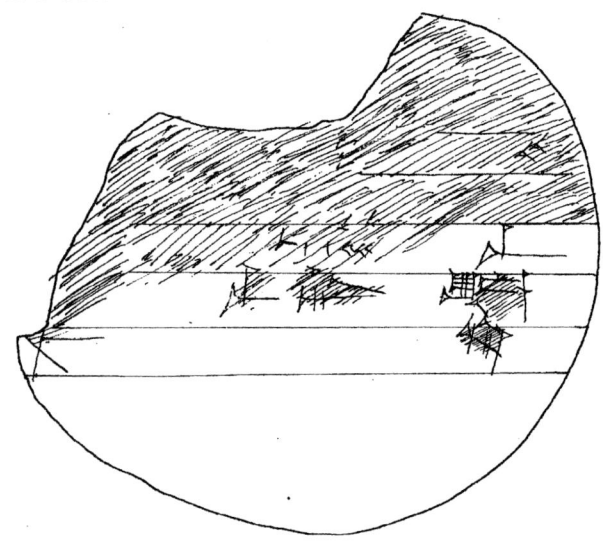

836 rev.

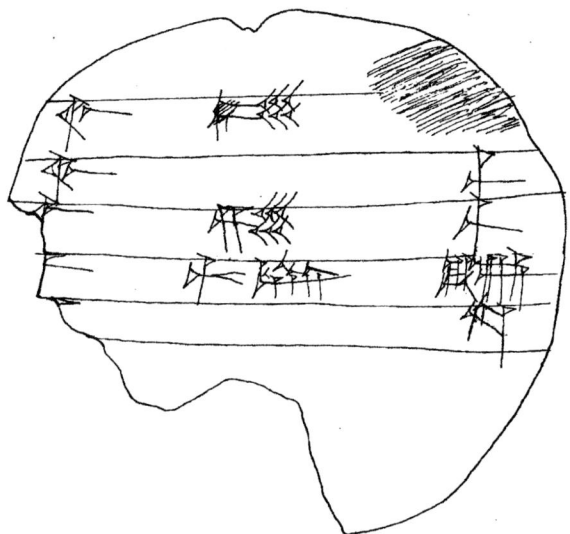

837 obv.

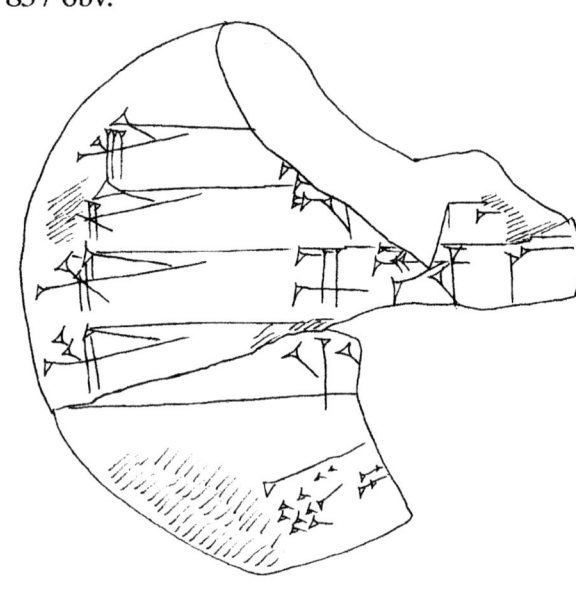

837 rev.

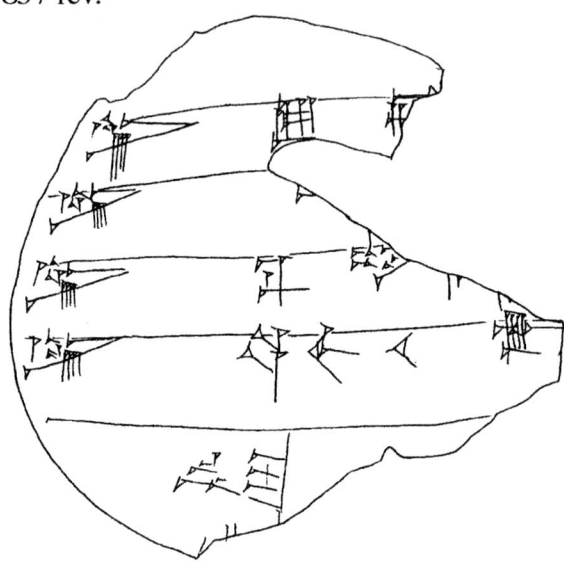

838 obv.

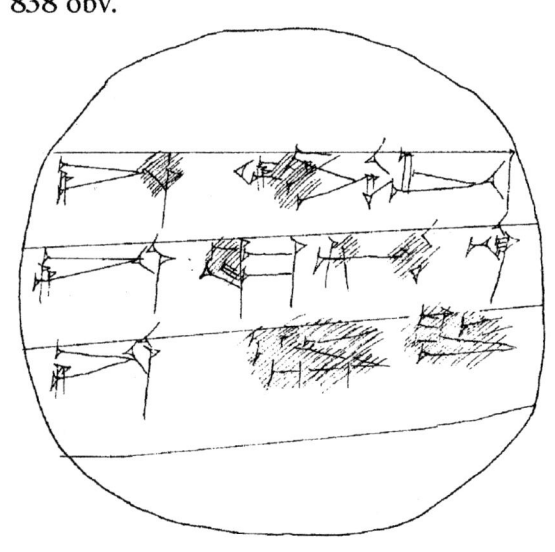

838 rev.

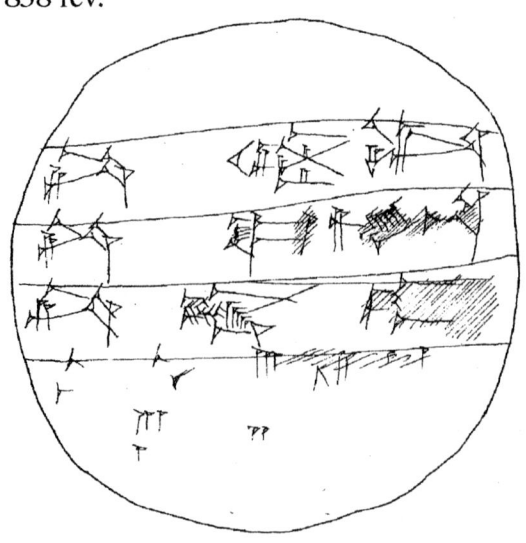

Plate 79

839 obv.

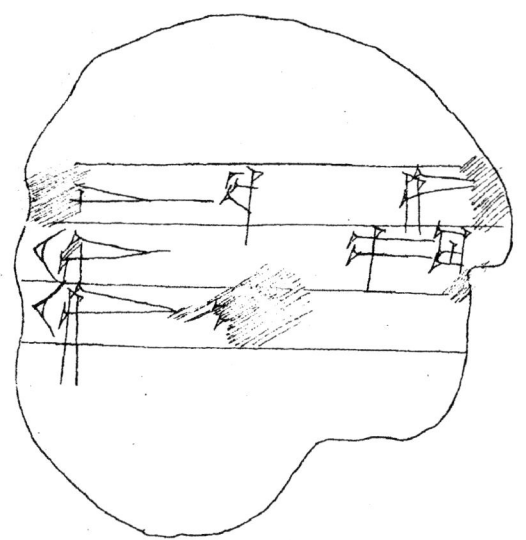

839 rev.

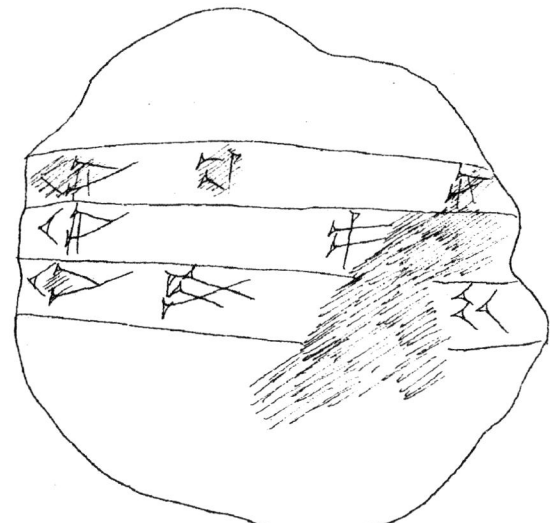

840 obv.

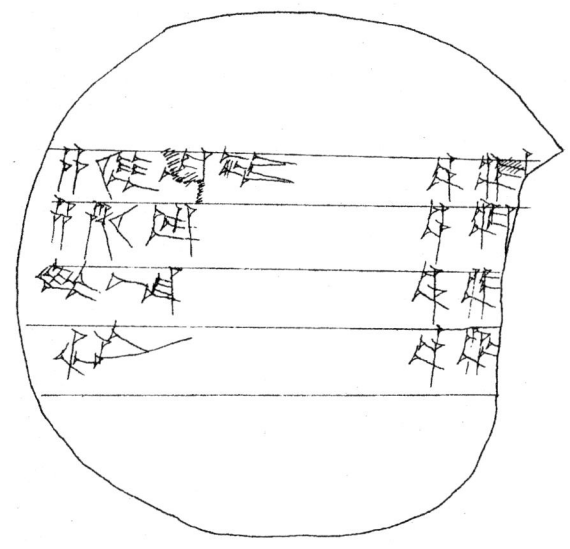

840 rev.

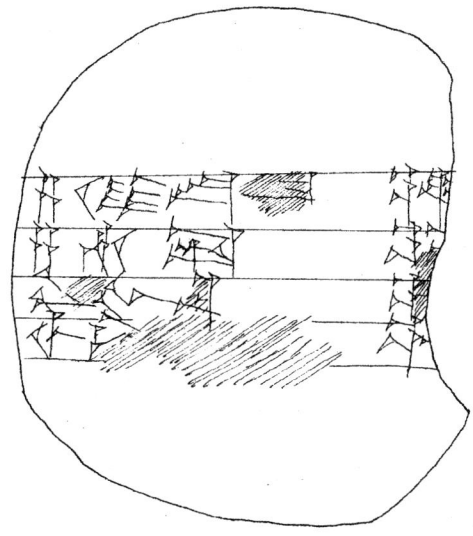

841 obv.

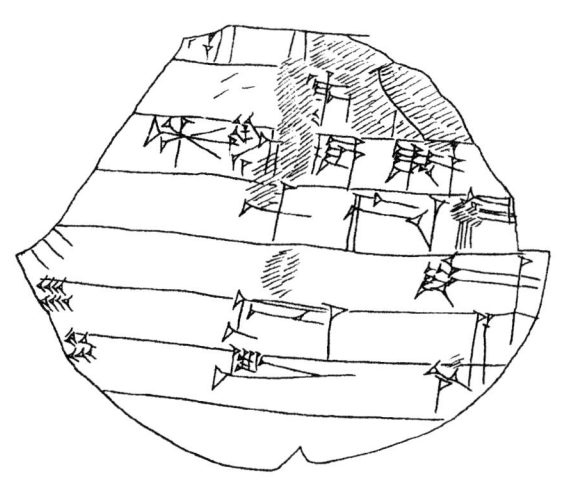

841 rev.

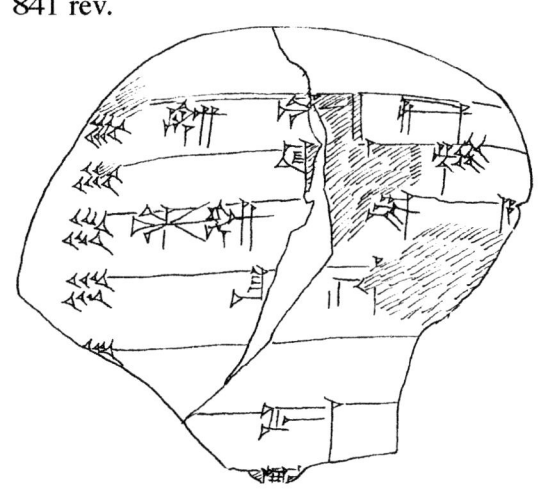

Plate 80

842

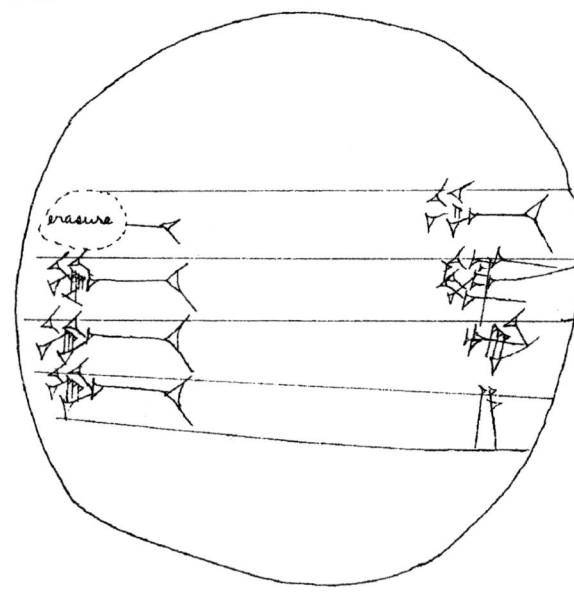

843

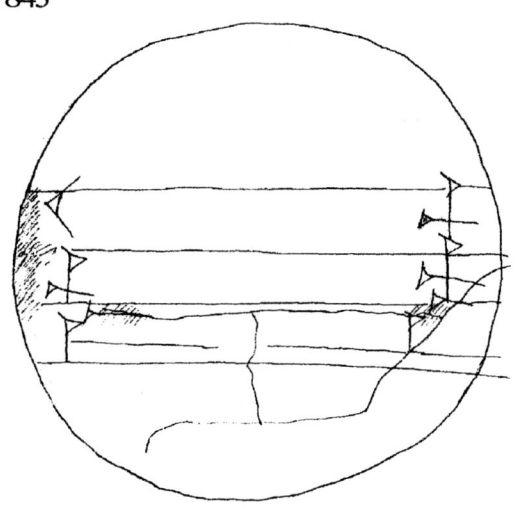

844 obv.

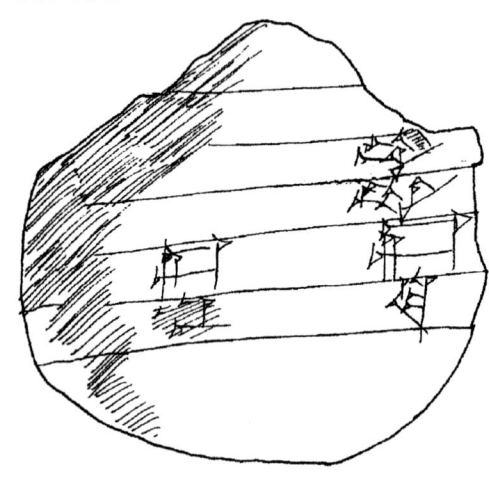

844 rev.

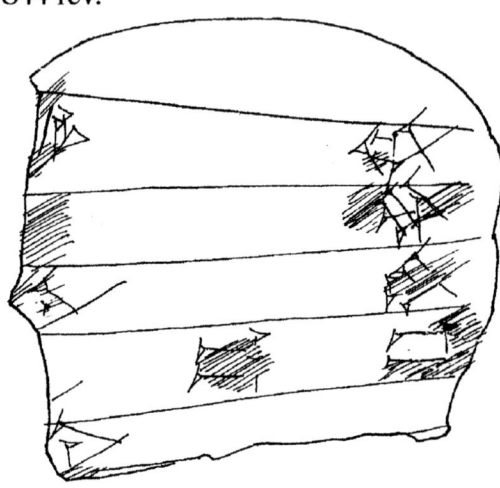

845

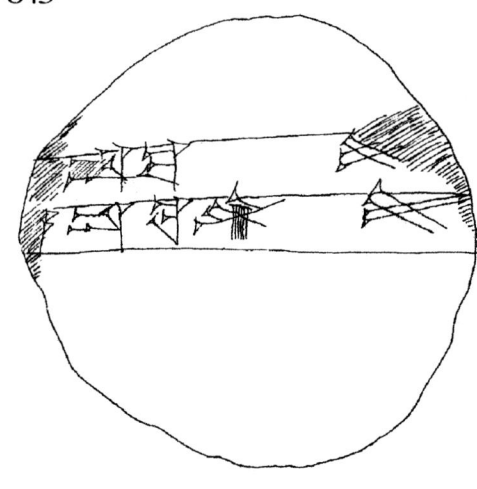

846

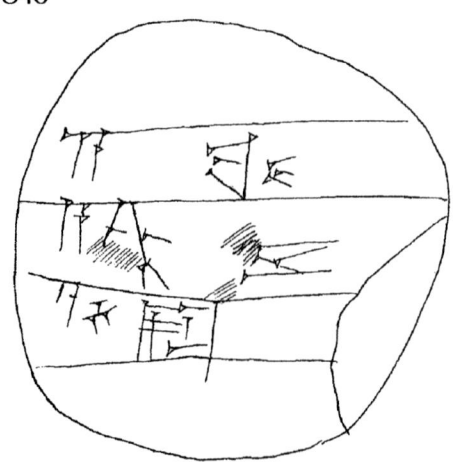

Plate 81

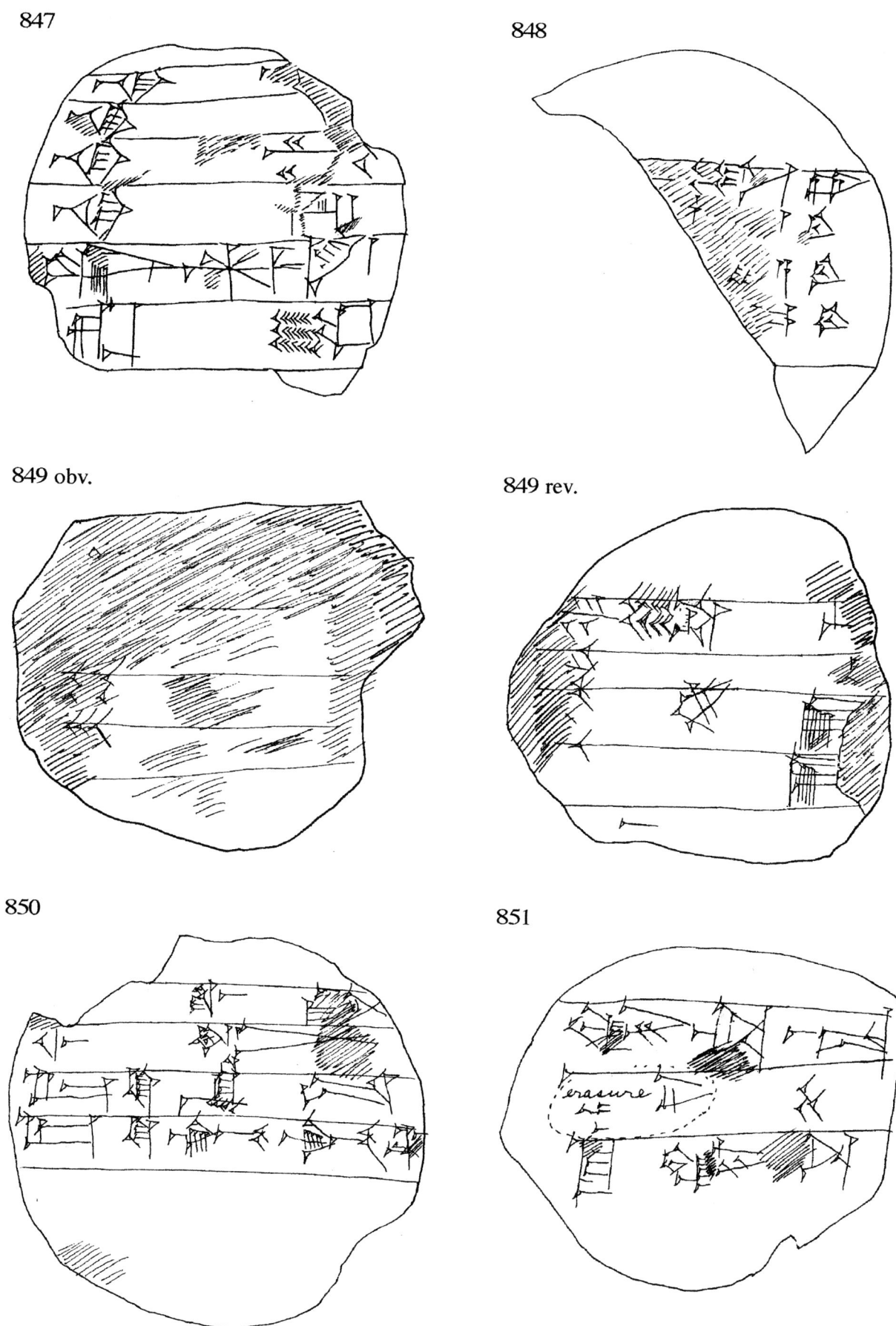

847

848

849 obv.

849 rev.

850

851

Plate 82

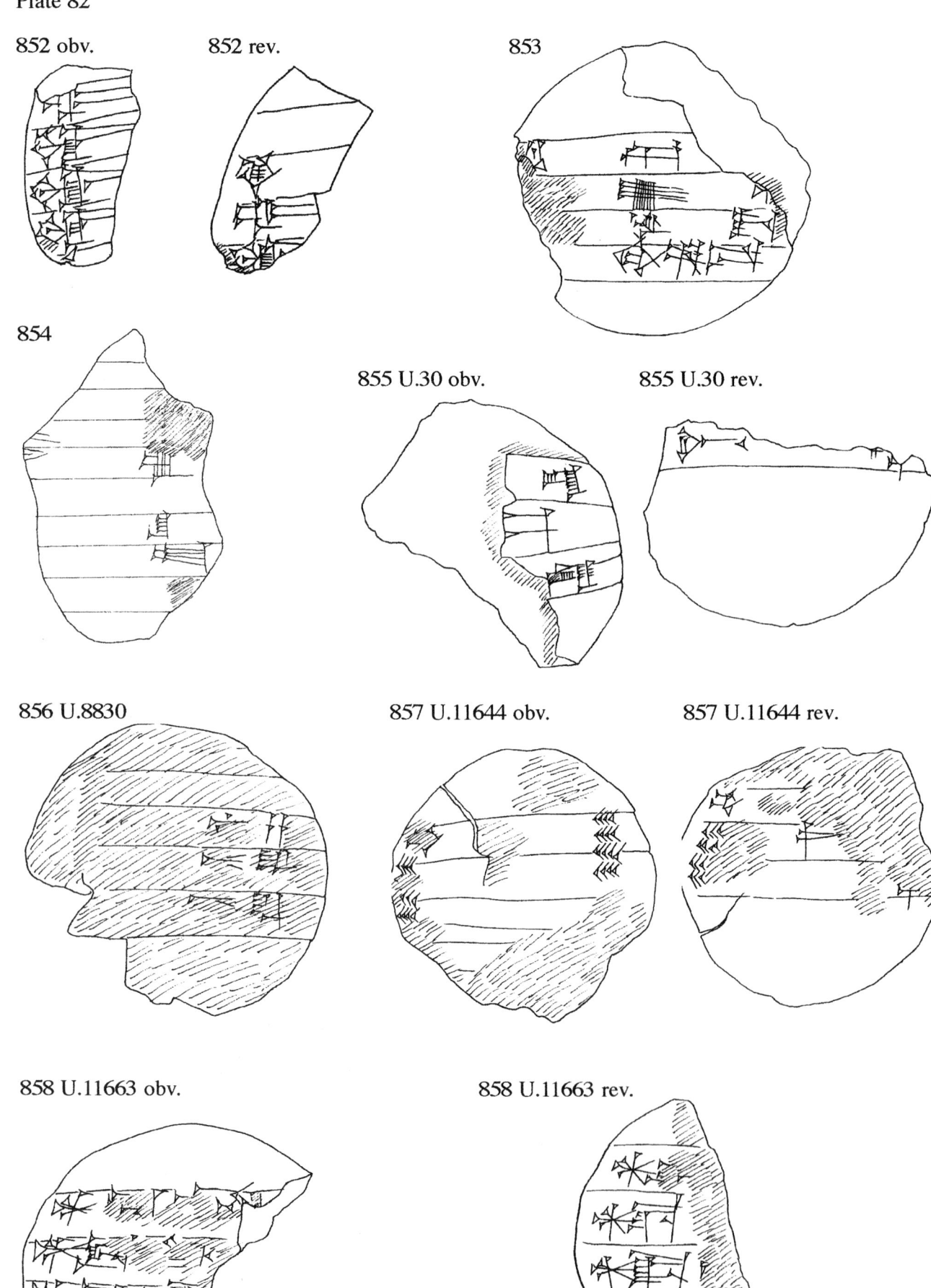

852 obv.   852 rev.   853

854   855 U.30 obv.   855 U.30 rev.

856 U.8830   857 U.11644 obv.   857 U.11644 rev.

858 U.11663 obv.   858 U.11663 rev.

Plate 83

859 U.13630

860 U.13631

862 U.17653 B

861 U.15027

863

864 obv.

864 rev.

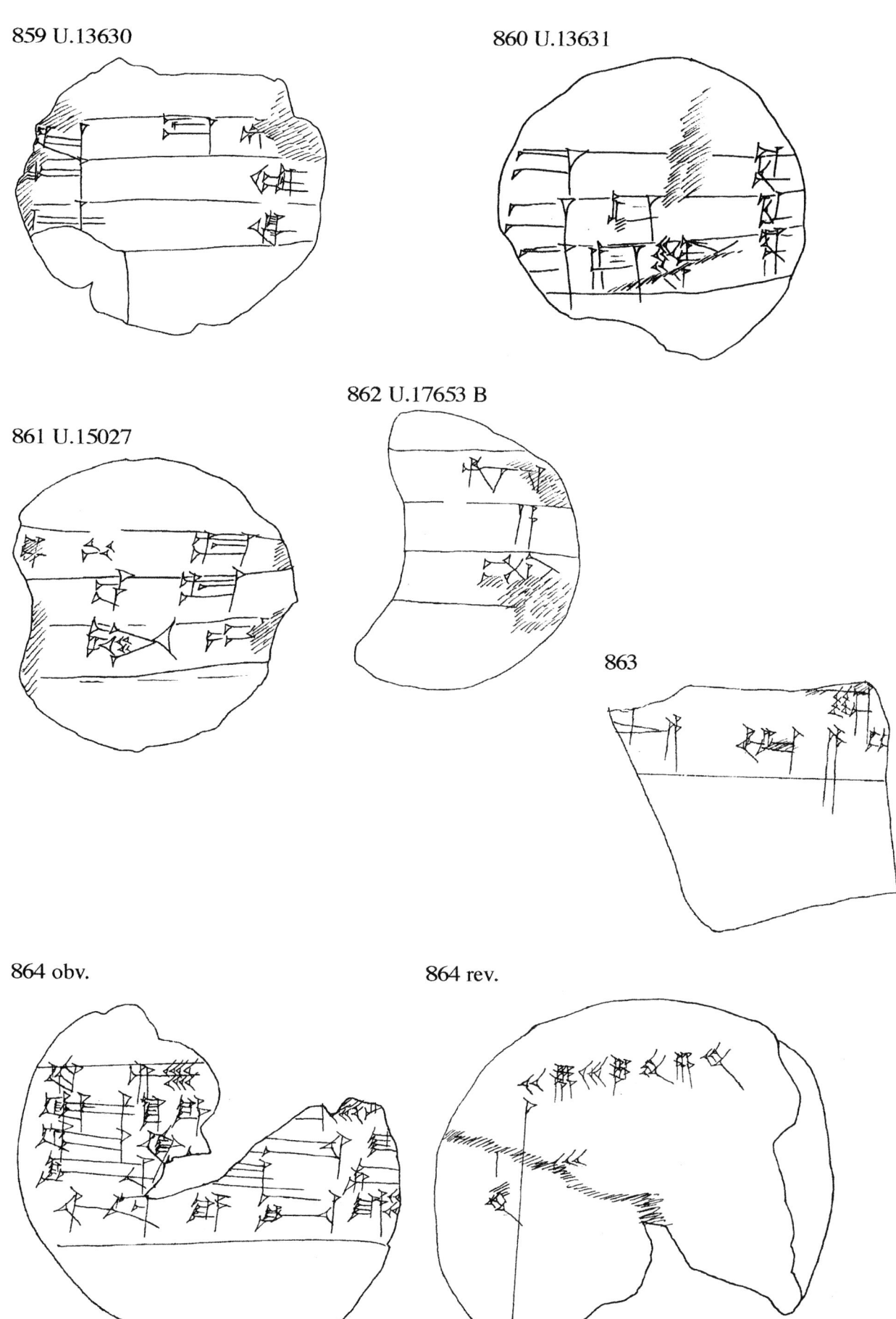

Plate 84

865 obv.

865 rev.

866

867

869

868 obv.

868 rev.

870

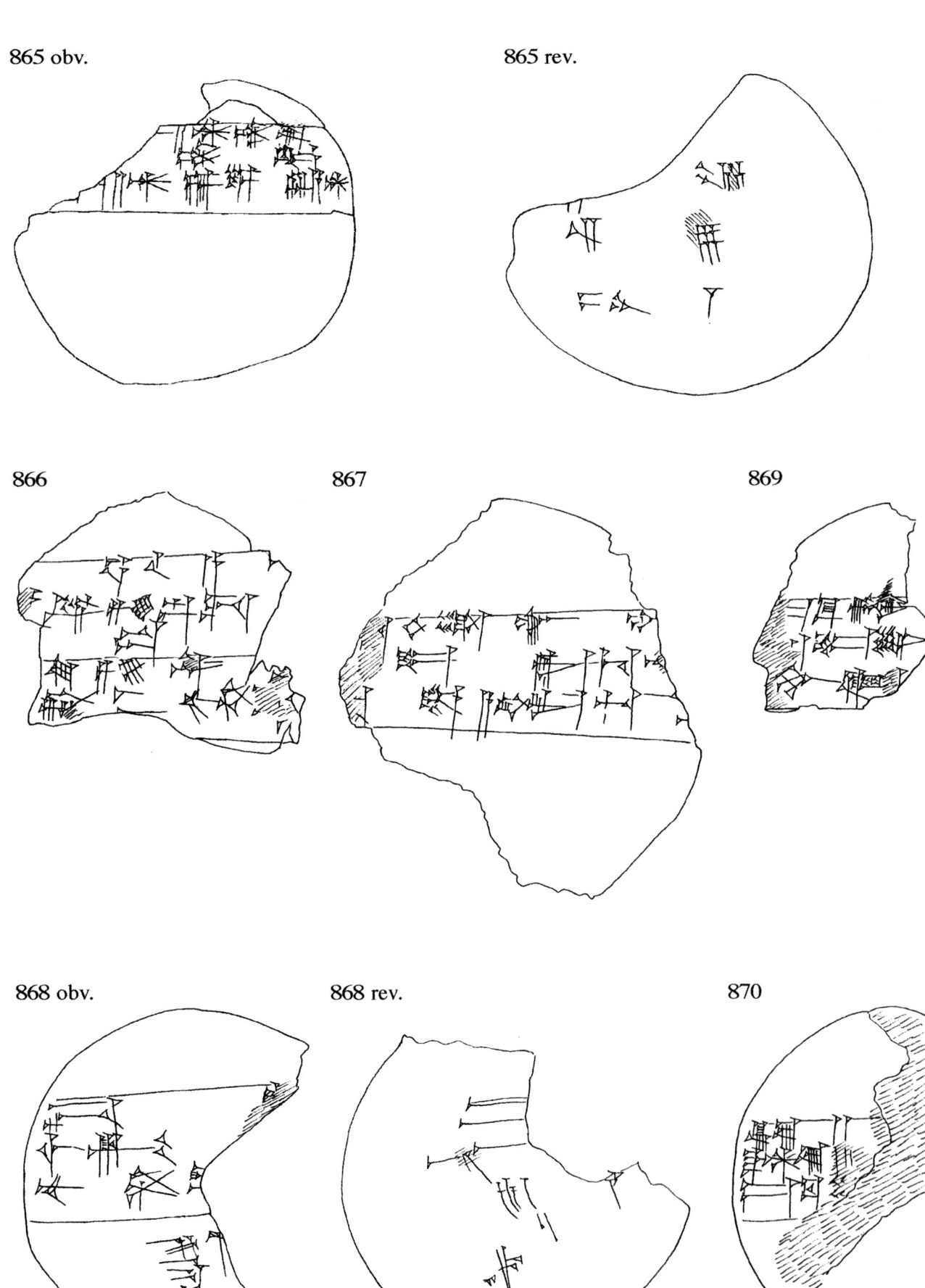

Plate 85

871 U.15084

872 U.8814 B obv.

872 U.8814 B rev.

873 obv.

875 obv.

875 rev.

873 rev.

874 obv.

874 rev.

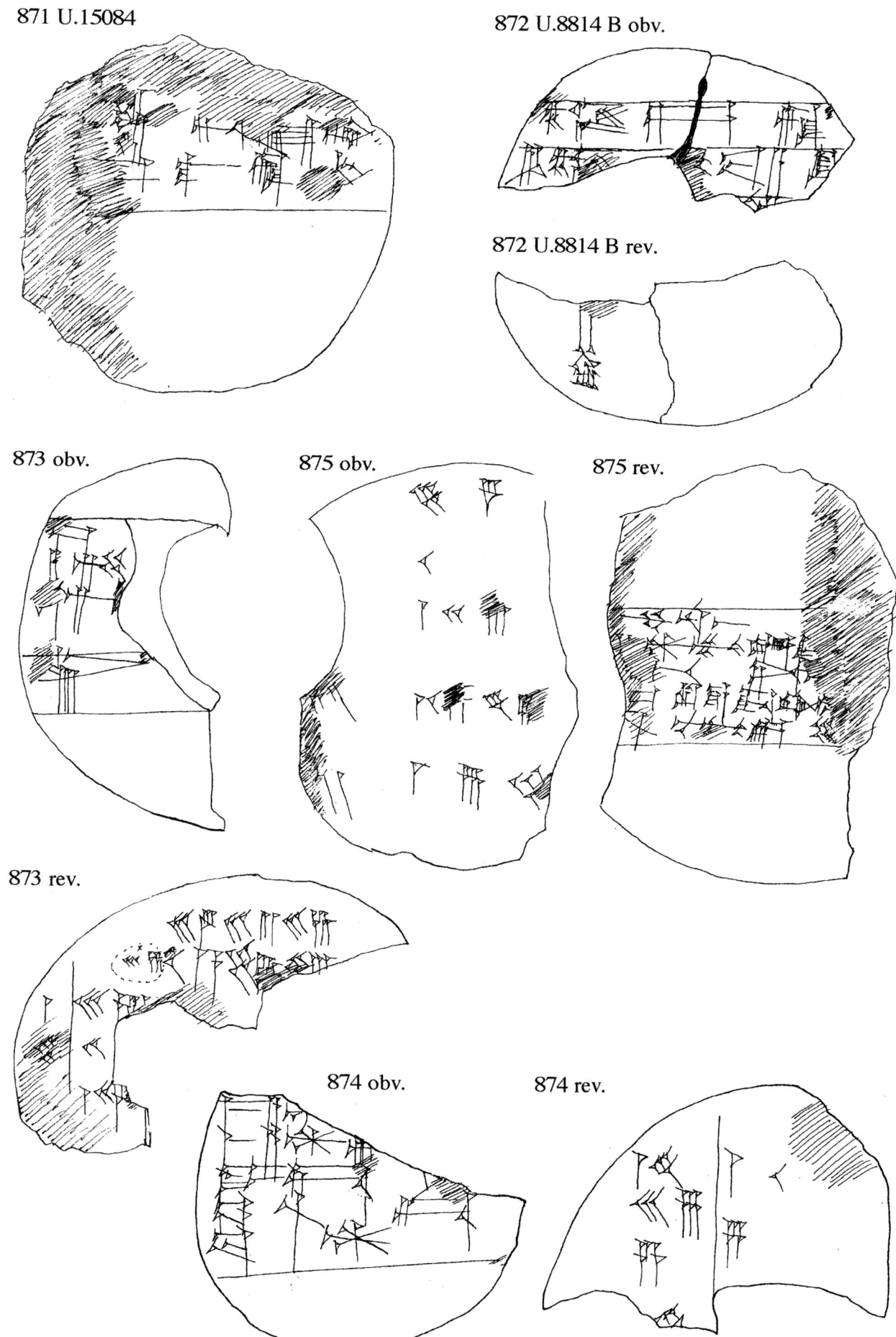

Plate 86

876 obv.

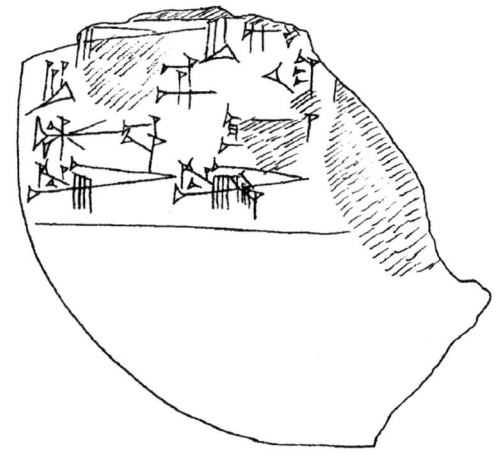

876 rev.

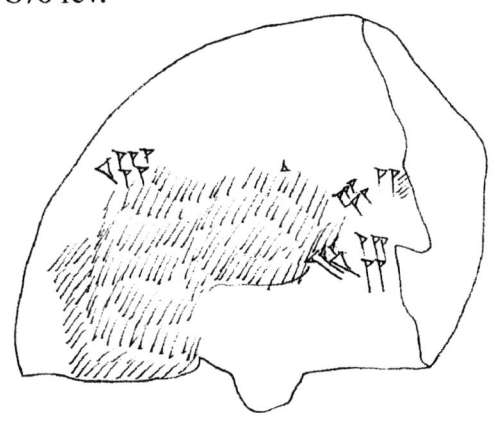

877 U.10144 obv.

877 U.10144 rev.

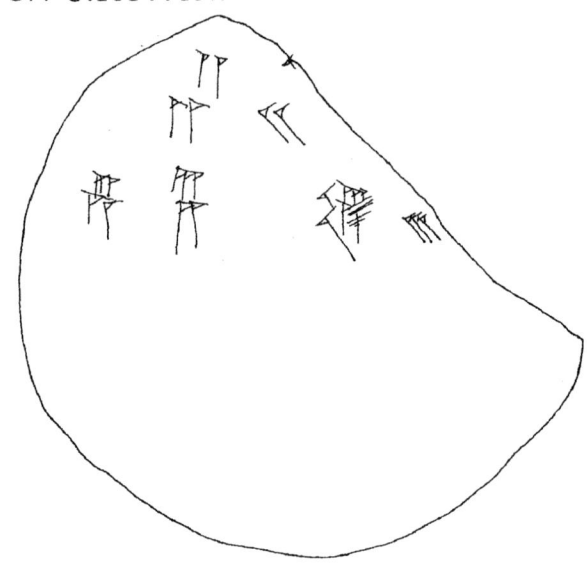

878 obv.

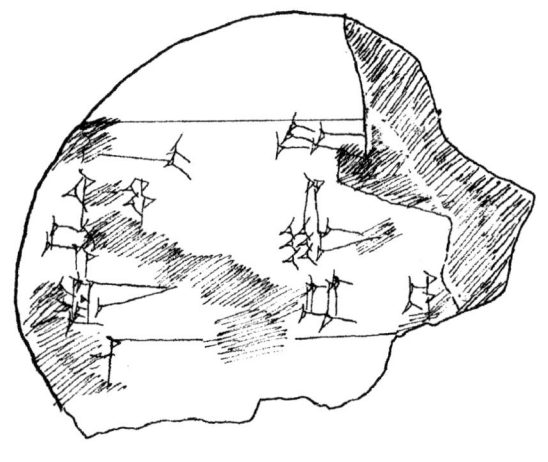

878 rev.

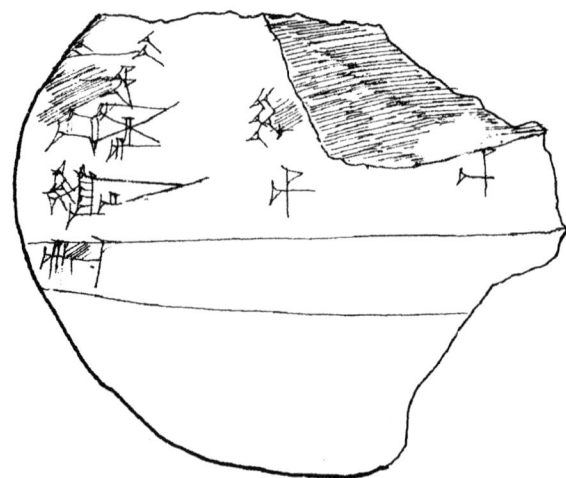

Plate 87

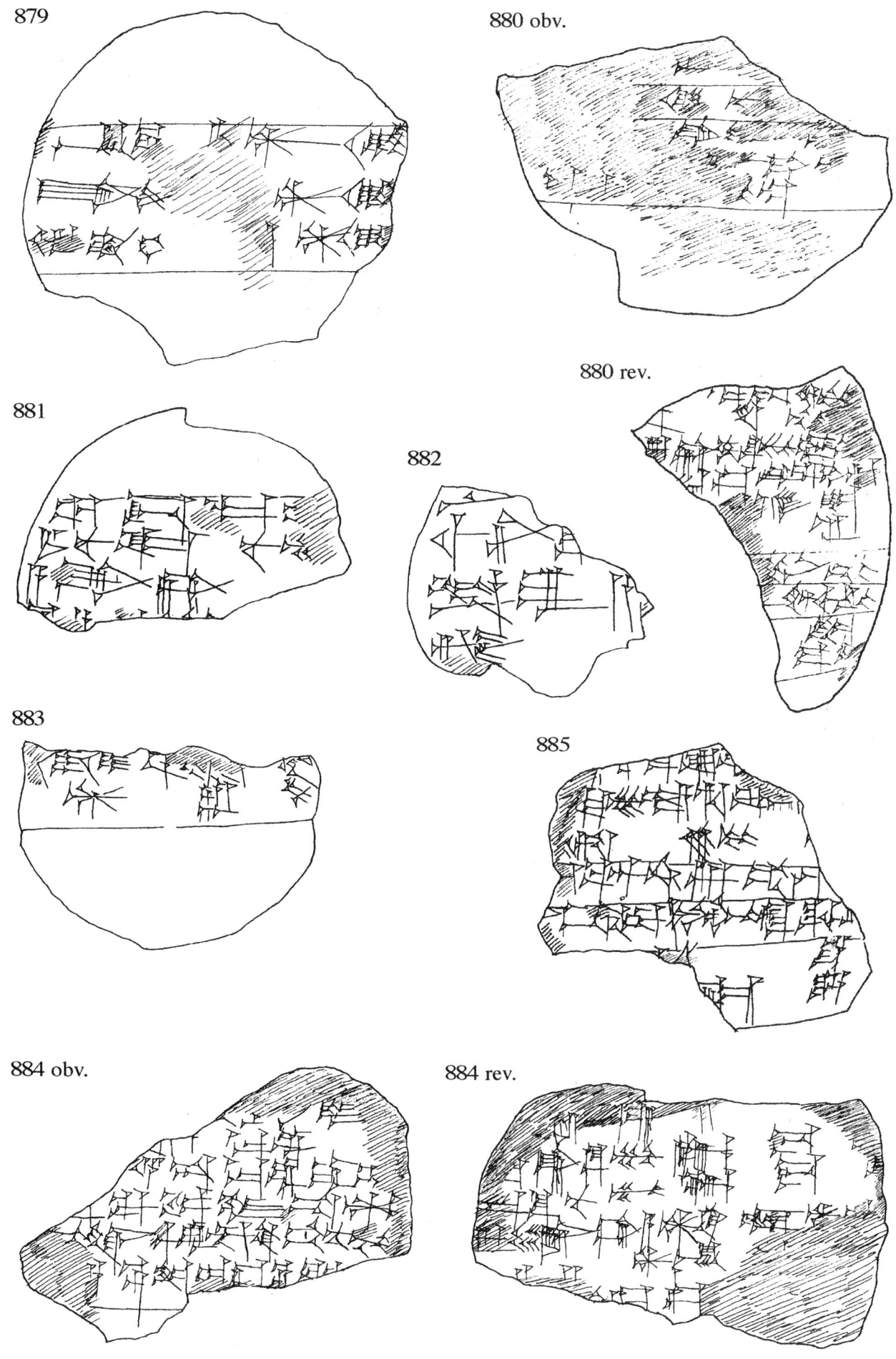

879

880 obv.

880 rev.

881

882

883

885

884 obv.

884 rev.

Plate 88

886 obv.

886 rev.

888 U.7703

887 U.7827 z

889

890

892
obv.
rev.

891

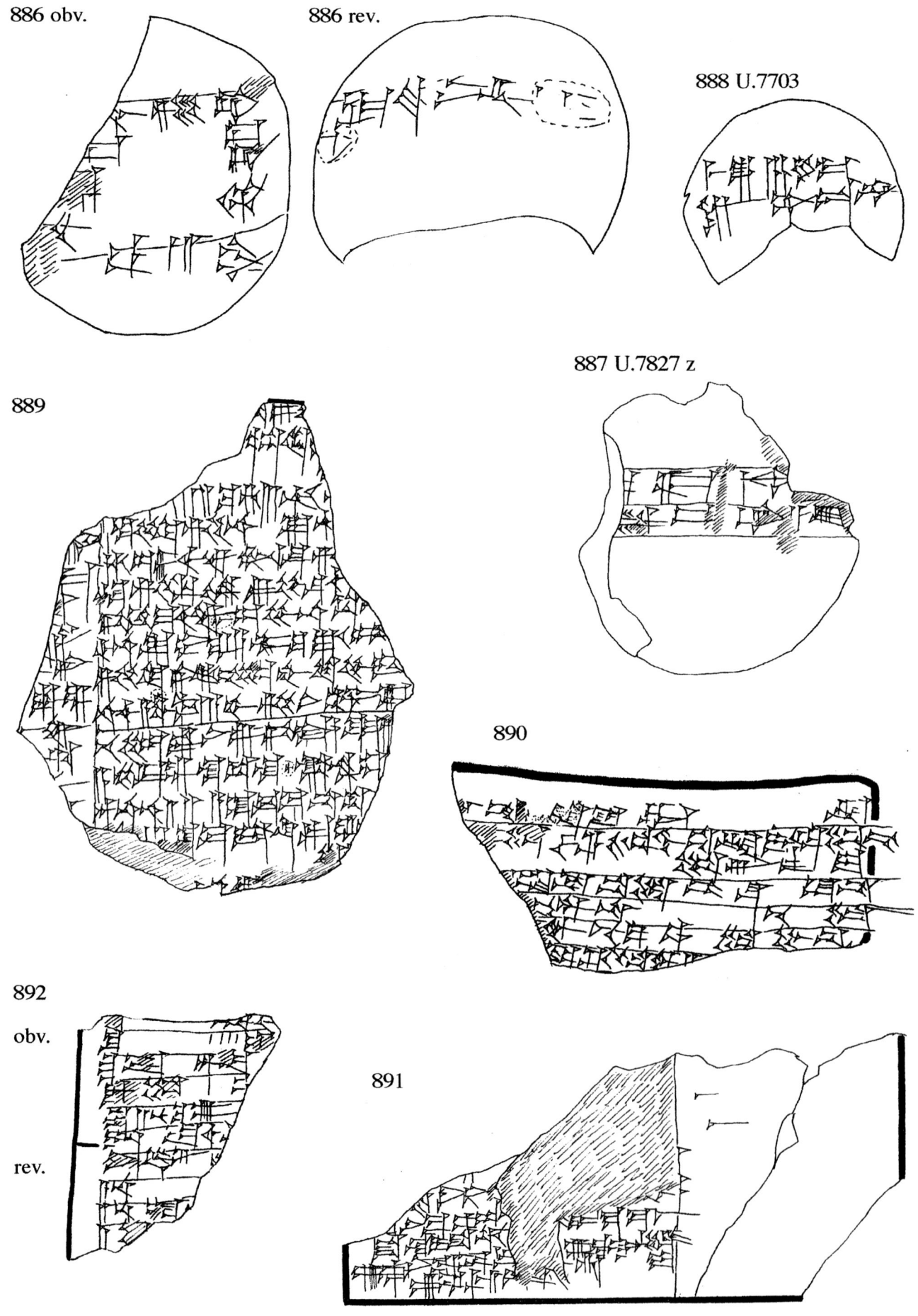

Plate 89

893 U.16523 obv.

893 U.16523 rev.

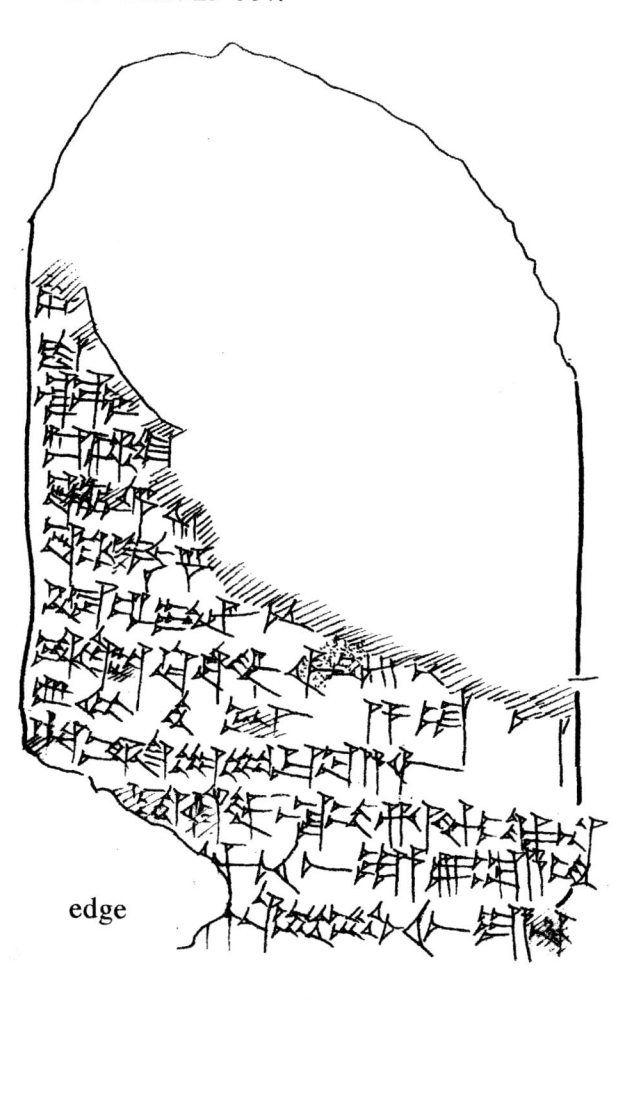

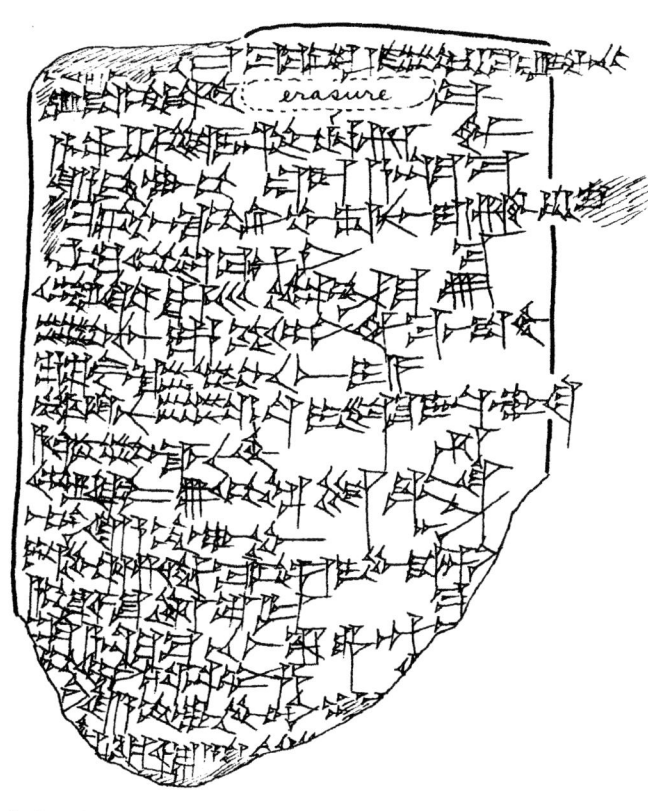

edge

left edge

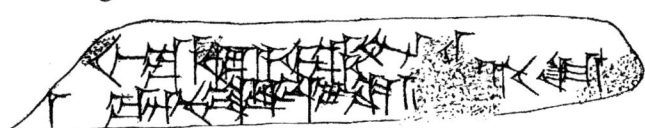

894 rev.

894 obv.

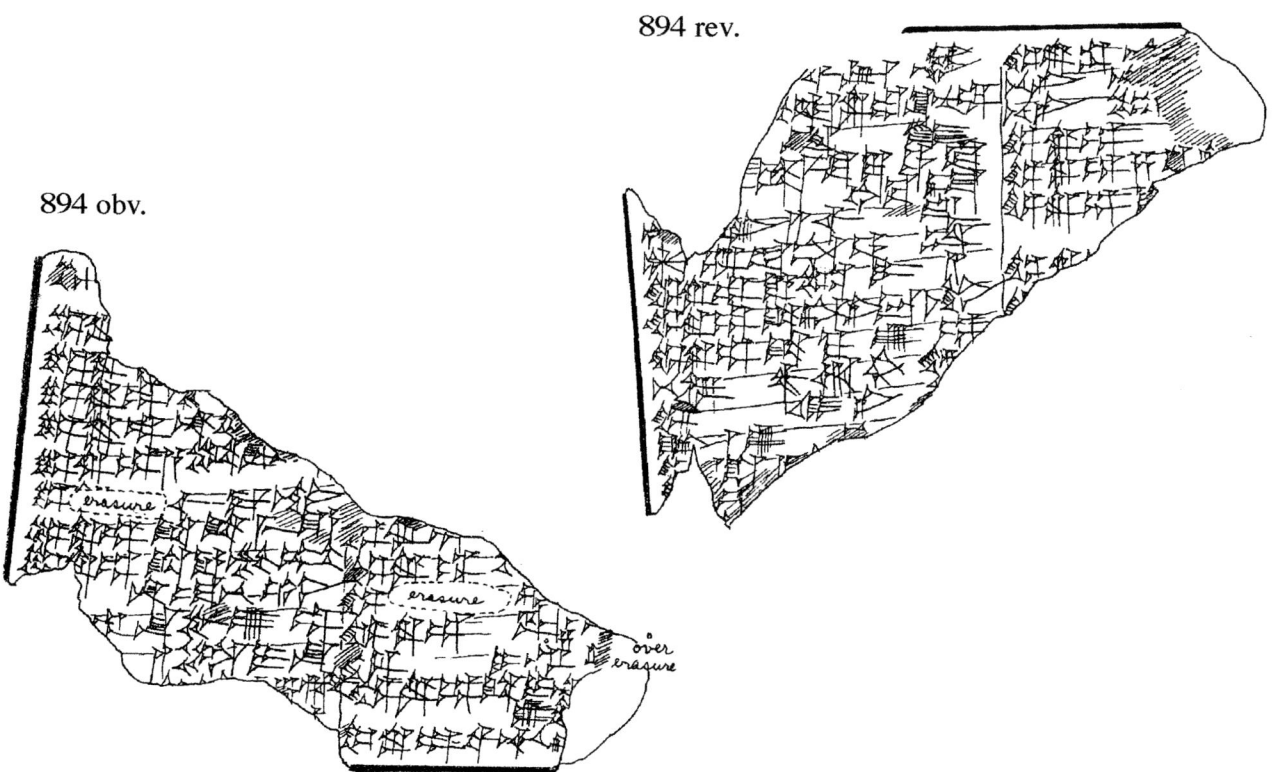

Plate 90

895 U.16856 obv.

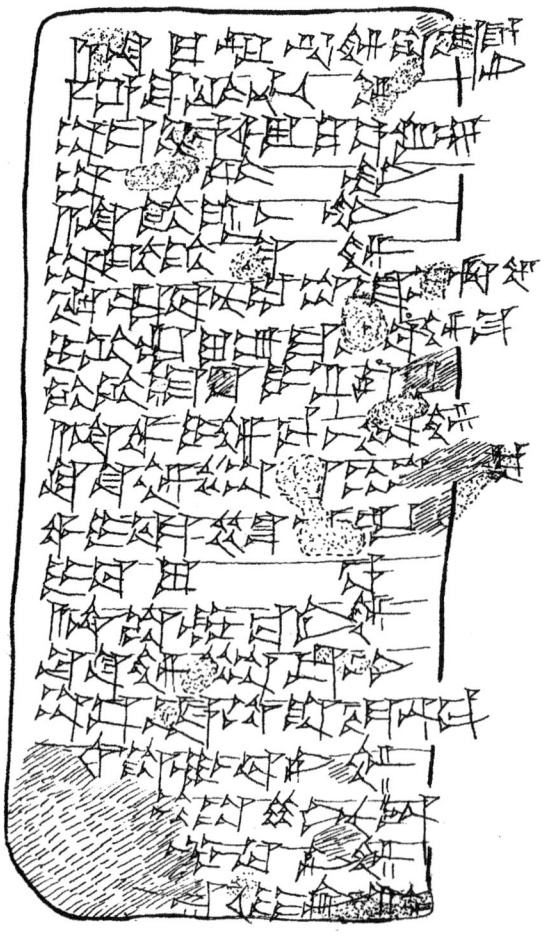

895 U.16856 rev.

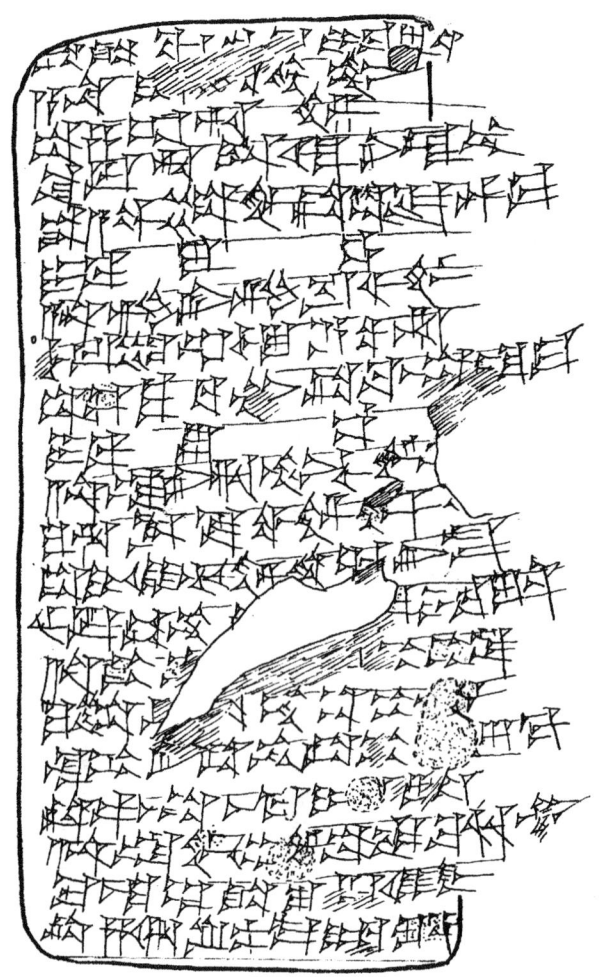

896 U.30655 obv.

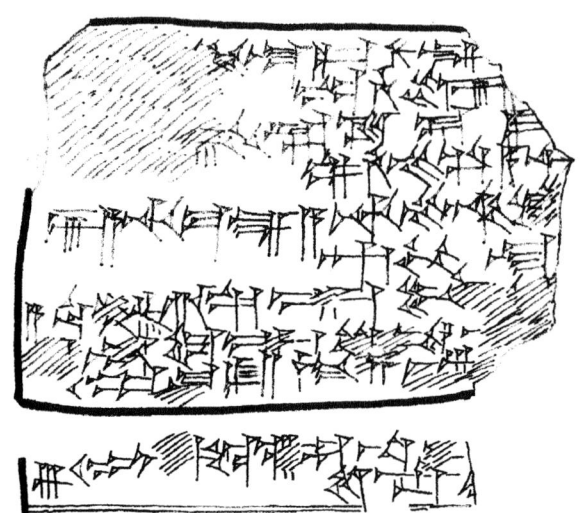

896 U.30655 rev.

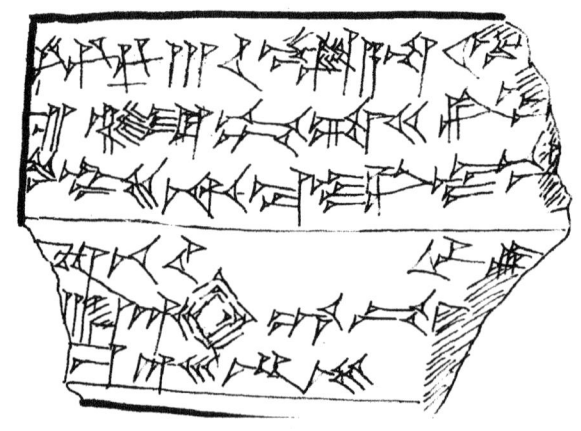

Plate 91

897 U.30654 obv.

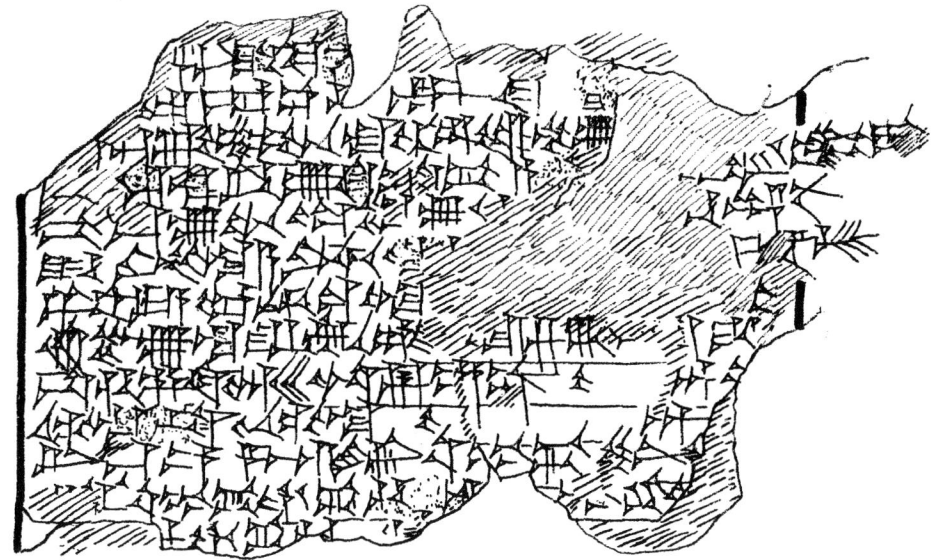

897 U.30654 rev.

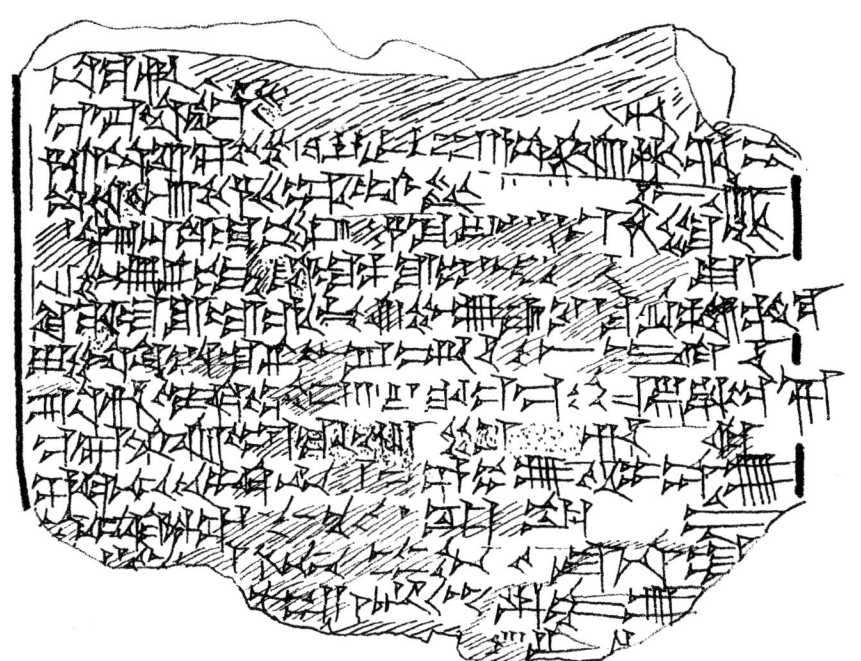

898 obv.

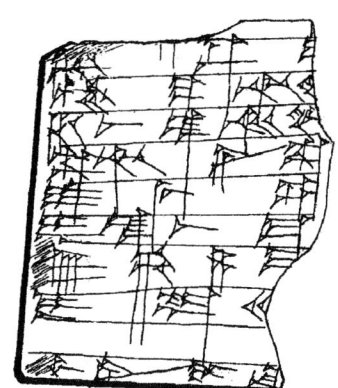

898 rev.

Plate 92

899

900 obv.

901 obv.

900 rev.

901 rev.

902 obv.

902 rev.

903

907 obv.

907 rev.

904 U.8810

905 U.5629

908

906 obv.

906 rev.

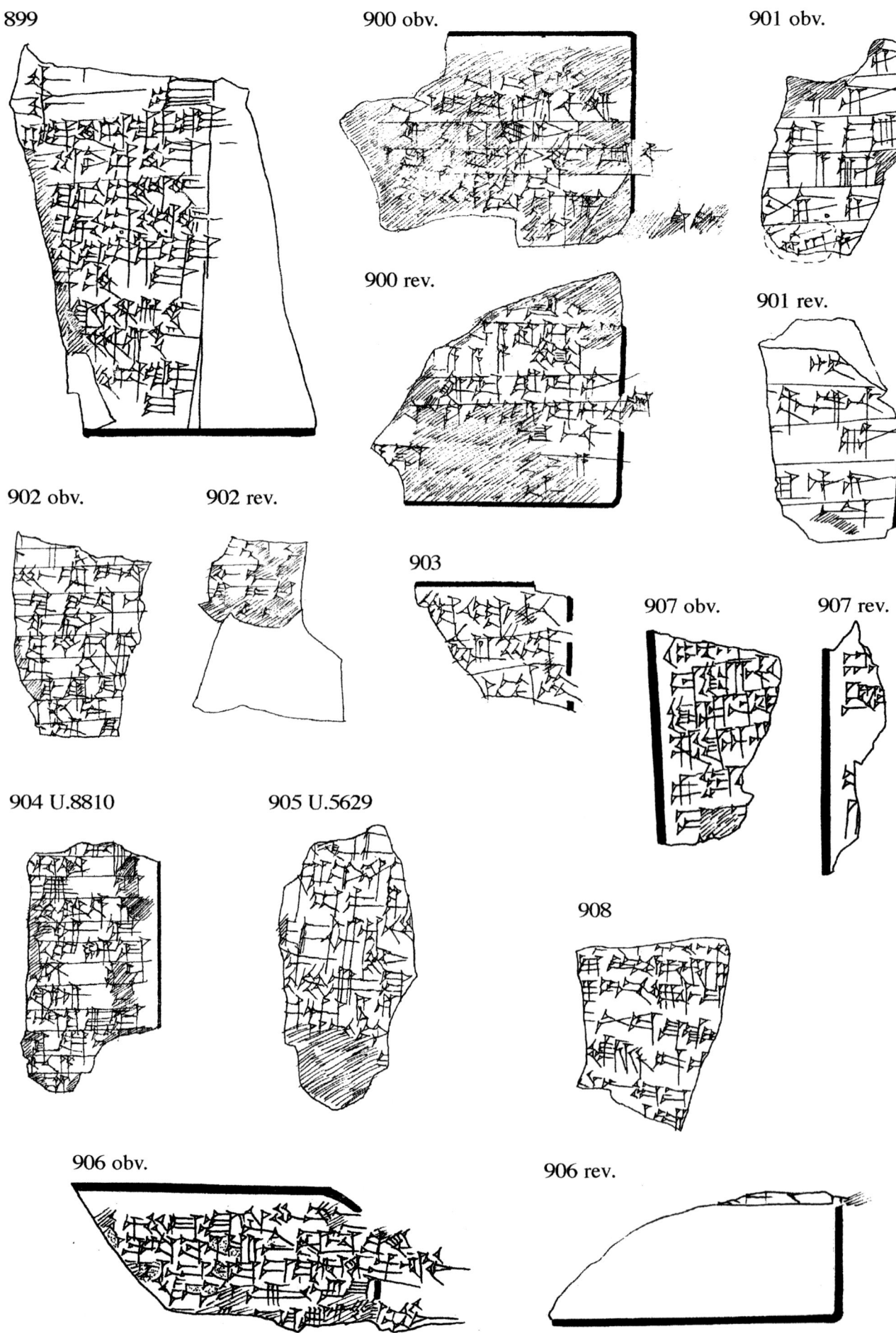

Plate 93

909 obv.

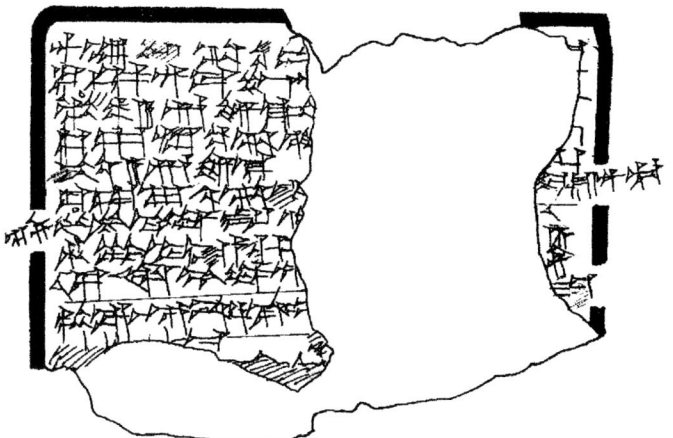

909 rev.

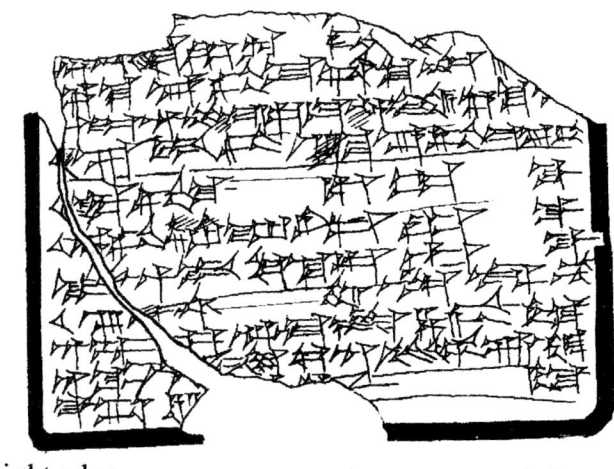

right edge

910 obv.

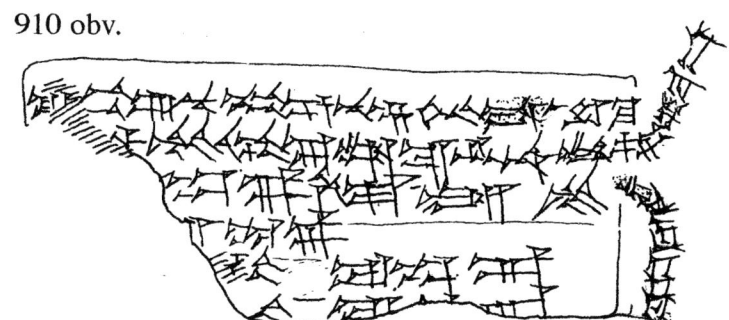

910 rev.

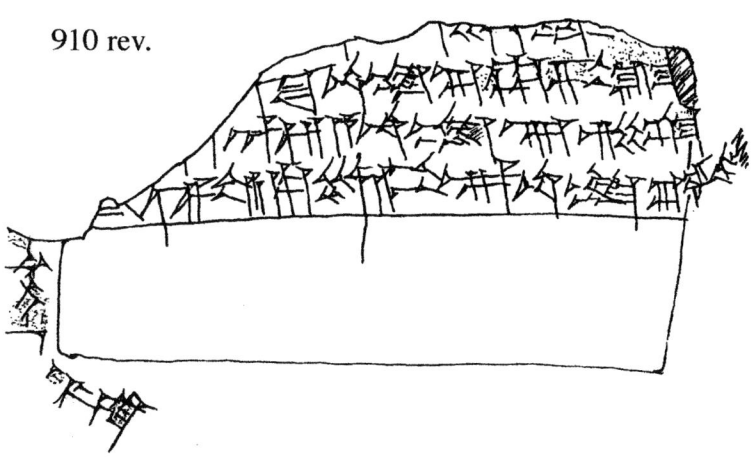

Plate 94

911 obv.

911 rev.

913 obv.

912 obv.

912 rev.

913 rev.

914 obv.

914 rev.

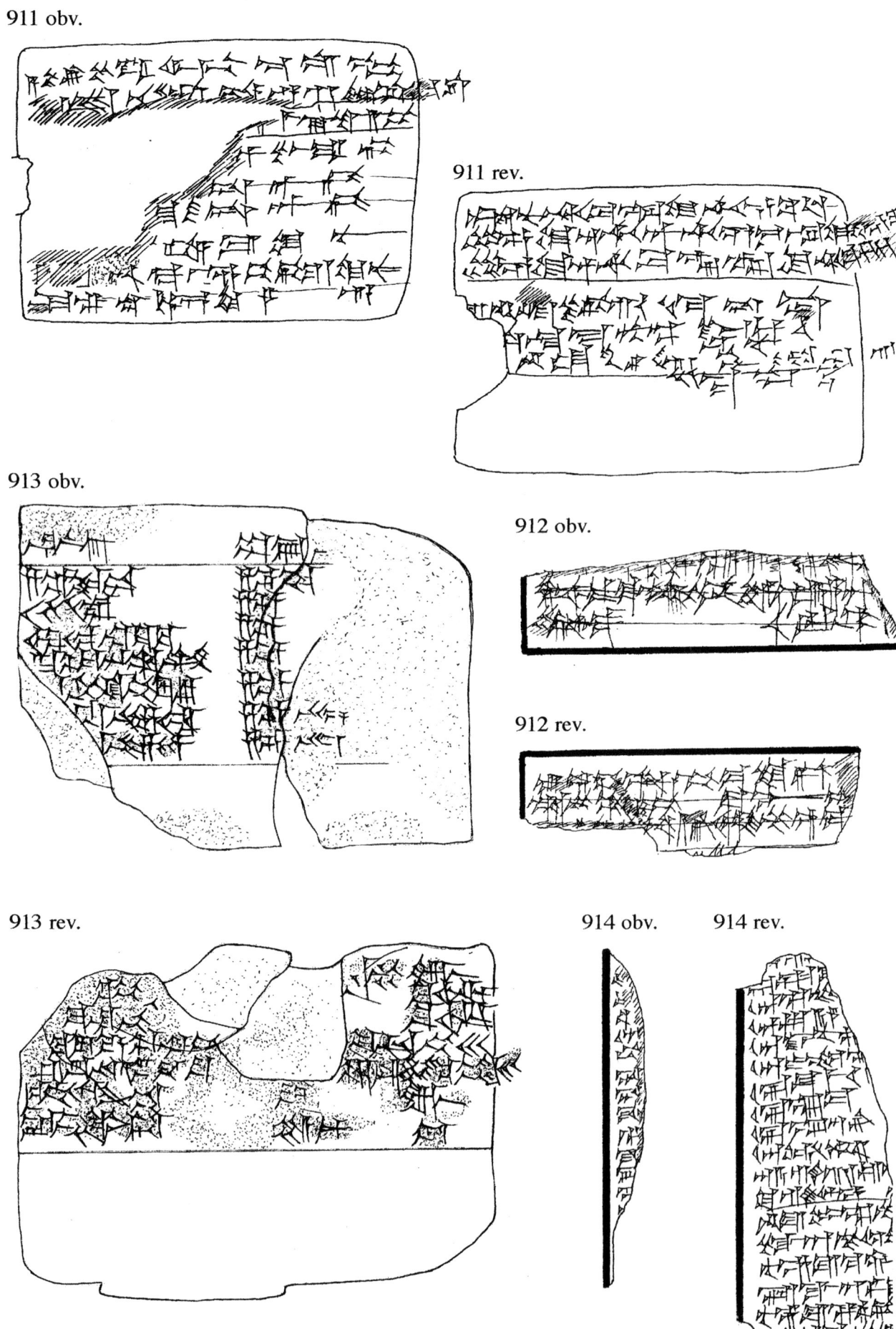

Plate 95

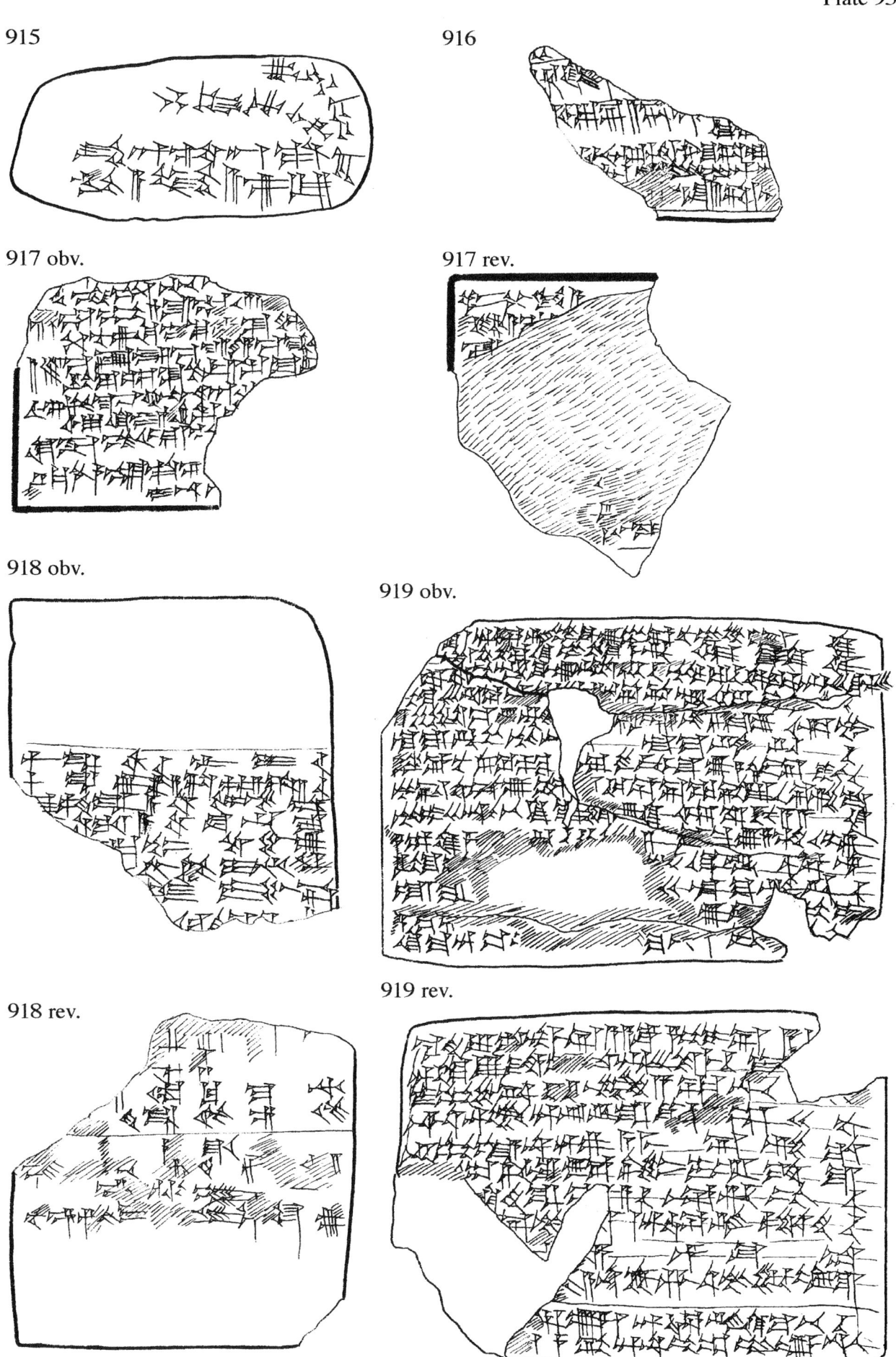

915

916

917 obv.

917 rev.

918 obv.

919 obv.

918 rev.

919 rev.

Plate 96

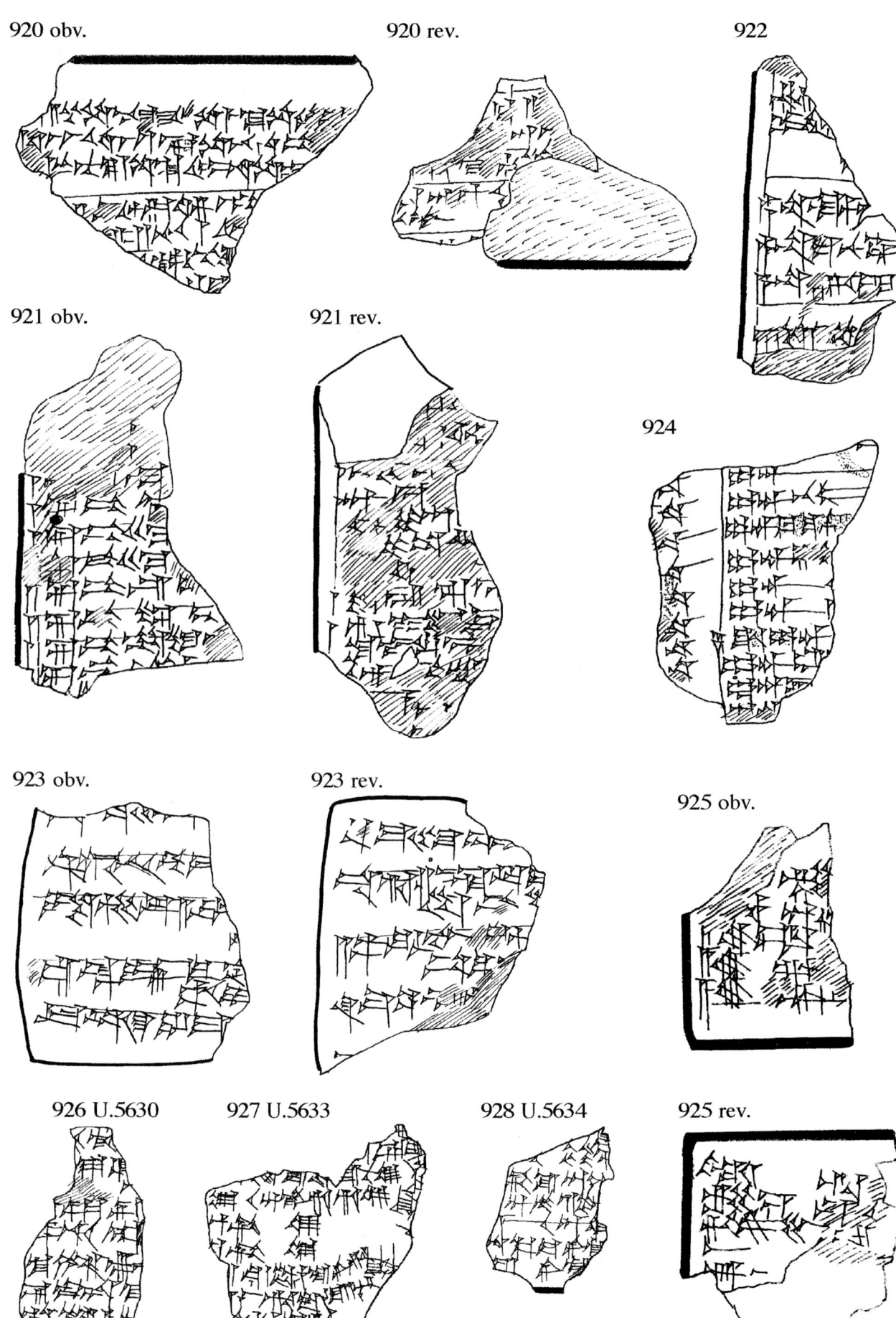

920 obv.

920 rev.

922

921 obv.

921 rev.

924

923 obv.

923 rev.

925 obv.

926 U.5630

927 U.5633

928 U.5634

925 rev.